The Freedom to Inquire

THE FREEDOM TO INQUIRE

Self Psychological Perspectives on Women's Issues, Masochism, and the Therapeutic Relationship

Esther Menaker, Ph.D.

with the editorial assistance of
Claude Barbre, M.Div., M.Phil.

JASON ARONSON INC.
Northvale, New Jersey
London

Production Editor: Ruth E. Brody

This book was set in 10 pt. Bodoni Light Antiqua by Alpha Graphics of Pittsfield, New Hampshire, and printed and bound by Book-mart Press of North Bergen, New Jersey.

Library of Congress Cataloging-in-Publication Data

Menaker, Esther.
    The freedom to inquire : self psychological perspectives on
women's issues, masochism, and the therapeutic relationship / Esther
Menaker.
        p.   cm.
    Includes bibliographical references and index.
    ISBN 1-56821-475-8
    1. Psychoanalysis. 2. Self psychology. 3. Women–Psychology.
    4. Masochism. I. Title.
    [DNLM: 1. Ego–essays. 2. Psychoanalysis–essays. 3. Women–
psychology–essays. 4. Masochism–psychology–essays. WM 460.5.E3 M534F 1995]
    RC509.M459 1995
    616.89'17'082–dc20
    DNLM/DLC
    for Library of Congress   94-49182

Manufactured in the United States of America. Jason Aronson Inc. offers books and cassettes. For information and catalog write to Jason Aronson Inc., 230 Livingston Street, Northvale, New Jersey 07647.

For Michael and Thomas

Contents

PART IV
PERSONAL JOURNEY 235

Foreword

One of the great temptations in all the psychologies is definition by category and, as its invariable adjunct, prescription by classification. One is united by cathexis, to use one of the jargon words with which this procedure is colorfully fitted out, to a determinism of language, image, and myth. Your patients come in familiar shapes and sizes. All you have to do is to check the appropriate volume in the *Gesammelte Schriften*, or whatever your particular vade mecum may be, and there it is—symptom, prognosis, therapy!

Esther Menaker never succumbed to the temptation, never, as this splendid collection attests again and again. Even as a young woman, when she studied in Vienna at one of the wellsprings of the temptation, where its vocabulary and rhetoric were polished to a dazzling shine, she was made uncomfortable by the ease with which one could slip into its reductions and simplifications. Well before Karl Popper's scorching criticism of the religion of psychoanalysis as a world in which dogma was all, Esther moved almost instinctively toward that understanding of her craft that insisted upon falsifiability as a canon of judgment. The story of Oedipus was a sometimes useful myth, not a periodic table of elements for the understanding and treatment of psychological dysfunction.

The opening words of the epigraph of this book, from Edgar Levenson, make the point: "Human language and perhaps human survival is dependent on an integration of the search for timeless pattern and the detection of imminent change." Esther's interest has always been in the "evolving ego," as she puts it, which all by itself would make her a potential dissident in the ranks, the result perhaps of that "inborn personality trait which," as she says, "has always eschewed an adherence to a dogmatic and limiting framework of thought." Hers has been "a search for a way to gain some freedom of thought within the confines of a rather constricted theory" that others in the field would do well to emulate.

This is not to say that one must throw over all that has been thought and done in the formulation of theory and practice in depth psychology. Esther can say, as she does in her essay on Anna Freud (Chapter 27), that she no longer feels "identified with classical psychoanalytic thought" and that its "literature and language seem remote" to her now. But she remains, trained as she was, fair as she is, open to what may still prove useful in the rules and procedures of the founding fathers and mothers. One sees this in her presentation of the case of the boys around whom she builds her "Contribution to the Study of the Neurotic Stealing Symptom" (Chapter 31), a case that was an important part of her personal journey. The analysis is an example, for the most part, of classical procedure; it could be used in training institutes as a model of its kind, without giving offense to the orthodox. But she is quick to dissociate herself from the shibboleths of mere orthodoxy. In the parents of the boys, she found "in each case what we have called a psychopathological family situation." But remember, she tells us, she is using the crunchy term "in a psychological and not in a social sense." Neither social delinquency nor economic stress was "in any sense" part of the family environment; the issue was subjection of the child "from the beginning of development on to trauma so constant and extensive that a normal emotional development" was impossible.

We see in this essay as in the closely related one on "Hypermotility and Transitory Tic in a Child of Seven" (Chapter 32), that closeness of observation that should make us profoundly grateful not only for the taste for the art but also the skill in it that Esther and an all too small number of analysts possess. She is a gifted painter. That gives her, some of us would say, that ease with her senses that makes hearing as well as seeing transcend the limits of ordinary observers, so that she can note with precision of phrase the little girl's "barkings and gruntings" as well as all the details of her "motor behavior," from her "throwing of herself about," to her pantomime.

It is such ease that makes Otto Rank so sensitive a chronicler of "the struggle of each individual to become an autonomous self," in Esther's words, and that "led him to incorporate an existential philosophical dimension into his psychological theory." When she says of Rank, the subject of so much of her theoretical work, that he "understood life to be a continuous process of emergence, both physically and psychologically," she is speaking of her own convictions as much as of his. Like him, she sees culture as "mankind's answer to the mortality-immortality issue since it can create a limitless world of invention and imagination outside the world of nature." This is a continuing preoccupation of Esther's, a direction of meditative inquiry that just the other day, so to speak, produced her memorable essay on "The Self-Object as Immortal Self" (Chapter 17).

Esther reminds us, in her summary of Heinz Kohut's self psychology in that chapter, that "the sense of self," which is to say "the feeling of self-esteem or its absence, depends on the inner relationship between the selfobject and the self." This reminder to herself as much as to us leads her to the summoning words near the end of the chapter: "While belief in a personal immortality is a matter of faith and lies beyond the realm of our certain knowledge, there is an aspect of immortality that, to my mind, exists within the province of psychology, is understandable, is connected to the phenomenon of the selfobject and adds greatly to the creation of meaningfulness in life." When we internalize our emotional experiences with those in our lives who have meant most to us, to whom we have become attached in respect and admiration, we store up "memory images," in Esther's moving words, which "are transmuted to harmonize with the original constitutionally given nature of the self to form a cohesive whole. Thus, the 'other' lives on—is immortalized—within ourselves."

Esther has herself become so attached to Rank, about whom she wrote a book central to our understanding of the man and his thought, and to Kohut, that it is easy to miss how often in her presentation of their ideas and accomplishments her own thinking and experience as an analyst and as a woman have become intertwined with theirs. She has in abundance the gift for empathic understanding that she sees, with some tutoring from Rank and Kohut, as a fundamental need in the prsent era, in which the "therapeutic task . . . often becomes one of reparation of self rather than resolution of conflict." This is a goal in which "the empathic stance of the therapist is of particular importance." It is also a gift that informs her pioneering work on the distressing subject of masochism in which she never forgets that the distress is felt by real persons living in a maelstrom of dysfunction and self-abandonment.

The chapters on masochism in this book (Chapters 18-21) make a significant addition to her earlier book on the subject, *Masochism and the Emergent Ego* (Menaker 1953). Like that collection of essays, they are the product of Esther Menaker's unceasing inquiry into the affliction, with special concern to develop some "understanding of the development and presistence of the self-image that characterizes moral masochism." One should pay close attention in this group of chapters to the way Esther adopts "the empathic introspective stance," which once again she credits to Kohut, at least as an identifying phrase. The risks of such a change of role for the analyst dealing with a severe case of moral masochism are unmistakable. They are less serious, however, than the alternative, a long journey to a "dead end in the therapeutic road." This way one may forge a "therapeutic alliance" and find some surcease from suffering for the beleaguered patient—and, it must be added, for oneself, for whether one is able to adopt an empathic stance or not, suffering of this kind is contagious and it can afflict analysts with an intensity almost equal to the pain of their patients.

Esther admires Charlotte Bronte's understanding of suffering as "a form of endurance, not as inevitably masochistic but as an opportunity for growth—growth in the capacity to love another human being." That, it seems to me, comes close to defining the textures of Esther Menaker's own evolution as we are privileged to witness it in this book. It was the element of love, growing within her in every way, that got her through feeling "somewhat frightened at the prospect of childbirth," when she was pregnant with her first child in her student days in Vienna. It is that same grace that permits her to say so quickly and so well, in the interview that concludes this book (Chapter 33), what must be said of her Viennese analyst's comment to her, unprovoked, with no apparent connection to anything except Esther's unmistakable sexual identity: "I don't know what women are complaining about, when they complain about being women. They have on the inside what men have on the outside!" Esther's comment is terse and to the point: "Please note the anatomical reference, the emphasis on structure rather than function; the concern with what one *has* rather than what one *is*."

In reading this book, we are bound to recognize and to prize both what Esther Menaker *has* and *is*. Both the having and the being offer eloquent testimony to the fruits of freedom of inquiry. See then, these chapters say to us from beginning to end, see what such freedom engenders. "One thinks one understood something and finds that one did not," Esther says near the end of the interview (Chapter 33). It is with that spirit of free inquiry that she finds herself involved in trying to understand, "to grasp," what it means to speak of a soul in and out of the vocabulary and concepts of modern psychology. "In other words," she concludes, "I think the soul plays a role, and an active role, in phenomena like empathy and love." My last word, in response to this, is from a language in which Esther has been adept since her student days: *Gewiss*!

                                                                                    Barry Ulanov

Acknowledgments

This book represents thought and work over a long period of my life. The major works cover a forty-year period in which there have been many changes in the external world as well as in my own inner life. Thus, in terms of the opportunities, influences, and encouragements that I experienced from the presence of family, friends, colleagues, and patients, I have much to be grateful for.

As the time was ripe in my latter years for collecting and preparing the works of these many years, I was fortunate in having the help of a talented editor and colleague, Claude Barbre. He read the papers carefully, grasping their import well, and helped organize them according to their major themes. His suggestions were always imaginative and creative; his work always conscientious and thorough, and attentive to detail. I wish to thank him for his efforts, for without his assistance my task would have been much more difficult, if not impossible.

Jill Carlen Kirby assisted Claude with the typing of the manuscript, adding to our work a keen knowledge of the computer. I wish to thank her also.

My good friend, Barry Ulanov, Professor Emeritus of Barnard College, deserves my deep gratitude for his tireless encouragement of my efforts through periods of difficulty and discouragement and for his laudatory remarks regarding the finished product, in his sensitive and understanding foreword. Many thanks.

The staff at Jason Aronson Publishers has been most helpful. I wish especially to thank Michael Moskowitz, acquisitions editor, Norma Pomerantz, assistant to Dr. Jason Aronson, and Ruth Brody, my editor who oversaw the final preparation of the manuscript.

Human language, and perhaps human survival, is dependent on an integration of the search for timeless pattern and the detection of imminent change. It is this out-of-balanceness that makes for movement and keeps us neither as ephemeral as the May fly nor as perfectly immutable as the shark. The same deceptively simple process motivates vast systems of biological and ecological change from genetics to evolution. Any analyst of any persuasion must follow this same dialogic process to be effective.

Edgar A. Levenson

Introduction

One of the advantages of reaching old age is the broad perspective that one achieves on the journey one has made. It is like climbing a mountain in order to experience the view from the summit: the details in the broad valley below become clear, and the successive mountain ranges in the distance stretch out against the horizon, becoming dim and misty as they fade into the sky. However, there is a flaw in the simile, for when climbing a mountain one is aware of one's goal, one knows when one has reached the top, and although the view from the summit may be majestic, one cannot always look back and see the way one has come. It is somewhat different with one's life. There are way stations along the path that are sometimes mistaken for the summit, and one is not certain about how much higher the mountain goes. But one can look back, especially if one has left traces— markers of one's journey—along the way.

It is precisely such a looking back at the markers one has left that a collection of professional papers represents. Although each chapter is an entity in itself, each is also part of an evolutionary process. The foci of one's interests stand out like details in the landscape, and one acquires a vista of the evolution of one's thinking. And like biological evolution itself there is continuity and change. For me the continuity was represented in the recurrence of themes that began with the first book that I wrote in collaboration with my late husband, William Menaker, entitled *Ego in Evolution* (1965). There, our departure from Freudian instinct theory as the primary and dominant explanation of human behavior began. We posited forces other than libido that propelled human development. In our view, a genetically determined characteristic of human beings, namely the ability to organize and integrate consciousness through the functioning of ego, superseded instinct as the power that in large measure controlled the psychic life. At that time, the psychic life, as we conceived it, was predominantly the mental life. We were aware that it was in a process of change, influenced by many factors—social, cultural, familial—and directed by ego that was itself changing and evolving .

After my husband's death in 1972 I continued to think and write about the evolving ego. However, the more inclusive concept of "self" had as yet not won precedence in my own thinking, although in a talk on "The Effects of Counteridentification" in 1975 I had already referred to the self and to the ego as its executive branch. In our attempt to describe the totality of the individual as opposed to the entity, ego, that was the executor either of an individual's libidinal wishes or of his or her superego demands, I began to realize that what we had referred to as Ego with a capital "E" was certainly closer to what Kohut thought of as Self than to the Freudian concept of *ego*.

The tendency to view the personality of an individual in its wholeness characterized my work from then on. It expressed itself in my interest in the self-image and especially in my writings on moral masochism. Two early essays published previously in a volume of selected papers (Menaker 1953) illustrated my concern to explain masochism in ego rather than drive terms and to see the importance of interpersonal interactions in its development. My interest in masochism continues and is represented in this collection in several chapters that relate it to self psychology (Chapters 18-21).

In reviewing my papers it was interesting to me to realize that in 1960, before I had made the acquaintance of Heinz Kohut's work on the self, I had described the defensive use of the self-image to safeguard the integrity and cohesiveness of the ego when it was threatened by annihilation through the loss of an introjected object. The important role of introjection was becoming clearer to me. I also experienced a growing awareness that the role of defenses in maintaining psychic balance was not solely to uphold repression of unacceptable drives but also to maintain and further the integrative function of the ego. Later I understood that this applied to the regulatory function of the entire personality, that is, to the Self.

The development of my deviations from Freudian theory and practice began early in my professional life and resulted from an inborn personality trait that has always eschewed an adherence to a dogmatic and limiting framework of thought, preferring to rely on observation of data from which to draw conclusions. My evolutionary outlook on all of life has resulted in an emphasis on growth and the optimal fulfillment of an individual's potentiality in my theoretical and clinical work, rather than on "cure" in the sense of the elimination of symptoms. Certainly I am not alone in this emphasis, for the general development of psychoanalysis has been away from "symptom analysis," largely, in my view, because the problems for which people seek help in the contemporary world are rarely symptoms like those described in Freud's early cases, but rather problems in living, in interacting felicitously with other people, in having at least an adequate sense of self-esteem, and in finding it difficult to overcome anomie and depression. These are important issues for modern men and women. The historical and social characteristics that are responsible for the appearance of a different set of psychological problems call for changes in therapeutic philosophy and procedure. The chapters that follow represent such changes in my own development over approximately a 20-year period.

In introducing these works it is of the utmost importance to speak of the influence that the writings of Otto Rank have had on my development both theoretically and in therapeutic practice. This influence has been of a dual nature: first as an encouraging confirmation of some of my own views and second as a stimulus to further thinking. Rank's interest in ego phenomena as primary and central to the understanding of human psychology preceded Freud's own movement toward a concern with ego processes. He was a forerunner of ego psychology and certainly of self psychology. His emphasis on *will* as the manifestation of the life force is unique in the history of psychoanalysis. He perceived that the development of ego processes began in the mother-child relationship, thus deviating from the heavily patrocentric emphasis of classical psychoanalysis. By placing ego development in an interpersonal context he removed it from its secondary place in the psychology of drives where ego was thought to be a secondary phenomenon developing out of the frustration of instinctual impulses. These views as they were absorbed into and modified by my own thinking are expressed in several chapters in this volume dealing with characteristically Rankian themes: creativity, will, guilt, ethics, and the self.

In addition, the movement of my thinking throughout the years has been in the direction of self psychology, and the writings of Heinz Kohut have been an inspiration to me. Both his introduction of the empathic stance as a legitimate method of observation in the therapeutic situation and his conception of the importance of the selfobject for the structuring of the self and for its "restoration" in therapy are milestones in the evolution of psychoanalytic thinking. This development is reflected in this book in several chapters—for example in "Self, Will and Empathy" (Chapter 4) and in "The Continuing Search for the Selfobject" (Chapter 6).

In the course of my early training there was perhaps no area of Freudian theory that left me with greater dissatisfaction and as profound a conviction of its inaccuracy as the theory of the psychology of women. In Part III, "Women's Issues," the reader will find an expression of my own thoughts on feminine psychology.

If the bringing together of my work covering the last 20 years were to require some justification, it would lie in the attempt to illustrate a personal evolution. It is an evolution that began in 1930 by perceiving the importance of unconscious phenomena in the realm of drives at a time when psychoanalytic theory was akin to quackery in the minds of academicians and the general public, and moved to include an understanding of the profound significance of ego, will, and self for human psychology. The process of moving from a theory that seemed adequate at first to a new point of view without discarding what is valuable in the original theory is one of inner growth—a growth that takes place as the result of pondering the deeper meanings of one's clinical work and of allowing the influences coming from social, cultural, and professional changes and innovations to play upon one's thinking. Along the way there may even be some original ideas that evolve.

I

SELF PSYCHOLOGICAL PERSPECTIVES

The chapters that follow represent more than half of the work in this collection. Their emphasis, as the part title indicates, is on varying aspects of the self and fulfills the promise of the introduction to this book by representing my departure from Freudian drive theory. As my own theorizing moves more and more toward self processes, the influence of the thinking of Otto Rank and of Heinz Kohut is apparent. The chapters are replete with clinical vignettes and case histories that not only illustrate differences with classic theory but also emphasize the therapeutic importance of fundamental modifications in classic technique. Thus, as the forces of therapy shift from conflict resolution to the structuring of a cohesive self, the actual relationship between patient and therapist gains in centrality. Since change or cure for the patient is no longer a solipsistic process but depends on an interpersonal exchange between two individuals—patient and analyst—the affirmation of the patient's will as it represents an acceptance of the individual's total personality by the analyst is crucial. This is an outgrowth of the therapist's empathy and of the realization that he or she must become a selfobject for the patient to be introjected, thus aiding the restructuring of the self. Issues of self-esteem, values, idealization, and self-disclosure are important topics for discussion; the significance of culture in evaluating personality and behavior takes on a primacy that is in sharp contrast with its neglect in the earlier literature of psychoanalysis. This perspective challenges the universality of psychoanalytic theory and places great emphasis on the uniqueness of the individual.

1

The Self-Image
as Defense
and Resistance

The aim of this chapter is to describe a form of resistance and a corresponding defense structure that has as yet not been characterized. Originally Freud
(1985) described resistance as appearing in analysis in connection with the
attempt to nullify repression, which in turn serves the purpose of keeping
unacceptable instinctual impulses unconscious. Thus repression is the first
defense mechanism described (Freud 1915b). Other mechanisms of defense
(Freud 1915a) employed by the ego, either in connection with or separate
from repression, are also in the service of protecting the ego from the anxiety
aroused by impulses that are unacceptable to it.

The inner threats that the ego experiences do not all stem from the
instinctual life. There are the dangers of the annihilation of the ego itself
or of parts of the ego, especially when these represent the loss of introjected
objects. Against such dangers the ego builds defenses, and these in turn
appear as resistances in psychoanalytic treatment when they are threatened.

A highly intelligent young man sought analysis because of hypochondriacal symptoms and disabilities imposed by a rigid compulsive-neurotic
character that inhibited him in many areas of activity, most notably in his
love life. He was unable to combine sexual impulses with feelings of affection and tenderness and therefore could never find a satisfactory love object.

At the time of his entrance into analysis he was involved in a highly sadomasochistic relationship with a young woman whom he could not decide to marry. He also did not feel completely committed to the professional work in which he was engaged—neither to the actual nature of the work itself nor the particular company that employed him. He rationalized his continuation in that position on the basis of gaining good experience and had fantasies of finding more congenial work later that would more closely meet his standards and social values.

The patient was the youngest child in a moderately large family. The parents inculcated in their children the desirability of extreme intellectual ambition. The father was a brutal, autocratic patriarch who ruled the family. The mother was a semi-invalid throughout most of the patient's childhood and died when he was about 11 years old. There was little warmth or tenderness expressed toward the children, the orientation toward them being primarily a narcissistic exploitation in terms of the glory and honor that they might bring to the family name. The patient had had a lonely, isolated childhood during which he suffered extreme feelings of inferiority, both in relation to his siblings and to other children, which eventuated in deeply masochistic attitudes.

When the resistance with which we are concerned appeared, he had had a disappointing experience in his work: he had not been given the promotion that he had hoped to receive. For a number of years he had worked for the same company, and, although a great deal of prestige was attached to being employed there, the type of firm and what it stood for were inconsistent with his ideals. He had hoped to leave the company shortly after getting a promotion, but at no time had taken any active steps to seek employment elsewhere. Throughout his analysis he remained indecisive about what he actually wished to do as an appropriate lifework. When, therefore, this disappointment occurred it was mainly an overwhelming narcissistic injury. He resigned and attempted to find work in a related field.

For him, talking about his vocational problems was the expression of an endless series of obsessive doubts. At an appropriate time I suggested that had he been given a promotion he might have stayed where he was indefinitely. My remark was made toward the end of a session and was intended to direct his attention again to his passivity and his inability to mobilize his decision to the point of action. This comment precipitated an emotional storm. He came to the next session in a highly disturbed condition and said that he had scarcely slept the night before. What had upset him was the thought that I could think he might have made a lifework of his employment. Indeed, if I thought this of him, he could not continue his analysis with me. Obviously it was essential for him, regardless of whatever action he took or did not take, to maintain the illusion that I held an image of him that corresponded to his ego-ideal and his self-image.

Two important aspects of the patient's personality are represented in this seemingly small and unimportant incident: one, the narcissistic nature of his transference, and the other, the way in which the self-image is used as a resistance and as a defense against anxiety.

Regarding the attachment to the analyst, we can certainly speak of this reaction in the transference as the projection of an aspect of his psychic life onto the analyst. However, this is not a transference reaction in the usual sense since what is being projected are not unconscious instinctual impulses, but rather a conception of "the other" that demands that a conception of "the self" be included. The analyst is experienced unconsciously as perceiving the patient in such a way as to be consistent with the patient's own self-image. If this identity is disturbed by an unavoidable perception of a contradicting reality, a flood of hostility is released. It is clear that one function of the unreal self-image, and its alliance with the image of the analyst and the analyst's conception of the patient, is to serve as a defense against hostile impulses. The self-image is unrealistic because it is anchored in fantasy; it does not draw for its principal confirmation upon action in reality, nor upon the perceived judgment of another person. I have noted elsewhere (Menaker 1953) that the self-image that is masochistically colored derives this character from the unconsciously or foreconsciously perceived belittling attitudes of the mother. It is then tenaciously clung to as a way of maintaining the only possible relationship with the mother.

In this case we are then dealing with a self-image, or at least one aspect of it, that derives its content from the ego ideal. In my patient the ego ideal represents a precipitate of composite identifications and counter-identifications. Since the self-image is inevitably cathected with narcissistic libido, the reaction in the transference just described must be of a highly narcissistic character, as what is projected is a self-image shared with and included in the image of the analyst. It might be compared to an extremely narcissistic object choice in the real life of an individual, with the important difference that the phenomenon takes place within the transference and therefore points inevitably to a repetitive functional need within the personality.

In order to understand this need more clearly, let us review the development of the transference from the beginning. Suffering from a compulsive neurotic character, this patient had characteristic defenses of isolation of affect and strong negativism. Despite the operation of these defenses the patient developed very early in the treatment a strong mother-sister transference with an erotic coloration. This was manifested in dreams, fantasies, and reactions of jealousy toward the analyst's husband. Although these were analyzed, they could not be worked through to a point where they caused much change in the emotional life of the patient. He was still caught in the sadomasochistic love relationship with which he entered treatment. It was largely through insight into the masochistic nature of this relationship that he was partially able to free himself of it.

When the father transference appeared in the analysis, it was distinguished by its masochistic character. He invariably felt subordinate and inferior to all other male figures, and notably to his brothers and colleagues with whom he developed transference relationships. The hostile father transference appeared in displaced and very attenuated forms and was expressed only at fleeting intervals. What returned repeatedly and strongly in the transference was the incestuous sexual wish toward the mother. Even when its meaning had been made fully conscious, and it had been analyzed many times in its various and variable manifestations, it could not be sufficiently worked through and impeded further progress of the treatment. This is, of course, a classic instance of transference as resistance described by Anna Freud (A. Freud 1946).[1]

It was in such a period of resistance in the transference that the incident described earlier occurred. One may suppose, therefore, that what we commonly observe as transference of instinctual impulses may be superseded by another type of transference involving ego processes—processes of projection of narcissistic feelings, attitudes, and conceptions about the self. What is emphasized here is an essential and important difference between the projection of impulses in the transference in which the patient expresses, in effect, "I wish to" or "I wish that" and the projection of the image of self or of the self in the other in which the patient states, in

---

[1] It is important to bear in mind the date (1960) of this chapter. It was written at a time when my thinking was still largely influenced by a Freudian theoretical frame of reference and thus illustrates how readily one perceives what one is prepared to see in terms of one's background. However, the paper goes beyond the understanding of oedipal strivings to describe the patient's introjection of his fantasied image of the analyst's image of him and thus illustrates a mechanism akin to Kohut's concept of the mirroring transference—a concept not yet formulated in Kohut's writings.

effect, "I am the kind of person who" or "You are the kind of person who." The former are drive phenomena, the latter ego phenomena.

The difference between the two is of importance in the understanding of resistances and in the technical problems of analyzing them. The familiar resistance of the ego is to admitting into consciousness representations of instinctual drives from the unconscious because of the anxiety that they produce. What remains untouched when the drives persist after they have become conscious is the existence of another form of resistance in an isolated part of the ego, the self-image, which, by aligning itself with the image of the analyst and thus serving as a defense against separation anxiety, prevents dynamic changes in the personality and nullifies the possible gains from insight that permit understanding to be converted into purposeful activity.

The period following the patient's acknowledgment of his need to merge his self-image with that which he wished the analyst to hold of him was an exceedingly productive one. He realized suddenly that he had not thought of the analysis as his, as being for him, throughout his many years of treatment. He had always thought of it in terms of what would be my reaction to what thoughts and feelings he was producing for me This supply of information would then in some magical way effect changes in him without any other participation by him. He had also had the feeling that, if he did not please me by compliance and by holding my interest. I would terminate his treatment. He expressed this newly found sense of self by saying, "I feel as if I now had a rib cage." He pointed to his ribs and traced their form with his hands. "Before," he continued, "I thought of myself as just a spine and some stunted limbs. My heart was exposed and not separate from the world, now it is protected and belongs to me." It is interesting to note that gaining a sense of ego autonomy was also expressed in terms of body image (Schilder 1951).

He had conjured up in his mind the notion that his mother was a very passionate woman. However, there was nothing he knew about his mother that would confirm this image. It was a projection of his own oedipal impulses for purposes of denying his own feelings and of avoiding the attendant feelings of guilt. A similar process had occurred in the transference, with a corresponding loss of the sense of self, when he had attributed to my thinking an aspect of his own self-image.

During the period when the patient's ego was beginning to function a little more freely and independently he visited a sister about four years older than himself. In reminiscing about their childhood, she told him that he had been very difficult to wean from the breast and that a story was told in the family that even when his mother put mustard on her nipples he was not dissuaded from his purpose. His reaction to this story was very significant. He did not react to the traumatic aspect of the weaning and his own tenacious orality, but rather with great pleasure and relief to the knowledge that his mother had breastfed him: "I feel much better knowing that my mother nursed me. I don't have to feel like such an orphan." We are dealing here, then, not only with the consequences of instinctual deprivation but also with a self-image, "an orphan," which is inextricably bound to the distorted image of the mother upon which it depends for its existence.

Whether the image is at one time of being an orphan or at another the idealist who will not spend his entire life in the business world, the highly narcissistically cathected self-image is resistant to change or movement. This immutability is dependent upon and is maintained by a kind of symbiosis with a mother image that either reflects or complements the self-image. The projection of this dyad constitutes a resistance in the transference that is not easily perceived. This interdependency of mother image and self-image is but one aspect of dependency, that is, of an arrested and anomalous development of the ego. From our knowledge of ego formation and differentiation, it would seem that the ground is laid for this fault in ego development in the early oral experiences of infancy. What is relevant for our purposes here is that what is an anomaly of ego development becomes a defense against anxiety, and it appears in the analytic transference as a negative therapeutic reaction.

In a later session the patient talked about seemingly indifferent matters in a manner that was guarded, overprecise in the use of words, and overaccurate in pronunciation. When this manner of speech was called to his attention he paused and then suddenly realized what he had been trying to avoid. He had spent the previous night with his new girlfriend and had had an unusually gratifying sexual experience with her. It transpired that from the time he discovered his "rib cage," he had noted a marked change in his sexual experiences. Although he had never objectively had gross or prolonged disturbances of potency, the sexual act for him had been an affectively isolated, more or less mechanical discharge of tension with little awareness of the emotional needs or responses of his partner. This had changed to an emotional participation with reciprocal feelings of tenderness and passion. The resistance to telling me about his recent gratifying sexual experience, which expressed itself in anger, covered a deep fear of telling me about it. He believed I would be angry and disappointed about his new relationship and his sexual gratification. Had he only referred to anger one might assume that he expected disapproval by a projection of his superego, but the anticipation of disappointment had other implications. This fantasy would seem to be predicated on the assumption that I was dependent on his love and in this sense was a denial of his oedipal attitude. In part this was a projection onto me of his own anger and frustration in the oedipal situation. But there was more than this in the fantasy.

The seemingly independent act still took place within the framework of the transference. The patient related its meaning for him to its meaning for the object of his transference love. It was not entirely his own experience any more than his analysis was entirely for him alone. He could not therefore derive the complete and adequate gratification from it, nor experience sufficient narcissistic satisfaction that normally feeds the ego its narcissistic supplies and from which the sense of self-esteem is derived.

The transference fantasy of the analyst's anticipated reactions to the patient's experience attests to the still unresolved bond to the analyst and therefore to the original object, his mother. In this case the fantasy was not one in which identical imagery is attributed to the analyst, as in the case of the fantasy regarding the self-image. Here a partially independent act—the satisfactory sexual relationship—disturbed the oneness of imagery that inhibited action, and the fantasy revealed that there was still an unresolved tie. The feeling that the analyst would be angry and disappointed was multidetermined. It was a projection of the patient's own anger and disappointment at the time of his original oedipal conflict: a fear in fantasy that his mother would be jealous if he loved another and that he would lose her. The latter fear appears in the analysis as the resistance to communicating his independence in achieving sexual maturity.

This progress and movement in the life of the patient were short-lived and were followed by regression and resistance. He was tempted to go back to his old job, rationalizing this on the basis that there would be difficulties wherever he worked and whatever he did. He began to think of his new love relationship in terms of the old one he had when he entered analysis; to create parallels in his mind that were really very far-fetched. The need to deny progress is one aspect of the negative therapeutic reaction. This reaction was precipitated by the fear of the free and independent functioning of the ego, which was in turn brought about through the analysis of the unconscious bond with the mother via their oneness in sharing the self-image of the patient. This unconscious unity with the maternal object was essential as the source of narcissistic supplies for his ego. As a child who was unloved, his adult ego could not relinquish the only tenuous security it had gained: a symbiotic, narcissistic dependence. It is for this very reason that no matter how thoroughly we analyze the unconscious wishes, there is essentially little change in the patient as long as the unconscious, archaic, narcissistic attachment to the mother through the use of the self-image remains.

At this primitive level of development the ego is not sufficiently delineated to sustain a separate self. The fear of separation is the threat of the loss of the only source of supplies that the dependent ego has. Because primitive self and object are one, loss of object is the equivalent of annihilation. Annihilation in this sense is the complete loss of self-esteem.

For patients with a strong narcissistic fixation of this type, the fear of leaving the original source of narcissistic supplies, namely the mother, and of substituting for it achievement in reality is too great. Their defense against this fear is a flight into an unconscious fantasy, the content of which is that the mother has the same good, positive image of the patient as he has of himself because both believe that the ego-ideal will be realized in some indeterminate future. This defense is expressed in the analysis as a transference resistance in which the analyst is seen as the mother and the patient's self-image is attributed to her thinking about him.

The uncovering of this resistance is crucial for the progress of these patients in analysis, but the giving up of the defensive use of the self-image, which has been an attempt to deal with a fundamental separation anxiety, is a slow and difficult process. It involves the repeated analysis of the fantasy of oneness with the mother in the area of the self-image, the consistent analysis of the regression that follows each attempt at separation, and the simultaneous pointing up of possible sources of healthy narcissistic gratification in the real-life activity of the patient.

SUMMARY

A type of defense in the transference is described in which the patient's self-image is projected onto the analyst, who represents the mother as the source of his narcissistic supplies. This type of transference is a resistance to mobilizing energy for mature activity that arouses an anxiety of separation from the mother. It is through the analysis of this resistance that this negative therapeutic reaction can be overcome.

2

Heinz Kohut
and Otto Rank

Thoughts and feelings, as precipitates of past experience, are preserved in the reservoir of our minds, and current experiences make connections with them and reawaken their memories. For an Englishman visiting the United States the gentle hills of New England remind him of his beloved English countryside. Should he be a lover of the Alpine scene, he will make comparisons with our mountains of the West. The process of comparing a present experience with one of the past is no less true of philosophical or psychological theories than it is of esthetic enjoyment. We are reassured by familiarity and a sense of continuity.

It is precisely the pleasure in such continuity that leads me to make a comparison between the psychology of Otto Rank, propounded in the 1920s, and that of Heinz Kohut, developed in the 1980s: the former, a much neglected and misunderstood erstwhile disciple of Freud in the early years of the psychoanalytic movement, and the latter, ignorant of any debt he might owe to Rank, yet arriving at some similar conclusions.

Both Rank and Kohut began as Freudians, yet became self psychologists, although in Rank's time that designation to characterize a cohesive body of psychological theory as well as a therapeutic approach was unknown. In their philosophical orientation they could both be called existentialists, yet, as far as l know, neither one designated himself as such.

Otto Rank's name is generally associated with *The Trauma of Birth* (1924), which represented his attempt to develop a biologically based paradigm for anxiety within the Freudian system of thought. The attempt miscarried as far as the Freudian movement was concerned, although ultimately Freud himself subscribed to the notion that the birth experience was indeed the primary source of anxiety. However, *The Trauma of Birth* shifted the emphasis away from the Oedipus complex and castration anxiety as the foci of human conflict and replaced them with the destiny of the early mother relationship as crucial for psychological development. This shift in emphasis was inimical to the Freudian point of view, but it led Rank to a psychology of the will as the ultimate expression of the individual's separation from the mother. The will is the life force of the individual self. In Rank's own development as a psychologist he shifted from a literal conception of separation as biological birth to a metaphorical notion of birth as psychological separation. It is this shift that caused Rank to abandon drive theory as a primary determinant in human life and to focus on the development of the self. He is thus not a conflict psychologist, seeing life as a struggle between instinctual drives and ego and superego directives, but rather a process thinker viewing human psychology as a continuous growth of the self striving for ever greater differentiation through the expression of the creative will.

Kohut came to self psychology empirically through observation and interpretation of his clinical data. It was the observation of individuals with narcissistic personality disorders that led him to conclude that their lack of self-esteem as well as their feelings of emptiness and meaninglessness in life derived from insufficiencies in the mother relationship. These were not failures in providing instinctual gratification as Freud had thought, but the inability to serve as an adequate selfobject for the child, i.e. to provide that reflection of pleasure and affirmation of the child's personality through the mirror of her own personality that would normally result for the child in a good feeling about him- or herself, through the incorporation of the mother's attitudes,

Although both Rank and Kohut view the mother relationship as primary in the formation of the self and in the nature of the self-feeling, their emphases are different. For Rank the fear of psychological separation from the mother and of thereby becoming an autonomous individual lies at the root of malformations of the self as well as of neurotic inhibition—inhibition that paralyzes the will and its creative expression. Kohut is concerned with the qualitative nature of the interaction between mother and child and concludes that "bad" mirroring on the part of the mother, if not followed by other positive experiences, results in disorders of the self, both in its structure and functioning.

Rank's strong emphasis on the issue of separation and the struggle of each individual to become an autonomous self led him to incorporate an existential, philosophical dimension into his psychological theory. The arduous process of building a self takes place within the context of the knowledge of its finitude, of its mortality. Therefore, Rank concluded, there is in human life a powerful motivation to immortalize, to perpetuate the self. For the vast majority of people immortality is achieved by having children or by identifying with what Rank termed an ideology—religious, political, or cultural—that would outlive the mortal self. For the artist in the broadest sense of that term, immortality is achieved through the creation of a product that is an expression of the self, a bid for its perpetuity and a contribution to society. Ernest Becker, who had a profound understanding of Rank, expresses this well when he writes: "Modern man became psychological because he became isolated from protective collective ideologies. He had to justify himself from within himself" (1973, p. 191). In other words, the structuring of an autonomous self became ever more crucial. The creative personality is more able to become an autonomous self than the average individual.

Kohut's concern with existential issues expresses itself in a sensitive awareness of the importance for each individual of preserving a sense of the purpose and meaningfulness in life. As the center of initiative, the self seeks to fulfill the ambitions and ideals that, through interaction with selfobjects, have become part of its structure. It is these goals and ideals that lend meaning to life, and a failure to fulfill them may result in disillusionment and an empty depression that are not uncharacteristic of late middle age—a time when the self seeks an accounting of its performance. Kohut refers to the conflicts that surround the resolution of the Oedipus complex as those of Guilty Man, and the conflicts that concern the fulfillment of the self as those of Tragic Man. While Rank is focused on the perpetuation of the self through immortalization, Kohut seeks self-realization as the way to achieve meaningfulness in life. The two are related and interdependent for there can be no immortality without the creative initiative of the will that leads to self-realization.

We are now left with the question of how the self psychology and the existential philosophy of these two thinkers influence their therapeutic approach. Both are convinced that knowledge and insight alone cannot be curative. For both Rank and Kohut, therapy must provide an opportunity for a restructuring of the self. This restructuring can only be achieved in the relationship between patient and therapist. Rank speaks of the therapist's acceptance and affirmation of the patient's total personality as the crucial factor in liberating him or her from excessive guilt and freeing the will (self) to function, for in Rank's view it is extreme guilt for autonomous willing that causes the neurotic inhibition of self functions. Kohut emphasizes the importance of an empathic relationship of therapist to patient so that the patient can take into himself the therapist's attitudes toward him, thereby replacing the flawed ones of childhood and thus reconstructing what was essentially a damaged self-structure. In other words, the therapist must be a more loving mirror for the patient than was the mother and must permit idealizations of himself that were insufficiently allowed in childhood by the patient's father. The therapist thus provides nutrients for a new formation of the self.

With different emphases, in part the result of differences in the historical time within which they developed their psychoanalytic ideas, both Rank and Kohut eschew the notion of the primacy of drives and would agree that processes within the self as it develops through interaction with significant others are most fundamental to an understanding of human psychology. They would also agree that "cure" for the patient involves not primarily the resolution of conflict but rather the reconstruction, through the internalization of new experiences, of a self initially burdened and inhibited by guilt and low self-esteem that can now function autonomously and creatively.

3

The Ethical
and the Empathic

In contemplating the psychology of the individual, it is possible to focus
on intrapsychic mechanisms, dynamisms, and structure, as did Freud, or
to adopt an interpersonal perspective and to view human thought, emotion, and behavior in the light of interactions between people, as did Rank.
The two approaches are certainly not mutually exclusive; in fact they complement each other, and each yields its own measure of truth about the human condition. At a time when infant research in the psychological field
was unknown, Rank had an intuitive sense about the nature of the bond
between mother and child. He sensed the depth of the attachment and the
pain of separation. He understood the striving of each individual in the
course of growth and development to become autonomous, and he recognized that the price for this delineation of self was a certain amount of
guilt. Rank referred to the nature of human relatedness, beginning with
the mother-child relationship, as ethical. He did not mean moral; he meant
related. He had no specific content in mind; no code of morals or superego
directives were part of his concept. However, although Rank did not explicitly speak of empathy in connection with his concept of ethical relatedness, the very word "related" inevitably implies an identification with the
person to whom one relates. Thus, in the interaction with another individual, the ethical and the empathic come together.

The origin of the ethical attitude resides in the mother-child relationship, and the potential for empathic feeling and understanding of one for the other comes from the fact that at one time they were one organism. The gradual separation of the "I" from the "Thou," initially through birth, leaves a residue of feeling for "the other," as if he or she were still part of oneself. In the human condition, therefore, the ethical-empathic stance is inherent since we all emerge both physically and psychologically from the mother's womb, literally and metaphorically.

This is an interesting variation on the issue of narcissism if one chooses to view the ethical phenomenon in this light. In Freudian libido theory, narcissism—whether primary or secondary—refers to the investment of the self with the sexual energy (libido) that, in the course of development, will properly be experienced in relation to a love-object. Rank does not speak in terms of instincts and their energies, but of the total organismic feeling of unity with which life begins—a unity that must be disturbed for a new individual to emerge. But the echo of the original oneness is felt and is expressed in empathy for the mother or for the child, as the case may be. This empathic seeing of oneself in the other could paradoxically perhaps be called narcissistic. However, if so, rather than viewing it pejoratively, I would, with Rank, prefer to call it the inevitably human way of knowing "the other." The ethical relatedness of individuals, informed as it is by empathy, attests to the primacy of the self. It is in this sense that the self spawn empathy.

Rank understood life to be a continuous process of emergence, both physically and psychologically. One of its chief characteristics is striving—striving toward the emergence of unique individuality. In the psychological realm of human development this striving expresses itself through the will of the individual. Rank defined the will as the strength of the "cosmic primal force" as it expresses itself in the emerging self. The self is creatively seeking ever higher goals both to define itself and to provide meaning and continuity for itself. Yet, although the will is the ultimate expression of the autonomy of the self, there always exists in every act of will, by implication, the presence of "another." In the abstract this "other" may be the life force expressing itself as will against the inevitability of death, that is, the will against fate. When Beethoven lost his hearing he vowed defiantly to grasp fate by the throat—a monumental expression of will! More specifically and concretely, it is the will of the individual asserting its separateness and difference from the will of another individual. This "other" was, of course, originally the mother, and observation of small children confirms the fact that the earliest expressions of will take the oppositional form of willfulness. However, since acts of will throughout life are acts of separation and autonomy, they oppose the oneness, the merging that once existed between mother and child and that continues in the inner life of the individual through all the internalized representations of the original relationship. It is this opposition of the will of the emerging individual to the ethical relatedness to others that creates conflict and guilt because of the human empathic capacity described above. Thus, for Rank, guilt is not primarily the product of the discrepancy between impulse and superego directives— although such guilt can also exist—but is the unavoidable price for individuation because of the empathic nature of human relatedness.

The will is an expression of the life force, which in turn fuels a creative evolutionary process that "may give rise to equally various kinds of individuality, from the physical self-identity of a metabolizing cell to the intangible but impressive individuality of an exceptional human being" (Langer 1967, p. 310). Because the function of willing is the legacy of this creative process and is itself creative, Rank coined the term *creative will* to express a spontaneous and freely arrived at act of will that is uniquely individual and is not predictable by any laws of causality. The creative will is responsible for a definite product, be it for example the creation of the self, of a work of art or literature, or of scientific discovery. The creative aspect of the will is intimately connected with the problem of guilt since as an act of self-assertion it is guilt-producing, whereas by producing a socially acceptable product it offers an opportunity to the individual to expiate the very guilt that the self-assertion has created.

It is because of the *creative* expression of the will that we leave the purely individual aspects of relatedness and forge a bond between the individual and larger social and cultural units. For all individuals there is some conflict between individual self-realization and societal demands, not only in the realm of the impulse life with the resultant formation of the superego, as Freud thought, but also in relation to the need to carve out a differentiated identity that is distinguishable from the larger social whole. This need is especially strong in the case of the exceptional individual to whom Rank referred as "the artist," meaning essentially all creative individuals who find expression for their uniqueness in products that are more or less accepted by society.

At this point in our discussion it is important to understand another dimension in Rank's conception of the motivation that leads individuals to strive toward creative expression. It is not only the impetus to achieve a

separation and autonomy of the self through the individual expression of
will but also the wish to immortalize that self that motivates creative activity. Rank believed not only in the inherency of the will but also in the fact
that there is a striving quality in the will that seeks "to reach for and create
ever higher levels in the realm of values and thus to perpetuate ourselves
beyond our material existence, to immortalize ourselves. We must therefore believe that there exists a spiritual dimension—be it actual or illusory—
for it is this belief, this faith, that sustains us and gives meaning to our
existence" (Menaker 1982, p. 5). It is this spiritual dimension, fed by the
creative will with its wish to immortalize the self, that is responsible for
the creation of culture.

The human creature among all living beings is alone in the possession
of consciousness that includes an awareness of self. This awareness has its
own line of development in the course of an individual life span, from the
small child's sense of self, first as a name, then as "I," to all the qualitative
differences of self-perception, self-activity, and self-evaluation that separate
a particular self from that of another. This dearly bought autonomous self
becomes aware early on that it is mortal, that like all living things its time
on earth is finite. Yet the self, in the course of evolution. has taken the striving
impulse to perpetuate life that characterizes the instinct life of the animal
world and has found ways of transcending the knowledge of death. In addition to the repression of the knowledge of death, which in some measure is
universal since a constant awareness of this fact would make life impossible,
the self feels that it can create perpetuity: first, biologically through the creation of succeeding generations, and second through its own self-realization
in the products of its creative will, that is, in culture.

Culture, according to Rank, is mankind's answer to the mortality-
immortality issue since it can create a limitless world of invention and
imagination outside the world of nature. Within nature the laws of life and
death prevail; in a *super*natural world (not to be confused with the occult),
that is, one outside or beyond nature, there is infinite opportunity for the
play of enduring expressions of the self.

Initially, when Rank was still under the influence of Freud, he viewed
culture as the product of the human attempt—especially of the exceptional
individual—to gratify libidinal drives by sublimating them through the creation of cultural products. The creative expression of the exceptional individual, that is, the "artist" in Rank's broad use of that term, meets not
only his own emotional needs but also those of society at large; the average
individual through the inherently human capacity for empathy can partici-

pate vicariously in the artist's creative experience and in the enjoyment of
the product as well. An interaction is thereby set up between the creative
individual and the larger social unit, and it is out of this interaction that
culture evolves. Like biological evolution itself, the process of cultural evolution has its stable as well as its changing forms. It is well known that the
creative innovations of exceptional individuals are often—especially initially—
rejected by society at large. The artist is ahead of his time; he is in the
vanguard of cultural evolutionary change. Ultimately, in the interaction
between the individual and society the products of his inventive imagination are accepted and assimilated in the culture of his time and place. A
change has taken place, and for a time, a new stability has been set up.

This interaction between the creative individual and his society is akin
to that of individuation and separation in the development of an individual
personality, and it eventuates in similar conflicts. For the individual, the
conflict in emerging as a separate self is that this striving is balanced by
the opposite wish to merge, to lose the self in a larger whole, thus abdicat-
ing the responsibilities of a discrete self and avoiding the mortality that
inevitably accompanies the emergence of that self. Both wishes—to emerge
and to merge—are guilt producing: the first because separation is an unempathic response vis-à-vis the oneness wished for by the "other," from
whom the individual is separating, and the second because merging is experienced as a betrayal of the wish and need to individuate.

In the psychological development of the individual, guilt is not only
the outcome of the conflict that reflects the will toward autonomy but also
plays a universal role in the history of culture according to Rank. As the
individual defies the oneness of the womb, so the products of culture defy
the limitations of the world of nature—notably death—by creating another
world that exists "beyond nature." It is the creative individual who is most
instrumental in the building of culture and who carries the burden of guilt
for his or her creativity. But human creativity in challenging the finitude
of life is not only guilt-producing, it also offers the opportunity for the
redemption of guilt by giving to society (i.e. to other individuals) the chance
to share in the creative experience of the individual artist's self-realization
and thereby in his or her immortality. For in the course of his own development Rank understood creativity to be motivated not solely, or even
primarily, by the need to sublimate libidinal impulses, but rather by the
human need for immortality.

Thus, the role of the exceptional individual—the artist—can be understood in ethical terms, for despite the fact that its primary emphasis is on

individual immortality, it implies relationship to society by the very presence of guilt that is expiated through the creative gift to society. "The evidence for such guilt is present throughout cultural history in the superstitions and rituals calculated to appease the existing gods and divert punishment in the form of natural disaster or death. Also in his religious and heroic myths man strives to account for his guilt in relationship to his conflict with God" (Rank in Menaker 1982, p. 59) In Rank's own words: "The heroic myth strives to justify this creative will through glorifying its deeds, while religion reminds man that he himself is but a creature dependent on cosmic forces. So the creative will automatically brings the guilt reaction with it as the self-reducing depression follows the manic elation. In a word, will and guilt are the two complementary sides of one and the same phenomenon" (p. 59).

Rank's psychology, his perception of man's position in the world, is rooted in the reality of ethical relatedness, yet suffused with an awareness of the anagogic character of the will. For in the striving for differentiation, for a fulfillment of the uniqueness that is each individual's heritage, the will functions creatively to produce ever higher goals and ideals. In this sense Rank can be said to advance not only a developmental but an evolutionary psychology as well. It is in the name of the need to immortalize the self that the will, as the active agent of the self, attempts to transcend the values of the predecessors from whom it would separate.

The dynamics of the relationship of the individual in his or her struggle to separate either from the familial or societal whole by way of the creation of a new and personal value system are particularly palpable in the case of the exceptionally creative individual. The artist or creative scientist not only differentiates himself through his works or inventions from the traditional modes and values to which he was born but often, in the course of his own development, also separates from certain aspects of his former self. Cultural change is thus brought about not only by the talent or genius of exceptional individuals and by their need to immortalize themselves, but by their courage to separate. In some measure such courage flies in the face of the ethical relatedness to others and the empathic awareness of their need for oneness. The need for self-realization and immortalization, supported by their existing special abilities, enables such creative individuals to transcend the cultural mores and to be instrumental in the creation of new values.

However, it is important to bear in mind that the artist's inevitable guilt for transcending his society is redeemed by the work that he gives to the community. It is as if ethical relatedness is concretized in the creative product. This not only meets the individual's need for expiation for what would classically be known as narcissism but also satisfies the need of the members of the community for identification with the exceptional individual's creativity, and ultimately with his or her immortality. Throughout cultural history, mankind gives us evidence for this communal need in the form of the heroic myths that all societies create. The hero, who is immortalized, is the carrier of the transcendent values to which the societal group aspires. In this sense the artist and the hero coincide. The former, however, expresses the individual will to autonomy; the latter, the collectively projected ideal figure with whom each individual can identify and can attempt to emulate.

The actual content of the ideals and values that are embodied in the person and behavior of a culture-hero vary and change with historical time and place. Thus, they are not absolute, but are relative to a particular cultural milieu and are a response to the collective need of the group at a given time. Rank was keenly aware of this relationship between the societal need for particular values at a given historical period and the collective creation of a heroic figure to meet that need. He illustrates this process in his profoundly moving writings on the origins of Christianity in which he understood the messianic need of the Jewish people as an important cultural root of the emergence of Jesus. The appearance of Christianity out of the collective need of the Jews was a revolutionary event and ushered in not only a new religion but also a new psychological dimension—a sense of individual personality that had scarcely existed previously. Rank writes: "Like the Jews, the early Christians put faith above everything—state and country; but with the important difference that instead of a realistic deliverance through the Messiah *an inner experience and change in the individual self was the salvation.*" It is as if a *change* in the self in terms of new values expressed as a new faith created the awareness for the individual of the fact that he or she had a self—a unique personality—to begin with. Like Albert Schweitzer before him, Rank attributes the development of Christianity, and with it the sense of self for the individual, to the conversion of Paul at Damascus. In becoming Jesus' ardent disciple, Paul experienced a new spirit of life and was imbued with the belief that "Christ was actually living in him." This "was not merely psychological identification, but real identity" (Rank 1958). Paul was born into a new sense of self and became an ideal for others who, as he taught, could, through faith, be awakened to a new self.

This "living in Christ" is akin to the oneness that Rank described as characteristic of the mother-child relationship. In the realm of religion such oneness with a spiritual ideal becomes the source of a collective ethic. It is interesting and seemingly paradoxical that the oneness, be it in a religion or other ideological experience, delineates the self, creates the person as it were, while at the same time the merging with a collective ideal enables the individual to lose himself within a larger whole, thus guaranteeing him a measure of immortality.

Of all the early psychoanalysts and depth psychologists, it is Otto Rank who understood the ethical nature and inevitability of the human conflict between self-interest—the will to be and to express one's unique self—and the will of another person. This conflict stems from the capacity for empathy and eventuates in guilt. Yet, Rank was not pessimistic about human destiny. He thought that the human creature could carry the burden of a certain amount of guilt and that the will when expressed creatively could expiate the rest. But more than this, the will can be implemented creatively to accept life's inevitabilities. He called this implementation "the volitional affirmation of the obligatory." The ethical conflict falls within the category of the obligatory as does death itself. But humankind has the capacity voluntarily to say "yes" to the nature of human interaction and to life itself. Rank's understanding of life goes "beyond psychology" to a profound philosophical acceptance of the human dilemma.

4

Self, Will,
and Empathy

When I mentioned the title "Self, Will, and Empathy," to a friend as a subject I would be writing about, he remarked, "Does anyone combine such formidable subjects into one paper?" My answer was that although these concepts are indeed formidable, they are interconnected, and it is to their relationship that I wish to address myself. In fact, it was a sudden understanding of the interdependence of self and empathy, a kind of "aha" experience, that alerted me to the importance of exploring the interpersonal, as well as the cultural dimension in each of these concepts.

I was viewing a documentary film about recent archeological finds of the Maya civilization in Tikal in Guatemala. I had been there a few years ago when much less was known about Mayan culture, largely because the fuller deciphering of their hieroglyphics had not yet been accomplished. Now we know much more about the structure of their society, their economy, and their religion. It has been clearly documented that in their religious rites they practiced human sacrifice. The altars and artifacts as well as the writings concerning this practice have been preserved. To us, whatever our present barbarisms, this practice is savagery indeed. We cannot identify with it; in fact, we are repelled by it. Whether it was because of the scientific detachment of the young curators reporting the findings, or the facts themselves and the projection of my imagination into that time and place, I was suddenly struck by the extent to which the ritual of human sacrifice, at least from our vantage point, seems to connote a complete lack of empathy with the victim. Perhaps this seems fairly obvious; yet it raises questions about the nature of the self, its relationship to empathy, and the relationship of both to culture.

First, what do we mean by empathy? It is the capacity, through sensitive perception and understanding, to feel what another individual is experiencing emotionally. Weigert cites Max Scheler's definition of "empathy as a form of emotional contagion based on a process of identification" (Weigert 1962, p. 146). It is characteristically a human quality, although domestic animals have been known to show signs of empathic relatedness. However, although animals, infants, and small children react to the emotions of those on whom they are dependent, such reactions are forerunners of empathy since they precede a clear and consolidated sense of self. Emotional identification with another individual requires an awareness and functioning of self in order for the process of creating analogies, which is essential to empathic relatedness, to take place. Such identification combines an imaginative projection of oneself into the emotional life of another with an introspective awareness of analogous experiences and emotions in one's own life. On this basis one might correctly assume that although there are great individual differences as well as a variety of other factors that determine a person's empathic capacity, in general, empathy increases with age and experience. It is a function of the maturation of the self—mostly in the sense of its autonomy.

Still the individuated sense of self and the capacity to make analogies and thereby to identify with another person are not enough to bring about an empathic response. There must be the will to create and implement the empathic understanding of, relatedness to, and communication with another individual. It is *will* that activates the self. But before we enter into a discussion of will, let us go back to my reaction to the primitive ritual of human sacrifice. I assumed a lack of empathy on the part of the religious community with the sacrificial victim. My assumption was subjective, based on values that respect individual life more than the religious ideology of the Mayans. But suppose this was not the case; suppose I was committed to their religious beliefs. What would it tell me about myself, about them, and about empathy? I, as well as the Mayans, would be merged in a communal cultural ideology. As a result we would all identify with the blood ritual. Perhaps even the victim, as a product of that culture, would not feel entirely victimized. And what happens to empathy under these circumstances? It seems to become greatly reduced, if not to disappear entirely;

for the identification that is essential to the empathic response is consumed in the commitment to the common belief. It would seem that empathy requires a clearly individuated self that is able to identify with and value the individual experience and feeling of another.

It is interesting to compare and contrast speculatively what might be two very different approaches to and interpretations of the mass phenomenon of a religious ritual involving human sacrifice: that of Freud and that of Rank. In "Group Psychology and the Analysis of the Ego," Freud (1921) clearly understood that emotional contagion can occur in a collective experience. He interpreted it as a regression to an earlier phase of libido development—in this case, to a sadistic phase—that is triggered by the need for dependency on a parental leader or a leading idea or common ego-ideal. Although Freud speaks of a loss of rational orientation, he does not speak of a loss of self. Otto Rank on the other hand would interpret such a mass phenomenon in terms of the needs of the self. The individual self, so dearly bought through lifetime processes of separation and individuation, fears its own finitude and seeks ways to immortalize itself. The creative individual does so through his or her creative products; parenthetically, it is important to note that Rank saw creativity not only in the artist but also in the ordinary individual, in fact, in the very creation of the self. Thus, the fulfillment of the creative potential of the self was for Rank a major path to immortality. But there was another way to immortality: the merging of the self with what Rank called a communal ideology. In the belief that the ideology will survive beyond the individual, the mortal self identifies with and merges in a common belief in the name of immortality. This was as true for the Mayan religious rituals as for any current ideology. The merging meets a basic need of the self—the need for immortality—but it also causes a partial loss of that self in terms of autonomy. Thus, both in Freud's and in Rank's explanation of a mass phenomenon there is a regression—in one case in terms of instinctual need, in the other in terms of self need. In either case there is a loss of self with a resultant loss of empathy.

In modern times the loss of empathy as a result of the loss of self in a mass movement is clearly and brutally illustrated by the German Nazi movement and the extermination of the Jews. All the rationalization that made such inhumanity possible—the theories of racial superiority, the xenophobia, the paranoid fears—served to create an identification with a communal ideology that enabled the individual to merge with the mass at the expense of the individual autonomy of the self, with an accompanying and inevitable loss of empathy. It is almost axiomatic that mass movements, which by their very nature invite a loss of self, also create a loss of empathy for those outside the movement unless an ideology of empathy is specifically built into the philosophy of the movement. Such is the case in certain religious ideologies, for example, Judaism and Christianity, wherein love and charity are taught as part of the religion. Yet even then, as history so unequivocally confirms, the empathic features of the teachings are often overshadowed or completely lost in favor of other aspects of the ideology. So great is the human need to give up the self, certainly a large part of the self, in order to be guaranteed meaningfulness, belonging, and perpetuity through identification with a mass ideology.

What characterizes the self that so paradoxically seeks to lose itself while also aiming to delineate itself, and how is it to be differentiated from the ego? In early psychoanalytic theory ego and self were not clearly distinguished. In fact Freud often used the terms loosely and interchangeably. However, the emphasis was on ego functions—on reality testing, on ego as the seat of anxiety, as the executor of the censorship on impulses and especially on defensive function. The self as representing the total personality was rarely considered, although Erikson (1950) wrote about "identity," a term akin to the concept of self. Later, as exemplified in the work of Hartmann (1950) and Jacobson (1964), the ego was understood to be the active agent of the self that represented the total personality. I would like to add that it is the will that activates the ego.

It is often difficult to express such interrelationships without giving the impression of the reification of static entities. Instead, I think of self, ego, and will as processes in continuous developmental movement throughout life. From its original emergence from the maternal matrix, through various phases of life during which many environmental influences play upon it, the individual self is constantly growing, changing, and choosing.

I wrote "individual self" because perhaps the single most important and distinguishing feature of the self is its uniqueness. For although generalizations can be made about the emergence of the self and about the anxiety that accompanies processes of growth and separation-individuation, it is the specificity of each individual as expressed in the nature of the self that is of utmost importance for his or her self-image and that is crucial for the expression of empathy in the therapeutic interaction.

Except in the work of Rank, the uniqueness of the self has been insufficiently appreciated in psychoanalytic theory and practice. Very early in psychoanalytic history he focused on the issue of separation: first literally in the individual's birth experience and later in terms of psychological birth, that is, the gradual emergence of autonomy from parental figures, especially the mother. Rank viewed this process as a creative one, and therefore the self that is thus structured is the particular product of original given characteristics interacting with the specific experience of the individual. The outcome in this conception of the growth of the self cannot be predicted. Like the created work of an artist, the self-created self is unknown and unknowable in its potentialities; although external influences impinge upon its growth and development, the final outcome, which actually is not final but rather a never-ending process, is the result of the operation of the individual's creative will. To understand the growth of personality as a creative process with limitless possibilities, resulting in a unique, individuated self, is in complete opposition to a deterministic viewpoint that applies general developmental principles—some poorly founded—as well as personality assessments to predictions concerning the health, viability, strength, and social and emotional functioning of the self. It was Rank who developed his creative conception of personality growth in opposition to the deterministic standpoint of classic psychoanalysis. And according to him it is the will that implements the individual's creative potential. Currently it is in the work of Kohut (1977), with its emphasis on an introspective-empathic stance that enables the psychological observer to regard the individual self as a center of initiative, that we find opposition to the deterministic viewpoint of classical psychoanalysis, which cannot account for the phenomena of choice, decision, and free will.

Yet, before embarking on a discussion of will, let me emphasize and illustrate the active striving of the self to continue the process of consolidating and structuring itself. The object relations theorists, for example Fairbairn (1954) and Guntrip (1964), speak of the ego as having a primary existence, however rudimentary, from the beginning of life. And contrary to the classical Freudian view I see this ego not as a derivative of the inevitable deprivations and frustrations in the early interactions of the child with the mother, but as actively "object-seeking," that is, searching for emotional relatedness to significant others who would provide psychological nutrients for the further structuring of the self.

In studying the case of individuals whose self is fragmented or lacks consolidation due to conflicting identifications or developmental arrests, we can sometimes observe the efforts of the self to effect such a consolidation. In a paper written in 1979, I described the effort of a young ballet dancer who suffered from anorexia to overcome her depression and apathy by implementing a particular fantasy as she awoke in the morning. In the fantasy she saw herself as a sort of Peter Pan character, wearing a moss green cap and dancing on a deserted beach. As she lived herself into this imagery, she came alive. She succeeded, through a volitional effort, in consolidating her otherwise fragmented self. The same patient, who at one point in treatment experienced a severe schizoid withdrawal that reflected a lack of cohesion in the nature of her "self," actively sought new identifications as a way of rescuing her personality from disintegration. This creative effort took the form of learning a new language—French in her case—which she learned within a few months and which she spoke fluently. She had established a close friendship with a French roommate and through her had not only acquired the language but also had completely identified with French culture, eventually going to France to live there for several years.

The acquisition of new internalizations to supersede the original conflictful ones with parental figures seems to be exemplified in the creative effort of my young patient to restructure her self. It is the work of the will—that force within personality that under normal circumstances is available for creative productivity, including the formation of the self.

The term *will* has come into ill repute in psychology. It is associated with the old facultative psychology and with the concept of willpower. Freud's discovery of a dynamic unconscious as a major determinant in human feeling, thinking, and action minimized the work of individual responsibility and effort to a great extent. The work of psychology and psychotherapy was colored by a deterministic, reductionistic point of view. In fact the word *will* does not appear in Freud's writings nor in those of his followers. It is not until the work of Otto Rank, who began his career as an analyst but who later deviated importantly from classical Freudian theory, that will became a crucial dimension in human life, one to be understood and reckoned with, especially in therapy.

It is not surprising that the will has been shunned by Freudian psychology since it is so intimately connected with the ego or self, and concern with the ego came late in the development of psychoanalytic theory and then largely as a derivative agent of personality caught between the imperatives of the drives and the superego. The function of "willing" depends on a conception of the self as primary. Later in psychoanalytic history, especially in the work of the object-relations theorists, for example, Fairbairn and Guntrip, there is room for a conception of ego as primary. For Rank, too, the ego, and one could include the concept of self, is primary. It is the agent of the cosmic life force, and the strength of this force represented in the individual that Rank calls "will." In referring to the "cosmic primal force" Rank does not mean some mystical power, but the energic nature of the universe, especially the living universe. This force manifests itself in the human because of consciousness and especially self-consciousness, not solely in adaptation to the environment but also in a psychological interchange between inner and outer reality that can result in a freely chosen modification of either or both. It is such action that Rank calls creative as distinguished from adaptive and that he considers a will phenomenon.

After a recent talk in which I dealt with Rank's theory of the will, I was asked whether will is conscious or unconscious. It is interesting that Rank was not especially mindful of this question; I would assume that he took it for granted that all psychic phenomena can be plotted on a continuum between the unconscious and conscious. In the writings of Brentano and Husserl (in May 1969), with the coining of the term *intentionality*, a bridge between the unconscious and conscious aspects of *willing* is created in that every act of will is in some measure determined by a matrix of meaning that is not usually present in conscious awareness. This issue is clearly dealt with by May (1969). However, the matrix of meaning or that which is "intended" is itself an accumulation of remembered experience, experience arrived at through innumerable acts of will. What interested Rank was the positive, creative aspect of the will as it represents the organizing force through which the uniqueness of the individual is created. In the individual act of will Rank saw a new source of causality within the individual. He wrote, "Only in the individual act of will do we have the unique phenomenon of spontaneity, the establishing of a new primary cause" (1945, p. 44). The emphasis here should be on the word " individual," for it is in the fact of differences in individuality that there is the possibility of a freely arrived at act of will, unbound by any predictable quality that identifies man as the creator of himself and defines his relationship to outer reality.

Thus, the will plays a major role in the formation of the self, as the example of the young ballerina, our work with patients, and our own lives confirm. But the achieving of an autonomous self is not easy; it is a lifelong struggle involving the consolidation of identifications with significant others, as well as a series of separations from them on the road to individuation. Primary among separations of course is the child's separation from the mother, first in the actual act of birth and then in all the subsequent phases of maturation. In addition, there are significant relationships throughout life from which the individual must part, again either in actuality or in terms of the emotional re-evaluation of internalized imagoes. These processes are often painful, and the individual is sometimes overwhelmed by a feeling of helplessness, especially in the final separation with which life faces us, namely death. Here it would seem the will of the individual has no function. The hard-won self must resign itself to the loss of loved ones and to its own extinction. Seemingly, one cannot will it otherwise. Yet, Rank had a solution that included the function of the will, a solution that to some extent at least, dispelled the feeling of helplessness. He expressed it in the phrase: "the volitional affirmation of the obligatory." Instead of resignation, the will is able actively to say "yes" to the nature of life—and to death. The "volitional affirmation" is an active function of the will; the obligatory refers to the painful tasks of life, especially to separations. William James, in struggling to overcome his severe depression, arrived at a similar point when he said: "So be it."

This view of the ultimate function of will, which amounts to a philosophy of life is of special importance in therapeutic work because it is the therapist's affirmation of the patient's will and therefore of the self that is a principal curative factor. The vehicle for such affirmation is empathy, and it is at this point that will, self, and empathy meet. Whatever the particular form or content of an individual's emotional disturbance, we can justifiably assume that the person who seeks out therapy is suffering from some deficit in self-structure and is therefore inhibited in the function of the will. And experience teaches us that the resolution of the separation conflict is crucial for the emergence of an autonomous self. But before separation can occur successfully, there must be an opportunity for union, for identification. It is the empathic understanding of the therapist that enables the patient to identify with him or her, thus creating the oneness from which the patient can then separate to become an individuated self without undue conflict.

Sometimes one can make a point by describing an event that is the opposite of what one would regard as appropriate. I would like to illustrate the importance of empathic understanding by describing a therapeutic session in which I failed in such understanding. It concerns a young woman in her late twenties whom I shall call Margaret. She has aspirations to be an actress and has done well when she has had an opportunity to perform, but gets into difficulty with directors, acting teachers, and colleagues whenever there are disagreements about acting techniques. Needless to say her career has not proceeded smoothly, and at the time of this incident she was quite depressed. She is an only child of parents who are both extremely ambivalent in their reactions to her and had always been so throughout her childhood. She recalls an incident when she was about 3 years old when her mother left her in the care of her father for a few hours. The little girl, seeing her mother leave, began to cry. This so enraged her father that he spanked her mercilessly. He has never been a comfort to her, is unsympathetic with her ambitions, never encourages her, and is in fact often withdrawn and uncommunicative. Her mother vacillates in her reactions. At times she is helpful and supportive; at other times she can be tactless, detached, and critical.

Recently Margaret had put on a performance of her own: producing and acting in it, arranging the stage set and the costuming as well. A young man of her acquaintance acted as director. The performance was successful, and he has continued to be in contact with her and to be generally helpful. However, he can be somewhat temperamental, and recently, in an early morning phone call he commented that she sounded "horrendous." Margaret took profound offense at the terminology and in reporting the incident to me in the session began to inveigh against the young man. Instead of maintaining a noncommittal attitude I commented that at times her voice was indeed so depressed, so lacking in energy as to be irritating. I was referring to the way in which she announced herself on the intercom when she came to her session. Naturally she became furious, accusing me of insensitivity, of taking her friend's side, of failing to understand her. She was right; I had not understood her need—a need to unite with me in her anger toward her friend. But dimly I perceived that she was repeating something out of childhood, and I mentioned the incident that had occurred with her father when she was 3 years old, emphasizing his failure to understand her fear of separation from her mother. In reply she told another story that clarified the issues still further. When she was a child of 6 or 7 some children with whom she had been playing teased her and, in the hostile exchanges that took place, tore her dress. She ran home crying but her mother, instead of sympathizing with her plight, blamed her for the incident, saying that she must have done something to the others that provoked their behavior. Clearly I fell into the trap of her repetition in the transference of the emotions that characterized her interaction with her mother. She sought affirmation from and a oneness with her mother then; she sought the same from me now. The fact that indeed she may have provoked the rejecting reactions of others then and now becomes important analytically only after she has experienced·the affirmation. For it is the empathic understanding of her needs and reactions as they express themselves first in the therapist's acceptance of her "self" as it *is* that strengthens it sufficiently to liberate the function of her will, the will to choose growth, change, and separation.

Fortunately I was able, despite my initial error, to retrieve Margaret's trust, and with great relief she experienced my making the connection between her childhood memory and her interaction with me as an empathic act on my part. Certainly Margaret has as yet not achieved sufficient emotional autonomy. But this brief encounter illustrates the need for oneness of the self with the other in an atmosphere of acceptance before there can be a consolidation of individual and separate identity.

Empathically affirming the self and will of another represents an emotional understanding of his or her intentionality, that is, of the matrix of meaning out of which he or she functions. We feel ourselves into the other's meaning by analogy with our own experience. The use of analogy is often productive in our therapeutic work when we hope among other things to change or modify the patient's structure of meaning, so that in the case of Margaret, for example, she would not continue to relate to others out of the need to merge nor to resort to all the strategies that would make the realization of such need possible.

Paradoxical as it may seem, it is essential to affirm the self as well as the will of another individual before insight and understanding can contribute to change and growth. Such affirmation is the outgrowth of empathy, and the capacity for empathy is, in turn, the product of a clearly and securely delineated self.

5

Empathy in the Therapeutic Situation

Many years ago when Molière, the seventeenth century French dramatist, wrote *Le Bourgeois Gentilhomme* satirizing the attempt of the newly rich to acquire culture, he created a scene in which the central character is being taught the difference between poetry and prose by his tutor. Suddenly he is overwhelmed by the discovery that he has been speaking prose all his life. It is something like that with empathy. All our lives we have been using empathy in our interactions with people, especially in our attempts to understand them. But it is to Heinz Kohut that we owe the attempt to formalize our understanding of empathy itself—to define it, to describe its role in the course of human development, and to point out its indispensableness in the psychotherapeutic process.

In the development of psychoanalysis the awareness of empathy appears early in its history: first in the writings of Freud himself. In *Group Psychology and the Analysis of the Ego*, Freud (1921, p. 42) speaks of "a path [that] leads from identification by way of imitation to empathy" and concludes that it is the way to the comprehension of another's mental life. Ferenczi and Rank were aware of the importance of empathy in the therapeutic process, and in 1962 Edith Weigert wrote an important paper called "Empathy, Sympathy and Freedom in Psychoanalysis."

Is the ability to feel ourselves into the situation, the feelings, and thoughts of another human being an exclusively human phenomenon, or is there evidence for its existence in the animal world? We have all heard anecdotes that reveal the empathic understanding of domesticated animals for the emotions of their masters. But this begs the question of the psychobiologic precursors of the capacity for empathy. What about animals in the wild? In reading Susan Langer (1967), for example, in her study called *Mind: An Essay on Human Feeling*, one has the impression that empathy is an archaic evolutionary mechanism of perception and communication among socially organized animals such as wolves or subhuman primates who live in groups. The attunement to the emotional state and behavior of others is essential for survival since it prevents the attack of individuals upon one another. They are in tune with one another as a group and are programmed as a unit to respond to the behavior of the leader. Thus, we must conclude that the ability to feel oneself into the mental state of another has its forerunners in the animal world.

In humans, infant research shows us that this ability is most likely present at birth. R. W. Restak (1984), in an article that attempts to explore possible neurophysiological correlates of empathic reactions, describes the attunement of an 8-day-old infant to a parent's (in this case the father's) receptivity to the infant's need to relax and fall asleep. The interaction that leads to this result is not only, and obviously nonverbal, but is also so subtle and finely tuned that it can only be perceived in the slow-motion replay of the videotaped recording of the event. Restak (1984) calls this kind of synchronization of behavior and feeling on the part of parent and child *mutual entrainment*, and sees it as a rhythmical process: "where formerly two rhythms existed, now there is only a single rhythm . . . the infant-parent pairs come gradually into 'synch' with each other. It is this tendency toward the formation of a shared rhythm that yields the best metaphor for the empathic process" (p. 63). Personally I have often thought of this human ability to synchronize separate units of experience into a cohesive whole as a kind of dance—a pas de deux or a tango—in which each individual perceives the message of the other through an empathic process and, in responding, creates a whole.

Kohut perceived the importance of the empathic process for the field of psychoanalysis. For him it is a tool of observation, a mode of cognition, a vicarious introspection. In order to grasp the patient's emotional dilemma, the analyst must feel him- or herself into the reality of the world of the patient's self. There are analogous experiences in the field of aesthetics. For example, in a recent radio interview Claudio Arrau, the celebrated pianist, spoke of the task of interpreting music. Referring to a Beethoven sonata that he had just played, he said, "One must feel oneself in to the music; one must not become Beethoven but—" and then he hesitated. Clearly he did not wish to suggest that the interpretive artist must achieve an identity with the composer, nor that he should be solely and entirely himself. The task is an empathic and seemingly paradoxical one. The performer must empathize sufficiently with the composer to grasp and convey his meaning and yet retain enough of his or her own reaction to lend the interpretation the stamp of his own personality.

It is not very different in the analytic situation. The analyst must use his empathic ability to feel him- or herself into the life and feelings of the patient in order to understand him or her, and yet retain the boundaries of his own personality so that he may express his understanding in his own unique way.

However, in regard to the use of empathy in therapy as a tool of observation, more is involved than understanding. Although Kohut mentions the unfortunate possibility that the understanding acquired through empathic in-tuneness with the patient can be used destructively in a confrontational way, he emphasizes the need to respond compassionately if one wishes to avoid repeating the very situation in the patient's family that, in early childhood, gave rise to the deficiencies in self-structure for which the patient seeks help. Thus, although empathy may be viewed as a method of observation, the very fact that it creates a oneness—however limited or transitory—between patient and analyst also makes it a communication of caring and concern. Kohut (1984) conveys his meaning clearly in a small example.

> If a patient tells me how hurt he was because I was a minute late or because I did not respond to his prideful story of a success, should I tell him that his responses are unrealistic? Should I tell him that his perception of reality is distorted and that he is confusing me with his father or mother? Or, should I rather say to him that we are all sensitive to the actions of people around us who have come to be as important to us as our parents were to us long ago and that, in view of his mother's unpredictability and his father's disinterest in him, his perception of the significance of my actions and omissions has been understandably heightened and his reactions to them intensified. [p. 176]

Kohut definitively opts for the latter response. This is clearly an empathic communication because it respects the patient's narcissistic vulnerability, and because in such phrases such as "we all are sensitive" or "has understandably heightened" your reactions, the emphasis is away from pathology; and through the emphasis on the commonality of experience an opportunity is created for identification with the analyst, thus promoting growth and change. The empathic response produces an empathic echo in the patient, which is directed toward the analyst. The result is a mutuality of empathic observation, and the therapeutic situation begins to resemble a dialogue between two individuals in which one of the participants does indeed have a framework of psychological knowledge that helps organize and make more understandable the communications of the person seeking help, but in which the analysand is also an active participant.

Let me describe to you the ongoing therapy of a middle-aged woman in which the role of empathy is clearly the driving motor of the undertaking. Carol is a professional, unmarried woman in her early fifties who consulted me because of an almost total paralysis of all her activities that was accompanied by severe depression. I have rarely encountered such a complete manifestation of inertia. She had worked in the field of computer science, but was unemployed at the time that she consulted me. She reported that her home was in disarray; there were projects that she had begun in an attempt to eliminate the chaos in her apartment and to create more space for her belongings, but they all remained uncompleted. She could not look for a job because she could not organize or write up her resume, and she could not get help with this task because her pride would not allow her to ask for help—even professional help for which she would pay. That she did, of course, come to me for help must be an indication of the extent of her despair.

Mistakenly, I began by trying to help her at least think about how to go about getting a job. We discussed the putting together of her curriculum vitae. I consulted a friend of mine who had had experience in my patient's particular area of expertise, endeavoring to get help with how best to set up the resume. I told Carol about this consultation. My patient made a few feeble attempts to put her resume together, but it was clear that my help was not taking hold. However, it is important that Carol was aware of my good intentions. It set the stage for what was later to become the empathic exchange between us. We began by talking about her apartment, and she told me about some carpentry work she was doing. She needed shelf and cabinet space, but her inertia kept her from working efficiently and from completing the job. I know something about design, about wood, about the difficulties that her job might present. For several sessions we discussed veneers, glue, stains, and measurements. The job was proceeding, if somewhat slowly. But a growing relationship was developing between us; in fact Carol became so sensitive and perceptive to what was going on in my mind and to what I was about to say that often she would pre-empt my remarks. We both enjoyed the humor in this situation. It is perhaps important to mention that Carol had some psychoanalytic therapy previously; most of it was of a traditional nature, and I was careful not to hand down stereotypic interpretations with which Carol was all too familiar (which I was not inclined to do in any case) and that had not been particularly helpful to her.

One day, something changed. Carol reported that a few days previously she had had a new awareness of her emotions and of her body. She had been doing the carpentry work in the evening, When her usual bedtime approached she realized that she did not want to go to bed. She gave in to her wish, stayed up, and continued to work. She said she actually *enjoyed* the time she was awake. She emphasized the word "enjoyed" as if at other times she would either have been too guilty or too unaware of her feelings and of her body to be able to enjoy herself. In this state of enjoyment a childhood memory came to her. She recaptured an image of herself in kindergarten as a little girl of 5 years wearing a little smock, standing before an easel with a paint brush in her hand. She fancied herself an artist, although where the image of an artist came from in her life we have not yet discovered, for she never drew or painted outside of the kindergarten experience nor was her family in any way connected to the world of art or artists. The memory was an extremely happy one, primarily because of the awareness of self. At that moment in front of the easel she had a sense of who she was—in fact, of being someone at all—for most of the time she lacked a sense of self. In the grip of these recollections Carol told me more about her efforts as a child to achieve some sense of self.

In her childhood home there was a large canvas bag like a laundry bag in which photographs that had accumulated over the years were kept. She remembers as a child going through these pictures one by one looking for pictures of herself as a child—or at least, any picture. There were none. There were photographs of siblings—an older sister and brother. She once asked her mother why there were no pictures of herself. The reply was that she was so beautiful that her parents had sent all her pictures to relatives in Europe. Whether there is truth in this statement or whether it is an invented excuse is irrelevant since in either case it attests to the indifference of Carol's parents to her as a person. For them she was apparently an object for their narcissistic gratification.

"How do you know who you are, what you are, how you look, if no one tells you?" added my patient. "Your mother failed to hold a mirror up to you," I replied.

Carol responded with another story—a story of a learning experience in which, metaphorically speaking, a mirror was held up to her for imitation. She had always been athletically inclined, but in learning to ski she had had some difficulty with certain movements. Once, when she was taking some lessons, she encountered on a ski slope a particularly patient and persistent teacher. Over and over again he tried to show her how to achieve a particular maneuver, but to no avail. Finally he instructed her to follow him as closely as possible—the tip of her skis almost touching the back of his. At first she was afraid, but as she did what he had instructed her to do and imitated his every move, thereby achieving her own mastery, she felt exhilarated, even ecstatic. The feeling returned as she told the story.

What does this story tell about the self and about empathy? We know from Kohut's work that the cohesion of the self depends heavily on what he calls the positive mirroring experience, i.e., the pleasurable in-tuneness with her child that the mother conveys to him or her in every aspect of their interaction. Her face is the mirror in which the child sees his or her worthwhileness. It is largely through the mother's empathic affirmation that the child—through the internalization of the mother's image of him or her—is born psychologically, that the self is consolidated and that he or she acquires the right to a separate existence. My patient Carol had an insufficient or faulty experience of positive mirroring within her family and probably especially in relation to her mother from whom it was most needed. At an early age, in a smock and with a paint brush in hand she created an abstract identity, the artist, which she experienced primarily through pleasurable body sensations—sensations that she re-experienced when she chose to assert and follow her own inclinations and to stay up into the night to do her own work.

This is a small beginning in the break in her inertia and her depression. In empathic resonance with what she feels to be my affirmation of her activities, of her lifestyle, indeed of her very "self," she is able to affirm her own wishes—to work into the night on her own project.

It is important to note that I began my interaction with Carol with a somewhat faulty empathy. I began pragmatically with the job issue, hoping that if she got a job and felt psychologically more secure we could then work on other issues. It is good that I did not impose my agenda on her, for her basic sense of security depended not upon a job (although she desperately needs this too), but upon her perceiving my capacity to be interested in, encourage, and affirm these activities that were of primary importance to her. This was the true expression of my empathic understanding. I cannot tell you how I perceived the hunger of the fragile, undernourished self for nurturance from someone who would understand the nature and content of the need and be able to respond to it. It was certainly not expressed verbally, especially by someone who could not ask for help in preparing a resume! We rely so much—probably too much—on verbal communication that nonverbal understanding seems somewhat mysterious to us. Yet, my perception must have been based on nonverbal cues, as is so often the case with empathic responses. However, in the therapeutic situation the empathic resonance is like a chemical equation that describes a reaction that goes in both directions. The patient empathically perceives the therapist's attunement and capacity for empathic response; the therapist resonates to this perception with his or her own empathic understanding much as a mother responds to the needs and expectations of her infant. And so the process of mutual empathic interaction is set in motion. Kohut alludes to this process when he writes "in the course of successful analyses [the analysands] became increasingly able to evoke the empathic resonance of mature self-objects and to be sustained by them" (1984, p. 66). It is Kohut's great contribution to have pointed out the central role of the empathic stance in the therapeutic analytic situation—beyond insight and beyond interpretation. It is also crucial in the interaction of individuals as they seek to live with others.

6

The Continuing Search
for the Selfobject

The introduction of self psychology into psychoanalytic theory represents a monumental evolutionary advance. Heinz Kohut shifted the emphasis from a conception of human psychology as developing under the aegis of the pleasure principle to a view of personality, and specifically the self, as motivated by a primary driving force to fulfill its potentiality. Although drives exist and play a role in human development, their gratification is not the prime mover in human affairs. It is the fulfillment of the optimal structuring and cohesion of the self that provides the overriding motivation for the growth and development of human life. This process takes place within the context of interaction and communication between individuals; indeed, social interaction is essential for the structuring of the self.

The importance of communication with others for the development and continuing mental health of an individual was brought home to me very dramatically through a television program that moved me very deeply. It was an interview with Winny Mandela. She described the history of her involvement with the anti-apartheid movement in South Africa, but above all she gave a detailed account of her imprisonment by the South African government for 16 months in solitary confinement. She was confined to a cell that was so small that she could touch its walls on all sides with outstretched arms. The cell contained the barest necessities for the maintenance of life. Food was kicked along the floor into the cell by a guard. There was no contact with another human being. "It is the absence of communication that is so devastating," she said. "It is impossible to imagine what happens to the mind. I found myself talking to my children as if they were there. If an ant or a fly entered the cell it was a good day."

This tragic description of the effects of isolation from human interaction not only touched me deeply but also turned my thoughts to the issue of communication in psychoanalytic theory and practice. Classically, psychoanalytic treatment was to take place in the context of abstinence: there were to be no instinctual gratifications either in life or in the treatment situation. Few analysts held to this principle of abstinence when it concerned the patient's life situation, although in the early days there were some, like Herman Nunberg (1932), who tried to forbid sexual activity of any kind during analysis. The purpose of creating this frustration was to elicit expressions of unconscious instinctual need and fantasy. However, in the treatment situation, "abstinence" was achieved through the absence of the analyst's response or interaction, through his or her relative silence. The function of the analyst's unresponsiveness was supposedly to induce expressions of the unconscious, i.e. to "break" the controlling, governing function of the conscious ego. Inevitably for the patient, the analyst's unresponsiveness is experienced as hostile and punitive. Although the patient can *learn* that the analyst's silence is not his or her doing and can therefore be tolerated as a technical device for revealing the unconscious, one might legitimately wonder whether these mini-isolations are of therapeutic value or whether, like the solitary confinement, they are destructive to the integrity of the self. The comparison is, of course, extreme and exaggerated, but it makes clear the universality of the need for human contact and communication.

With the increasing impersonality of human interaction in the workplace and the detachment of sexuality from emotions of attachment—affection and love—the primary need of patients today is precisely for human communication. It was different in the early days of psychoanalysis when patients came to treatment to be cured of symptoms—hysterical conversions, obsessional thoughts, or compulsive behavior. Then the uncovering of unconscious impulses, which were in large measure responsible for symptom formation, was helpful and appropriate. But social change has brought new problems and new needs. Individuals now seek help because of depression, of alienation, of a loss of purpose and meaning in life, and because of difficulty in getting along with people, of finding a mate, of making a commitment, of deciding on a career. The replacement of symptom analysis by what initially was called character analysis came about gradually, for even in the early 1930s when I was a student of analysis, the cases that came for treatment were already varied: there were some symptom analyses, especially compulsion neuroses, but there were also cases of individuals whose personalities revealed more general problems in living.

However, the therapeutic philosophy of treatment for classical Freudian analysis remained the same, although the problems that patients presented differed from those of the past. In fact there were analysts who denied any change in the problems for which people sought psychoanalytic help, and there are still those who view human problems as so uniformly universal that they cancel out the influence of social and cultural factors. I do not share this view, and the advent of a psychology of the self and the prominence of the search for selfobjects, as we see this clinically, reflect and confirm the close relationship between the nature of the individual self and the larger social matrix with which it interacts.

Kohut, in his writings, often refers to the social and historical dimension that determines the energy and urgency with which the selfobject is sought. He writes (Kohut 1984): "Man of our time is the man of the precariously cohesive self, the man who craves the presence, the interest, the availability of the self-cohesion-maintaining-selfobject / The self's autonomy is only relative . . . a self can never exist outside a matrix of selfobjects" (p. 61); moreover, "the self needs selfobjects not only in infancy but throughout the whole span of life" (p. 50).

For those of us who have accepted the idea of the selfobject—that is, the imprinted image resulting from communication and interaction with the "other"—as essential for the building of psychic structure through transmuting internalizations, the notion that this process takes place in infancy, initially with the mother, is not so foreign. But when we project this process into the future, we might wonder why it persists throughout the entire life span.

The answer might best be given if we contrast a self psychological view of self-structuring with Freud's view of the formation of personality in terms of his structural model. Beginning with an undifferentiated "id" that is instinctual in nature, the other entities that form the psyche, the ego and superego, emerge as the result of frustration and deprivation. In this connection Freud uses the well-known analogy of the grain of sand that has gotten into the oyster shell, setting up an irritation that is responsible for the formation of the pearl. Psychic structure, like the pearl, is laid down as a finite entity that is more or less immutable once it has been formed. Such change as may occur, occurs only as the result of therapy, for example, within the relationship of the parts of the structure to one another. Thus, the psychic structure, in Freudian terms, is the product of a reaction to an obstacle.

For self psychology, on the other hand, psychic structure is laid down within the context of a continuously unfolding growth process. Like the body, which continues to grow and change throughout the human life span, the psychological structures strive to fulfill their growth potential by constantly developing and changing. To make this possible, however, there must be psychological nutrients, and these are found in the selfobjects with whom an individual will have contact in the course of life's activities. The selfobjects are internalized and worked over to adapt to the unique personality of the individual. This process of taking in and reworking the experience of contact with the outside world is the very nature of life itself. The health of the mind and the emotions depends on the availability of objects that can become selfobjects; that is, those that can be used in the service of the self to maintain the cohesion of its psychic structure.

That is why deprivation of human contact, of human communication, is devastating. However, even when deprivation is not as extreme as in the case of Winny Mandela's solitary confinement, but is temporary and an aspect of a normal work situation, there can be palpable emotional distress. I had a patient once who was a radio announcer and complained of feelings of depersonalization in the midst of broadcasting. "There is no audience, no response," he complained. This seems to confirm the need for the selfobject, as well as to point to the relativity of individual autonomy. The need and search for response and affirmation from another do not necessarily constitute neurotic dependency, but rather a normal aspect of psychic life.

The survival need of the self is so powerful that in its search for sustaining nutrition it does not and cannot always rely on individual or personal selfobjects; instead it turns to what Kohut refers to as "cultural selfobjects." Thus, religion, a value system, an ideology, a national identity can serve as a selfobject in that it supports and helps to maintain the integrity of the self.

In an early paper of mine ("A Daydream in the Service of Ego Formation" in Menaker 1979), written before there was a psychology of the self, I described a young ballet dancer whom one might diagnose as very nearly schizophrenic, who had withdrawn from the world but had found her way back by adopting a new identity. She had met a young French woman with whom she developed a deep friendship; she learned French in a remarkably short time, identified with French life, and went to live in Paris for several years. Gradually, through the use of another culture and language as a selfobject, as well as through the relationship that had inspired the new cultural identification, she made a more or less normal adjustment to the world of reality.

Although the need of the striving self for a selfobject that can maintain its cohesiveness is often met by cultural artifacts, the fact that the values, customs, and goals of a society are constantly changing poses a special problem of adaptation for the self. Culture and society are in continuous movement, especially in the modern technological world, and the rate of change, the acceleration, is on the increase. Technological and scientific advances and changes in sexual mores, in family structure, in gender role, in occupational opportunity—to mention only a few areas—have inevitably brought about changes in goals and values. Either the nature of the new cultural values is too amorphous or too unstable to provide adequate selfobjects for the striving self of individuals, or the changed values come into conflict with those that they have already incorporated from parental figures in their early development. Such factors account to a large extent for the fragmentation, alienation, and even emptiness that are so often characteristic of the self structure of the modern personality. For the individual, the social instability and ferment not only make the choice of a cultural selfobject difficult but also the familial figures who normally are the primary selfobjects are themselves products of sociocultural unrest that has left them with a somewhat fragmented self structure. Therefore, they are not adequate selfobjects for the succeeding generation.

The striving self, which is at the heart of human psychic life, behaves like all living things: it forages constantly for life-sustaining nutrients in the form of selfobjects that aid in the building of psychic structure, support the cohesiveness of the self, and provide the means for its further growth and adaptation. The self encounters the opportunity for finding such nutrients through emotional communication and interaction with individuals and with society. Two powerful forces propel the self in the course of its development as it searches out selfobjects: first, its own striving to fulfill its potential and continue its growth, and second, the need to adapt to ongoing cultural change. The deficits and conflicts that may arise for an individual as these forces impinge upon the striving self become the subject matter of a therapeutic endeavor. In the course of that endeavor it is mandatory for the therapist to maintain the kind of contact and communication with the patient that will enable the therapist to become the needed selfobject for the rebuilding of the patient's self structure.

7

A Case Palpably
Illustrating the Growth
of Self through a Change
in the Selfobject

Selfobject! Through this rather awkward term and all that it implies, Heinz Kohut has given us a new perspective on the dynamics of the human psyche and has added a new and essential dimension to the theory and technique of psychoanalytic psychotherapy. He called the new perspective self psychology. Instead of attributing human motivation in a primary sense to the instinctual drives—especially to the sexual drives—Kohut's observations led him to conclude that the development of the individual self was primary and that the self was the prime mover in human behavior, thought, and feeling. Certain requisite responses of the familial environment to the child from the beginning of life were essential for the normal development of the self. When these responses were lacking, abnormalities in the self-structure resulted—abnormalities that had in earlier psychoanalytic thinking been attributed to libidinal deprivations. Kohut spelled out the requirements for normal self-development: the experience of unequivocal affirmation on the part of the mother from earliest infancy, the opportunity to idealize at least one parent (often the father), and occasionally the chance to enjoy one's similarity to another human being, These early emotional experiences with parents, their surrogates, or others with whom the growing child is close are internalized and form the nucleus of the child's self-structure. The persons who provide the nutrients for the structuring of the self by being available for internalization are known as the selfobjects. If the mother's affirmation, expressed by the reflection of her feelings about her child that Kohut called *mirroring, is* positive, then what is internalized is positive. It supports the child's self-esteem and promotes the consolidation of the self. If it is negative, inadequate, or absent, the cohesion of the child's self-structure is threatened. The same is true of the internalization of selfobjects that have been idealized.

These processes that participate in the formation of the self are strongly influenced not only by the nature of the parental personalities that impinge upon the child but also by the culture or subculture in which they are embedded. If a child is exposed to conflicting values that grow out of the differing cultural ethos of adjacent cultures or subcultures in which he or she is brought up, especially if there are in addition important deficits in the parents' ability to relate to the child, the self-structure of the child will be profoundly threatened.

The following case illustrates the power of the impetus toward the consolidation of a cohesive self in a highly intelligent young woman who grew up under extremely adverse familial circumstances to which was added the disadvantage of subcultural conflict. Louisa was not my patient, but that of one of my supervisees. She was of Hispanic origin and had come to New York from a large midwestern city to pursue graduate studies toward a master's degree at a university. She had earned a graduate fellowship that provided her with tuition and housing and required of her a limited amount of work for the university. Her brilliant mind and scholarly interests had already attracted the attention of her teachers at college, and one of her professors in her chosen field of history became her mentor. It was he who persuaded her to continue her studies and encouraged her to apply for a fellowship. In self psychological terms, he became her selfobject.

Louisa came from a poverty-stricken family. When she was a small child and after the family had left their native land to emigrate to the United States, her parents had divorced. After the divorce her father left the family and moved to another part of the country, and although he was a skilled worker and might have been able to support the family had they been together, he no longer sent them any money. Louisa, her severely emotionally disturbed mother, and a psychotic sister who had to be institutionalized from time to time were left to fend for themselves. They survived on welfare.

The family was not only poverty stricken economically but also emotionally, culturally, socially, and intellectually. In Louisa's description of her family life, as one heard it in her therapy sessions, there was little relatedness, little communication among the family members. Her mother and sister were withdrawn and isolated. There existed among them only a fierce attachment based on dependency and the bonds of likeness in a hostile world. The attachment grew out of fear and distrust of the outside world, which was dangerous because it was alien; the patient's culture spoke another language, had other customs, and seemed secure in a reality of its own. It was a culture of its own. In her home, with its emotional poverty, there was no one to emulate, no one from whom to learn, no one who understood or appreciated her. Louisa was different from the others. She had a powerful mind, great intellectual curiosity, and the ambition to escape the grinding poverty in which she had grown up. She escaped from the emotional desert in which she lived by losing herself in scholarly pursuits— by entering the world of her intellectual interests. She worked so diligently and so productively that she attracted the attention of her professors with whose help the doors to higher education were opened to her.

However, it is important to remember that, although Louisa structured herself almost exclusively on the basis of her native intellectual abilities, she had no adequate selfobjects to internalize. Neither her mother nor her father, with whom she had kept in touch, understood, appreciated, or shared her intellectual interests. In fact, they tended to disparage her academic strivings as impractical and unnecessary.

Louisa's academic work went brilliantly, but her knowledge of how to live a day-to-day life in practical terms was sorely limited. In the early stages of her therapy much time and effort were spent in simply educating her in how and what to feed herself, how to cook some basic, nutritious dishes, and how to observe certain rules of cleanliness and order. She had trouble getting along with roommates because of her extreme messiness and because she demanded complete quiet since even minimal sounds of another person disturbed her in her studies. She lived exclusively to fulfill her scholastic goals

It was clear that in her childhood home there had been no one who might have taught her how to live, no one to act as mediator between herself and the outside world. Had she not been so unusually gifted intellectually, she would probably have drowned in the swamp of the chaotic emotions of her semi-psychotic mother and sister—emotions that expressed little understanding of or relatedness to her.

The extent of her own detachment was apparent in her reactions to her therapist, an attractive, capable young woman with considerable life experience and an outstanding capacity for empathy. For many months after the beginning of her therapy, Louisa did not perceive her therapist as a person, but related only in terms of her function as a therapist, complaining of her difficulties and expressing her anxieties. This became clear when the time came for her to apply to graduate schools for further study in a Ph.D. program. She applied to many schools throughout the country, with no regard as to whether she would be able to continue treatment with her current therapist. Apparently one therapist was as good as another. The issue was never mentioned, never brought up for discussion.

In the meantime her therapist was outstandingly supportive, helpful, and encouraging. One university to which Louisa had applied required that the score of a special examination be submitted along with the application for admission to the Ph.D. program. Louisa resisted taking this examination, but her therapist encouraged her to do so, assuring her that she could not only pass it but would also do well. This expression of faith in her abilities, which Louisa had never experienced except for the encouragement on the part of the professor in her undergraduate college, was of extreme importance. It paved the way for the formation of a relationship between Louisa and her therapist—a relationship through which the therapist ultimately became a selfobject for Louisa. Louisa studied for this examination from a particular book that was recommended for preparation. She had studied so avidly and had exhausted the possibilities that the book offered so completely that one day she told her therapist that she dared not take the book home with her or she would obsessively continue studying the material she already knew. It would drive her crazy, she believed. "Would you like to leave it here?" asked the therapist. Louisa agreed, and the book was placed on a shelf in a bookcase that Louisa faced as she sat opposite the therapist during her sessions. Below the bookshelves was a desk on which there was always a vase of fresh flowers. If Louisa had even seen them, there had never been any indication that she had perceived them, much less enjoyed them.

Some months after she had left her book with the therapist, had taken the examination, had done well, and had been accepted with a generous stipend into the Ph.D. program at an outstanding university, she looked up at the bookshelves during one of her sessions, noticed her book, and commented casually that it was still there. Her glance then fell to the desk level. She noticed the flowers and exclaimed, "What beautiful flowers!" This is the moment when it became palpably clear that a change had taken place in her relationship to her therapist, as symbolized in her ability to remember the therapist's encouragement, faith in her, and helpfulness, and to perceive the therapeutic environment positively and to respond to it. It was the beginning of an internalization of her therapist as selfobject—the beginning of a formation and consolidation of her self-structure. She had certainly suffered during her development from a deficit in available selfobject relationships. She was almost never affirmed, nor were there individuals to idealize. She had survived psychologically primarily on the basis of what Kohut termed "compensatory mechanisms." Her outstanding intelligence, her determination and persistence in doing everything possible to escape from the prison of her subculture with its emotional and economic poverty were used in the successful pursuit of her goals.

However, her acceptance by one of the universities of her choice—a university with world authorities in her field of study on its faculty—did not yet signal a secure victory over the tendencies toward fragmentation that characterized her self-structure. In her mind and feelings there arose a great surge of hate and resentment that she directed at the department within the university where she was currently studying. In her therapy sessions she complained of a sort of bottomless fatigue that she felt would make it impossible for her to complete the two more courses required for the master's degree. She might do the master's thesis, but she was adamant about her need, in the light of her weariness and the fact that she had already been accepted for Ph.D. studies, to be excused from the courses. Needless to say, her professors who felt they had already done so much to help her did not take kindly to her request. They felt that in view of the financial aid that she had received she should be responsible for completing the entire course of study. From the point of view of an institution, this position would seem justifiable. From the point of view of her therapist, Louisa's insistence that the university make an exception for her and excuse her from the two courses, because of her lifelong struggle to come this far that had resulted in a tiredness she could neither explain nor overcome, was a self-destructive act.

I held a different view. In my supervisee's account of the happenings in Louisa's life pertaining to the completion of her work for the master's degree, I had noted the remark of one of her professors. It was a simple answer to Louisa's complaint that she was so tired that she could not imagine how she would write the two papers required for the courses. (Parenthetically, whenever Louisa had written course papers in the past they were like mini-dissertations, extensively researched, original, and profound.) The professor had unempathically answered, "Everyone is tired." I was offended for Louisa by his answer and determined to try to understand the meaning of her strange fatigue. I tried to find the echo of an analogous feeling in my own experience, and I remembered that when I had put out great effort to achieve something or to overcome some great anxiety or conflict, and that when the crisis had passed, I had wanted to do nothing, to rest, perhaps even to indulge in a pleasure unrelated to the task I had accomplished. I even remembered some anger at not having had, in my eyes, sufficient support for my endeavors. How minor these feelings must be compared to a whole lifetime of crisis and effort without affirmation, support, or understanding of her goals. When Louisa had been accepted at an Ivy League university and had won a large stipend in addition, she had called her father to try to share her joy with him. It proved to be a futile effort. He could not understand why she had to be studying at all or why she had to be so far away from home. I understood the rage Louisa felt because she had had to create herself by herself. An unusually insightful patient of mine, who had received insufficient support while growing up, said recently as she was expressing gratitude for my support of her efforts to extend her education, "When the self feels unsupported, it destroys itself." This is the destructiveness of psychological marasmus analogous to that of institutionalized infants (described by Spitz 1965) whose need for physical contact with another human being is not met, and so the body withers and dies. The self too needs nourishment in order to grow, and its capacity to feed itself—that is, to live on compensatory mechanisms—is limited. Louisa's exhaustion was the result of her seemingly endless effort to feed herself emotionally. She needed that kind of understanding from the professors for whose indulgence she had pleaded. When she failed to get it, she still made one final effort: she sought out the director of a consultation center for minority students on the campus of the university she was currently attending. He was himself a "minority person," an African-American. He listened to her story, an account of her life's struggle. He understood and promised to try to educate the faculty members whom she had approached as to the nature of her fatigue and therefore to the legitimacy of her request. At this writing, I still do not know the outcome.

What have we learned about the selfobject from this segment of a life history? First, Louisa's experience of emotional deficit in her family confirms Kohut's discovery that the internalization of a selfobject is essential for the formation of a cohesive, normally functioning self. Second, when an individual is subjected to the transition from one culture or subculture to another, the effect of the familial deficits is augmented and accordingly the self-structure lacks cohesion because the differences in values, goals, customs, and mores of the impinging cultures create conflict in processes of internalization—especially in relation to the choice of selfobject. Most often the developing generation seeks to identify with the dominant culture. Louisa's effort to get out of her subculture, to make use of the opportunities that the dominant culture offered was heroic. It was made possible by her unusual intellectual gifts, by the immense power of the life force within her, and by the empathic understanding of some of her teachers and of her therapist. Louisa began to internalize the therapist, to choose her as a selfobject, when, in response to the therapist's faith in and admiration of Louisa, she perceived the beauty of her surroundings, the flowers, and saw them rightly as the symbol of her therapist's empathy.

8

The Ego-Ideal:
An Aspect of Narcissism

The concept of narcissism in psychoanalysis is an energic one and, true to its mythological origins, refers to the concentration of libidinal energy on the ego (Freud 1914). As our knowledge of the ego, of the processes of introjection and identification upon which much of it is built, and of its various substructures has grown, so our understanding of the role of the investment of narcissistic energy has deepened. It is with this energy that the ego nourishes itself and those of its component parts whose successful and integrated functioning maintain that inner psychic balance that normally guarantees the individual a goodly measure of self-esteem. The distribution of narcissistic energy—whether it is vested in intrapsychic structures or in internalized representations of the self and of others or is projected onto others in the outer world—is often an important indicator of the nature and extent of the psychic balance or imbalance of the individual.

The ego-ideal, of all the substructures of ego, is perhaps most heavily invested with narcissistic energy and from a very early point in development. An exploration therefore of the role of the ego-ideal in relation to individual issues of emotional health and of its significance as the vehicle for social cohesion, as well as for change and progress, points to the vital importance of normal narcissism in human development.

The fact that the study of human personality involves an attempt at understanding individual intrapsychic dynamics and the relationship of the individual to his outer environment and to other individuals in the areas of his most significant involvements, and recognizes that these factors impinge on social and philosophical issues, is never more clearly exemplified than in the study of the ego-ideal. In the early psychoanalytic literature there was but minimal concern with the ego-ideal, which was often not clearly differentiated from the superego. Within the last 10 to 15 years, however, this focus has changed. Perhaps a greater concern with a refinement of concepts of ego structure and dynamics has brought about this shift in focus. But growing interest in the role of values in human psychology, resulting from social, cultural, and moral changes that are worldwide, has also played a large role in an increased concern with the ego-ideal.

If we forget for a moment the issues of the derivation, development, and maturation of the ego-ideal in the course of an individual's life and shelve momentarily the issues of its content and the sources of its energy to formulate a common-sense definition of the ego-ideal, we would say that it is the experience, generally perceived in some verbal form, of the individual's aspirations, of the broadest framework that gives meaning to his life, and from which he or she derives self-esteem and a sense of worth relative to his capacity to fulfill these aspirations. Such a definition refers to the maturing or mature ego-ideal, since the idea of aspiration does not belong to early childhood years. Yet, it is the very factor of the motivation toward aspiration, toward striving, which remains insufficiently accounted for in psychoanalytic literature on the ego-ideal. However, in his article "Geneology of the Ego-Ideal," Blos (1974) has expressed a keen awareness of the scope and significance of the ego-ideal for human life beyond its ontogenetic development. He says that the ego-ideal spans an orbit that extends from primary narcissism to the "categorical imperative," from the most primitive form of psychic life to the highest level of man's achievements. Whatever these achievements might be, they emerge from the paradox of never attaining the sought-after fulfillment or satiation, on the one hand, and of their never ceasing pursuit, on the other. This search extends into the limitless future that blends into eternity. Thus, the fright of the finity of time, of death itself, is rendered non-existent, as it once had been in the state of primary narcissism.

Potentially, the ego-ideal transcends castration anxiety, thus propelling man toward the incredible feats of creativity, heroism, sacrifice, and selflessness. One dies for one's ego-ideal rather than let it die. It is the most uncompromising influence on the conduct of the mature individual: its position always remains unequivocal.

The question then arises: are these feats, these creative achievements arising out of ego-ideal motivation, an expression of man's need to master the anxiety that the giving up of his position of primary narcissism—oneness with the mother—has induced, or are they in fact manifestations of a kind of immortality? To formulate the question in this way is to lay oneself open to the criticism that the issue transcends the field of psychological concern and enters the realm of philosophy and religion. Yet is this really the case? In biological terms, we have become accustomed to regard the genetic material and its reproduction as an expression of species, if not individual, immortality. Would it be so farfetched to regard the transmission and perpetuation of psychological traits through the vehicle of internalized dynamic structures such as the ego-ideal as serving psychosocial immortality?

This would then be a phylogenetic understanding of the ego-ideal, its origins lying in man's potentiality for psychological internalization; its function, the psychological survival, continuity, and advance of human society; its meaning, to provide the individual, in the course of the ontogenetic development of his ego-ideal, with a future-directed meaningfulness for his life through participation in the ego-ideals—either through acceptance or rejection—of the ideals of the society with which he is identified.

Before we explore the deeper meaning of this dimension of the ego-ideal, let us review the psychoanalytic view of its development in the life history of the individual. Lampl-de-Groot (1962) has given us an excellent exposition of the Freudian view. The so-called hallucinations of early infancy, which are attempts to deal with the inevitable frustrations and deprivations of the child's life situation (hunger, cold) by reducing tension and restoring equilibrium, are described as forerunners of the ego-ideal. They take place in a narcissistic phase when self and object are not yet differentiated and are thus entirely self-centered. In the course of development, as self and object become more differentiated, but the problem of maintaining a narcissistic balance, of retaining self-esteem, is not solved in the face of frustration and deprivation, the child tries to maintain this balance through fantasies of omnipotence and self-idealization.

But these fantasies have little effect on reality, and the child then projects the omnipotent expectation upon his parents, who in fact have the greater mastery of the actuality of his world; secondarily, he introjects this idealization of them so that his own self-ideal partakes of their omnipotence. Finally, with the passing of the oedipal period, the attachment to parents becomes desexualized, and the ego-ideal, which is one legacy of this attachment, is also desexualized. In Freudian terms, this means that the goals and aspirations of the growing child shift from unrealistic, sexual goals to neutralized and attainable ones in the realm of learning, in the development of skills, and in the acceptance of norms and ethical standards.

To the extent that the individual lives up to these goals, his narcissistic balance, his self-esteem, is maintained. Thus, its forerunners and the finally structured ego-ideal serve wish-fulfilling functions in Freud's sense of tension reduction. The ego-ideal supports the ego in its attempt to deal with the inevitable disappointments and frustrations of life; it is a need-satisfying agency. The superego, by contrast, is a restricting, prohibiting, sometimes commanding agency, which can interact with the ego-ideal in an attempt to force the carrying out of its goals.

Jacobson (1964), too, sees idealization processes of parents and self as enabling the child to master sexual and aggressive tendencies. The ego-ideal is eventually molded from idealized object and self-images that are ultimately combined with more realistic self and other representations. It is this duality in the ego-ideal that reflects a split between the individual's acceptance of reality and his belief in magic.

There may be variations in emphasis in the writings of authors with a Freudian orientation regarding the genesis of the ego-ideal. But all are in agreement that the function of idealization is defensive, that it is the human organism's attempt to deal with the frustration of instinct, be it sexual or aggressive. The instinctual drives of the individual are thus the nodal point of psychic development. The motivation for inner growth—even of the highest and most human of structures, the ego-ideal—as well as the motivation for action in the outer world of reality originates in the need for the reduction of tension.

When we consider that all the achievements of mankind—in art, literature, religion, philosophy, and social structure, and ethics—derive ultimately from the striving to fulfill ego-ideal goals, it hardly seems plausible to attribute the genesis of this unique capacity for culture to a defensive response to the frustration of instinctual drives. Surely there is more here than the purely biological life history of the individual, or perhaps it would be more accurate to say that the concept of the biological must be broadened to include the social nature of man as well as the larger phylogenetic, evolutionary perspective.

In the psychoanalytic literature all the authors concerned with understanding ego-ideal formation speak of two processes that are crucial for its development: idealization and internalization. Of the latter we know a good

deal from clinical observation and experience and from the theoretical formulations of many workers in the field. Later in this chapter I present some
clinical examples that illustrate the wide spectral range of such internalizations from seemingly simple suggestions to the intricate and complex relationships of identifications to other aspects of the personality as well as to
outer reality.

But what of idealization? The term is used with such ease as if its
meaning were self-evident. Do we really understand what happens in idealization and how it happens?

When a child idealizes a parent he is in the grip of a creative ego process, for he is taking the reality of his experience—as it exists in his memory
imagery, both conscious and unconscious—and embroidering, embellish-
ing, altering it to create illusion. But to create illusion he must have experienced reality, and he did so in the childhood emotions of love and hate,
of dependency and anxiety, of the wish to be autonomous and the fear of
separation. While the human capacity to create illusion through idealization of a love-object or of oneself (narcissism) may be placed in the service
of tension reduction, its main function is ego-building.

In the course of individuation and differentiation, the ego depends
for its development on the experience of the outer world of reality, on its
encounter with this world, and on the internalization of significant love-
objects. Were this internalization merely a duplication within the psyche
of outer reality—were the parents mirrored within as they actually exist in
external reality, without idealization—then the element of aspiration, of
progress toward higher goals, would disappear from human experience.

The history of humanity's cultural development contradicts such a
possibility. Humankind has always been characterized by striving; the human being in his struggle to become individuated is always future-directed.
It is because the child *believes* his idealization to be real that in the course
of the growth of his ego he has the potential to exceed his predecessors.
Thus, the capacity for idealization through the use of creative imagination
is a major factor in man's sociocultural evolution as well as in the psychological evolution of ego. Obviously not all idealizations are used construc-
tively in individual development, nor is the course of cultural history a consistently progressive one. Nevertheless, it is the ability to idealize that makes
for change in the direction of higher levels of organization, both in individual and social history.

In psychoanalytic practice we are accustomed more frequently to distortions of a negative nature. It is the image of the bad parent that is often

magnified and made the cause and justification for neurotic conflict. Just as ego-ideal formation is viewed, for example, by Jacobson (1964), as serving the mastery of sexual and aggressive impulses, so Fairbairn (1954) views the internalization of the bad object as the child's attempt to master the inevitable frustrations of his life by placing the source of control within himself, taking the burden of badness upon himself, and maintaining the environment—that is, the love-object—as good.

In either view, the ability to deal with reality by playing with its internalized reflection is seen as a defensive operation. It is because we deal with the pathology of internalized images and with negative distortions that idealization has been regarded too exclusively in its defensive capacity. Defense, in itself, although understood as an essential aspect of the life process, has nevertheless acquired an aura of disapproving condescension, and with this attitude, idealization, the creation of illusion, has come to be viewed pejoratively as an aspect of outmoded romanticism, as an escape from reality.

Let me propose that ego-ideal formation, through the ceaseless creation of illusion and the attempts at its actualization, is man's reality. In discussing the relationship between truth and reality, Otto Rank (1945) has said:

> To be able to live one needs illusions, not only outer illusions such as art, religion, philosophy, science and love afford, but inner illusions which first condition the outer. The more a man can take reality as truth, appearance as essence, the sounder, the better adjusted, the happier he will be. [p. 250]

By "reality" Rank means the actuality of feeling and its transformation into the creative products of his imagination, as opposed to "truth," which he equates with intellectual knowledge and understanding.

There is a wide range of ego-ideal phenomena, from simple suggestion to complex fragmentation of ego structure. The power of the internalization of words spoken by a much loved person in a highly charged emotional situation came home to me on a European trip some years ago when I met a survivor of the Holocaust. She was a middle-aged woman at the time, living in a central European country behind the Iron Curtain and, because of special circumstances, was able to take a short vacation in one of the neutral, more or less affluent, countries of Europe. Perhaps it was the contrast with her current, rather difficult lifestyle that brought to her mind the days of the Second World War when her family was caught between two invading armies.

She recounted the story of her anguished escape. In the hope that some members of the family would survive, they split up, each going to a separate hiding place. At the moment of parting from her father he had said to her, "Be brave." The words sustained her through countless trials and difficulties, through terror and despair. They were spoken by a deeply loved person whose image she internalized and whose words became, in content, her ego-ideal, and in their imperative form, her superego. Their impact was probably reinforced by the fact that she never saw her father again, and the idealization could be maintained. Thus, the idealized internalization nourished her ego and made possible her actual physical survival as well as her psychological survival.

Since this was for me but a passing encounter with a tragic life story, I had no opportunity to learn more of the dynamic structure of her personality. However, within the framework of my knowledge of these events of her life, the words "be brave," as they became part of her ego-ideal, functioned as a hypnotic suggestion. Perhaps the effectiveness of suggestion in general as it is a part of therapy rests on how closely, both in its form and content, it approximates an already internalized ego-ideal.

As we know from clinical experience, the internalized parental images are not always idealized to healthy proportions. The actual parents in their relationship to the child may be either so overwhelmingly critical or so narcissistic that the incorporation of their images becomes a source of profound conflict and of character disturbance. It has been my impression from recent work with patients that the fragmentation of the ego due to the pathological character of the ego-ideal and superego, and the conflict between them, is as responsible for much of the inhibition that we encounter in the area of sex and work as is conflict surrounding the gratification of instinctual drives.

Let me present a case in point. Lisa, an attractive and highly intelligent girl of about 21, came to me for analysis (which she recently completed) about seven years ago. She had just graduated from college and had returned to New York to live again in the home of her parents. She was depressed, unhappy, at sea about her vocational life, and was experiencing difficulty in her sexual and social life. I noted the length of her treatment specifically, because the analysis of conflicts surrounding the ego-ideal came only in the last year of her therapy—and could only have come after the analysis of what I shall call, for the moment, the family neurosis. This fact points to the extremely early formation of ego-ideal processes. They are therefore anchored in an early phase of narcissistic development, and in form, process, and quality, remain deeply unconscious. Their content is synthesized much later, is conscious, and is superimposed on the primitive, narcissistic, and unconscious form.

Lisa's analysis began with the struggle between her wish for autonomy and her extreme dependency on her parents, especially her mother, for although she had been away from home for four years she never entirely overcame her homesickness. The exposure of this infantile dependency and its partial resolution, in that she moved away from home, might have heralded the deeper intrapsychic dependencies of ego function on ego-ideal and super-ego processes, but much had to be analyzed in the realm of her instinct life before we could return to an analysis of her ego-ideal formation.

Prominent in her sexual conflict was her omnipotent wish to be both boy and girl. She grew up in a home in which her parents had ostensibly thrown convention overboard. Their goals and aspirations were expressed verbally in rebellion and criticism of the existing society; much of their behavior, however, conformed to the most conventional of social values. They were acquisitive, placed great importance on material possessions and social status, and were eager for their daughter to marry and have children in the socially accepted way. As a little girl Lisa went through a long tomboy phase. She wore overalls, climbed trees, and enjoyed sporting her leather jacket and being as messy and dirty as possible. But in the afternoon of the same day in which she played like the boys, she would suddenly run home and change into her prettiest, daintiest, party dress. Clearly, her sexual identity was not consolidated, and this was in large measure due to the contradictory and confused messages that she received from her parents, especially from her mother, who herself was not secure in her role as a woman.

Her normal oedipal wishes, her rivalry with her brother (her only sibling), her competition with her mother, her rebelliousness and hostility, her fear of abandonment, and her homosexual impulses all made their appearance in her treatment. All were analyzed and worked through to a point, with good therapeutic results. Her social relationships improved; her relationships with men became more stable and long lasting; there was less conflict with her parents and less demand upon them; she was able to—focus her intellectual interests and to choose a profession, attending graduate school and working at the same time.

But these gains covered deeper levels of ego pathology that she experienced, subjectively, as hypochondriacal anxiety, a low threshold for injured self-esteem in interpersonal relations, and a troublesome, relentlessly competitive attitude toward others in almost all phases of her life. It was in the detailed analysis of her competitive stance, which was at variance with her conscious social values, that we discovered the true nature of the fragmentation of her ego based upon the character of her introjects.

Lisa had always been competitive with her women friends. Was her boyfriend as good as Marjorie's? Did he love her as much? Did he make love to her as frequently? Was her sexual experience as fulfilling as her friend's? The constant comparison disturbed her. She was never able to immerse herself in experience, to live the moment. One day, in a self-created, competitive situation with a colleague, she suddenly became aware of the depth and extent of her self-centeredness. In the school where she had been teaching, a group of teachers had gotten together to discuss some professional problems. One of the teachers happened to mention that some students had a crush on her. Lisa was disturbed by what she perceived as the other woman's bragging, but was also jealous of her. In the midst of these emotions she suddenly realized that she thought of and related to others entirely in terms of herself. She was entirely focused on a comparison, to her disadvantage, of herself with the other person, struggling to retrieve her self-esteem. She lost judgment and a clear perception of reality in these situations and finally experienced a sense of loss of self.

There was something in the quality of the feeling of loss that she described that recalled to me her fear of and feeling of abandonment by her mother in childhood. Once, when Lisa was almost 5, her mother had gone into a store and had left her in a parked car, and she had become so certain that she had been abandoned that in panic she had left the car and was found some time later running distractedly along the highway.

She now experienced the same feeling of loss of self at the height of her hypochondriacal anxiety, when she feared imperfection in some part of her body. Or if her sexual partner did not make love to her when she wished it, she felt equally abandoned, lost, rejected.

The mother whom she feared had abandoned her in the parking lot is not only present in every competitor who might outdo her, in every lover who might reject her, indeed in her very body that might disappoint her with its illnesses and imperfections, but also resides within her. It is the part of the mother that failed to accept her unless she was perfect that she has introjected, and it is this introject that constitutes a major part of her superego and her ego-ideal.

A relative of Lisa's recently told her that soon after her mother was married, she said, "If I were to have a daughter, I would make her perfect." It is relatively unimportant what the content of the ideal of perfection was for the mother; perhaps it meant being both boy and girl, being both self-sufficient yet dependent on and devoted to her, being sexually emancipated yet adhering to more traditional sexual codes. Whatever the content, since an ideal of perfection is unrealizable, the child felt constantly criticized, either explicitly for overt behavior or implicitly for the very nature of her being. She was insufficiently accepted for who she was. She was the vehicle for the gratification of her mother's narcissistic needs, and the price she paid to retain her mother's love was to identify with these needs, to merge with her mother by internalizing the mother's perfectionistic demands upon the standards for her. The mother introject, because of its extreme narcissistic character, militated against differentiation of the child as a separate individual.

The mother's personality as it resided in her daughter consumed the girl's ego and rendered it powerless in the face of the relentless inner measuring of a perfectionistic superego against the realization and actualization of an ego-ideal of perfection. This continuous internal competition between discrete ego functions was projected by Lisa onto the outer world, so that her relationships with others were characterized by a constant measuring of herself against them. The function of this projection, however ineffectual, was an attempt, as is the case in paranoia, to rescue some relatedness to the outer world, to emerge from the undifferentiated narcissistic cocoon in which her mother introject enveloped her.

We must not neglect the hostile, aggressive impulses and emotions that accompany the imposition of perfectionistic standards, first from without and then from within, and that inevitably mean a failure in acceptance of self, at times even a hatred of oneself. In the course of our work on these issues, Lisa realized that her parents were frequently critical, often humiliated her in the presence of others, and were identified with her competitor. To the extent that she internalized the criticality in the nature of her superego, she failed to accept herself. She realized this and one day asked me, "How do I achieve an acceptance of myself?"

Before presenting a response to this question, it is necessary to return to the issue of idealization and ego-ideal formation. Early in this chapter I emphasized the striving, creative aspects of idealization as these processes eventuate in the formation of the ego-ideal. The ego-ideal, as it represents the individual's aspirations, gives meaning and direction to his life, and because the individual is part of a larger social unit, as he interacts with others, his ego-ideal may come to influence society as a whole and may ultimately affect the evolution of culture itself.

Although this may be an idealization of the ego-ideal itself, the important point here is that the effectiveness of the ego-ideal as an agent of individual psychic health and of social progress depends on its normal development. In the case of Lisa, we witness a pathological development of the ego-ideal. The root of the pathology lies in the developing ego's inability to become sufficiently individuated, to separate sufficiently from the parental introjects to structure an independent, autonomous value system. In Lisa's case, as in a number of other cases that I have observed, the most important impediment to the development of such autonomy is the overwhelmingly narcissistic character of the mother's love.

If the mother lives through her child and the child, out of the normal dependency needs of childhood, introjects an image of the mother in which the gratification of her needs predominates, the child lives for the mother. The fulfillment of the ego-ideal is for the mother, and because of the lack of differentiation between ego and object, the child has little opportunity to form a healthy ego-ideal based on the experience of an independent outer reality that can be idealized and woven into the fabric of useful, ego-building illusions. Thus, the ego is crippled, not only in its relationship to the ego-ideal and superego, since it is constantly concerned with the fulfillment of foreign ego-ideal requirements, but also in its functioning in the outer world of reality. Lisa expressed this sense of being crippled when she reported a loss of judgment and clear perception of reality as well as a feeling of loss of self in a competitive situation that aroused in her the fear that she could not meet the requirements of her ego-ideal and would thus be abandoned by her mother introject—an introject so closely attached to her own ego that in losing it, she would lose herself.

These considerations lead to my answer to Lisa's question, "How do I accept myself?" Since the issue of self-acceptance, of healthy self-love, hinges on being autonomous to begin with, the answer must lie primarily in becoming separate from the maternal introject. As a separately delineated personality, Lisa's ego would function not solely to fulfill the needs of an introject, which was too great a portion of her personality, but primarily in relation to the demands of reality and of her own needs as they could be adapted to reality. My answer to her, therefore, was that when she succeeded in detaching herself from her mother through insight and the experience of gratification in other relationships, the actual achievements of her ego in the fulfillment of realistic ego-ideal goals that she set up for herself would bring her the acceptance of herself that she failed to get at the hands of her mother.

What I advisedly did not say, but thought, was that the experience of my acceptance of her and of her goals and aspirations would help liberate her from the mother introject, thus helping consolidate her identity and formulate an independent ego-ideal. For just as the patient's ego—both superego and ego-ideal functions—must make an alliance with the analyst in the therapeutic undertaking—that is, pass critical judgment on his neurosis and seek to overcome it—so the analyst must make an alliance with the patient's realistic ego-ideal aspirations. It is this alliance that accepts and supports the ego's normal striving for growth and development and that is the effective therapeutic agent above and beyond the use of insight, the emotional working through of conflictful experience, or the analysis of the transference.

In summary the human mind, because of the survival value of planfulness, is future-directed; because it is capable of internalizing experience through memory images, it is imaginative; because awareness and self-awareness demand meaningfulness, continuity, and perpetuity, the imagination of man had to create ideal images. To maintain the meaningfulness of existence and to ensure a sense of his own continuity, man sought to fulfill in reality the idealizations that he created in his mind—that is, to actualize his ego-ideal. As an individual his self-esteem depends in large measure on the extent to which he succeeds in the realization of these idealizations. For society, its cohesion and survival may depend on the commonality of its ego-ideals, its progress on a flexibility that will permit viable modifications of its ideals.

We have explored the pathology of ego-ideal formation and function in an individual case and have seen its close relationship to the narcissistic involvement of a mother with her child. A pathologically narcissistic relationship of either parent with the child can have similar effects on ego-ideal and superego formation. Generally, however, because the process of individuation and separation begins in the mother relationship, it is this relationship, with its normal propensity for narcissistic involvement, that is more crucial for ego autonomy and therefore for the healthy development of the ego-ideal.

And so we must conclude that in the final analysis the ego-ideal, upon which man's achievements and aspirations depend and which is at one and the same time the carrier of tradition and the vehicle for innovation, depends for its healthy development in the individual, on the parental capacity to love and accept the child as a discrete individual—that is, to maintain a sound balance between narcissistic investment in self and other.

9

The Therapeutic
Significance of Uniqueness

This title is intended to introduce a perspective on the clinical application of psychoanalysis that is not often taken into account. Uniqueness! I was curious about how the dictionary would define that word. Its meaning as "one and only" was, of course, known to me; but Webster's dictionary also included a definition as "singular, unusual, extraordinary, rare," and in the latter sense it was "still regarded by some as an objectionable usage." I was reminded of a conversation many years ago with Edith Jacobson in which I was describing the not unusual unhappy reaction of an adolescent girl to the fact that she was not popular. "But in Germany," countered Dr. Jacobson, "no normal young girl would wish to be popular. She would wish to be unusual." Whether or not this is the case to the extent that Jacobson indicated is irrelevant to the fact that norms are strongly conditioned by social factors and that the uniqueness of an individual is both fact and societal norm. It is a fact first in the strictly biological sense of the term. For as the evolutionary biologist, C. Judson Herrick (1956), has written in discussing the uniqueness of individuals and commenting on the probabilities of genetic combinations when paternal and maternal chromosomes are paired, "no two people in the world (except identical twins) are alike genetically, and these innate differences are accentuated by the diverse cultural influences to which they respond" (p. 115). The cultural differences to which

Herrick refers create the societal norms that may value likeness or difference as the anecdote about Edith Jacobson indicates. The social value placed
upon uniqueness—that is, whether it is "objectionable" as the dictionary
terms it—or positively valued in its specialness—makes the very fact of individuality a potential source of conflict. The social attitude toward uniqueness becomes internalized and thus enters the domain of the psychological.

When a phenomenon enters the domain of the psychological, one seeks
to illustrate it with some empirical data—in this case with a clinical example.
In my attempt to do this by selecting an example from my practice, I was
having difficulty. I began to realize on a new level the truth of Herrick's
comment that no two individuals are alike; each is unique. But more, I
realized the extent to which in our therapeutic work we think in terms of
norms. Certainly, there are commonalities and similarities among individuals. Yet, each one carries some measure of uniqueness. The norm is a sta-
tistical fiction; uniqueness is a genetic, physical, and psychological reality
that is an attribute of every individual. In working psychoanalytically and
psychotherapeutically, optimally we must be aware of the norm in a half-
conscious way, but must search out the uniqueness of the individual, address it, and above all convey our acceptance of it.

As I was going through the exercise of selecting a specific clinical
example that might better illustrate the importance of addressing uniqueness in the therapeutic encounter, I turned to my own book about Otto
Rank (Menaker 1982), and as I leafed through it for some inspirational
stimulus, I unexpectedly made an important discovery. I caught an error
in the book, and I did so on the basis of the phenomenon of uniqueness.

There is a passage in the chapter on psychotherapy in which Rank,
speaking of the love-feeling as it appears in the therapeutic situation, describes the patient's response to the therapist's acceptance as one in which
he discovers his "true self" in the mirror of the other. This viewpoint is, of
course, reminiscent of Kohut's thinking. In this chapter I refer to their
similarity but continue to expand on Rank's views, especially on his description of an individual's psychological strategy in the case of unrecipro-
cated love when the rejected individual, in order to preserve a feeling of
oneness with the loved other, denies the reality and creates an inner illusion of oneness. I then quote Rank: "The feeling says this identity between
me and the other exists because it exists in me." But instead of correctly
attributing the quotation to Rank, the text attributes it to Kohut, in fact, to
his work entitled *The Restoration of the Self* (1977). As I reread it, I said to
myself, this is impossible. The quotation could not be from Kohut's book;

it reads like Rank. I looked up the references, and indeed it is Rank's statement, which appears in a chapter called "Emotion (or Feeling) and Denial"
from his book entitled *The Genetic Psychology* that is untranslated as an
entirety, but for which a translation of the chapter to which I refer appears
in the *Journal of the Otto Rank Association* (1968a). It is because of the
uniqueness of Rank's style both in the content of his thought and in his
way of expressing himself, as well as the very different but nevertheless
unique style of Kohut, that I was able to make the differentiation and catch
the error. Quite apart from content, a thinker's style of thought and his
way of communicating it are like signatures or fingerprints. They express
the uniqueness of the personality. The same is even more apparent in the
painting style of a particular artist. No one would confuse a painting by
Van Gogh with one by Renoir. Nor in music would one fail to recognize
the characteristic harmonies of Chopin, for example; although in the case
of music, the influence of historical time and national origin seems more
than in other art forms to leave a particularly clear imprint on the work of
individual composers, an imprint that sometimes blurs the uniqueness of
their individual products. It is, of course, in the products of creative individuals that uniqueness asserts itself most definitively, but it is an aspect
of the functioning of every individual.

    One might well ask: why is this of importance to psychoanalysis, both
in its theory of personality and its philosophy of therapy? The answer lies
in the fact that uniqueness is a source of conflict in several ways. First, as
the flowering of individuality it involves all the conflicts attendant on separation and individuation; for in human development, because of awareness,
normal developmental processes are often accompanied by conflictual
emotions. Inevitably, anxiety accompanies the awareness of separateness
for the small child, who experiences the temporary loss of protective physical comfort, as well as instinctual gratification, and the dim sense of uniqueness—of difference from every other self with whom the growing child has
contact. The developing child with the emergence of a sense of self becomes
aware not only *that* he or she is separate from others but also of *how* he or
she is different. This sense of uniqueness intensifies anxiety. In other words,
a qualitative factor is at play.

    In addition, the manner in which the environment—both familial and
societal—responds to an individual's uniqueness may become a potential
source of conflict, since the sense of self derives not only from the awareness of separateness but also acquires its specific character from interaction with the environment. Ultimately this sense of self is consolidated into

a self-image whose coloration will determine the extent to which self-esteem is nourished.

We know from psychoanalytic study, especially from the work of Heinz Kohut, that the self-conception derives in large measure from the reflected attitudes toward the self of parents and important "others," as well as those of society at large. These attitudes are internalized and serve to give the qualitative coloration to the self-image. If the sense of uniqueness as an aspect of the self-image has received a positive valence, an individual's self-esteem is sound; otherwise a feeling of uncertainty, insecurity, even worthlessness, and conflict results. These issues clearly place the problem of uniqueness in the realm of narcissistic phenomena—a term that, like uniqueness, has suffered a history of pejorative meaning from which it is just emerging.

However, neither an anxious sense of separateness nor the disparaged uniqueness within the self-image is the only source of conflict about differentiation and difference for the individual. It is to Otto Rank that we owe the psychological study of the will and the perspective on human existential guilt that is the inevitable by-product of the functioning of the individual will. The will is the ultimate expression of uniqueness. In the conscious act of volition, be it expressed in behavior, thought, or creative product, the individual expresses most clearly that which he or she *is* as different from all others. Yet, it is this very assertion of the particularity of self that makes for conflict, for the expression of will is an act of separation that is inevitably guilt producing. There is a seeming paradox in the fact that such differentiation that serves the growth principle should also produce guilt. It "arises in the wake of separation because the creative self assertion signals opposition to another part of the self which seeks oneness and merging with an internalized parental image" (Menaker 1982, p. 60). Duality of impulse, whether it arises from opposition within the individual or is expressed outside the self as separation from the self of another—as in the case of the separation of the child from the mother—always creates guilt. One part of the self, especially as it expresses the unique will of the individual, must inevitably betray the opposing wish to be one with the other. The separation thus becomes the hallmark of hostility and is accompanied by guilt. It is in this sense that uniqueness, as it is expressed in acts of will, fuels guilt, the inevitable by-product of growth and individuation.

Freud postulated that the driving forces in the psychic life of an individual are the pleasure principle and the reality principle. Certainly, there is no doubt that these are strong—in fact, often inevitable—motivating factors in the lives of individuals. Yet, they operate on a level that addresses the instinctual life of individuals rather than the basic nature of the life force itself, which strives toward growth, toward the unfolding and emerging of potentialities, and toward their expression in the uniqueness of individuality. The tree is in the seed in its generic being as "tree"—as "tree" of a given species—but also in its uniqueness as a specific individual tree. Its uniqueness will be further either tempered or enhanced by the effects of environment. How much truer and more complex is this in human life! The individual infant is in the embryo, and to some extent the man or woman is in the infant. Yet, in the case of human beings the effect of environment on development, and the interaction between what is constitutionally given and the environment are more crucial for the fulfillment of optimal potential than in the nonhuman world of life. It is to these effects of the environment that psychoanalysis addresses itself. Until recently, however, its main emphasis has been on the general rather than the specific and unique aspects of personality in conflict. Beginning with pathology, initially with hysteria, and discovering what it considered to be universal phenomena—for example, repression, the Oedipus complex, castration anxiety, and the stages of libido development—psychoanalysis sought to become a general psychology of humankind. In this endeavor some important general truths were discovered, but others were overlooked. The specific, as it expressed itself in the unique lives of individuals, was often neglected and was in fact in the therapeutic situation often judged aberrant, using the general psychological phenomena as a measuring rod.

It is little wonder that initially psychoanalysis eschewed a concern with the uniqueness of individuality, for it strove to formulate basic, general laws about the neuroses based on a theory of drives. Drives, although they may differ among individuals in intensity for example, represent that fundamental expression of human life that is common to all people. Even the appearance of object-relations theory and of the interpersonal dimension in psychoanalysis did not lead specifically to an interest in the unique. Benjamin Wolstein makes this quite clear in his paper, "Toward a Conception of Unique Individuality" (1974). It is in phenomena of the ego and self that uniqueness makes its appearance, and both ego psychology and self psychology appeared late in the history of the development of psychoanalysis. It is in Rank's will psychology, as I have already stated, that we find the first true expression of an interest in the uniqueness of the individual in psychoanalytic thought.

In the work of Wolstein (1974) we find a sensitive awareness of the importance of uniqueness, especially as a factor in the relationship between therapist and patient, where its acknowledgment leads to the possibility of intimacy; intimacy, in turn, is dependent on a mutual appreciation of uniqueness. Intimacy, rightly described by Wolstein as a much neglected theme in psychoanalytic thought, is essential in the therapeutic encounter for an understanding and experiencing of the ultimate depth of feeling that is necessary for a positive outcome of the treatment.

The omission of the dimension of uniqueness has had grave consequences for the therapeutic application of psychoanalysis. It is well known that Freud, out of his own unique drive toward discovery, was not primarily concerned with therapeutic efficacy. The fate of the individual patient was secondary to the uncovering of data that could translate into universal laws applicable to an understanding of human psychology. In his work with hysteria and in the study of his own dreams, he discovered repression—most specifically, repression of forbidden sexual wishes—and thus the dynamic unconscious. This was an appropriate discovery for the era in which he lived. Indeed, it would be difficult to make the same discovery today. But Freud was not alert to the effect of social, cultural, and interpersonal factors on the psychology of the individual. His own world was universal. Thus, when he posited erotic feelings and fantasies for the very young child and put together the puzzle of the Oedipus complex, he conceived of it as a universal human experience. Now while it is probably true that children at a specific point in development experience quasi-sexual emotions toward the parent of the opposite sex, the specific form, intensity, and destiny of such feelings are highly individual. In the sophisticated urban culture of our time, psychoanalytic theory in its broad, general, and simplistic form has become so much a part of acceptable thinking that the therapeutic effect of "discovering" oedipal feelings in the course of treatment has been all but negated. As therapists, if we make such interpretations, we usually get an answer that says in effect: "I know that; so what!" Aside from the fact that interpretation *alone* is not curative, although it helps integrate the self, to point to oedipal impulses as such is far too general. It is only in the detailed exploration of the possible genesis of the unique and specific emotions or their derivatives that the interpretation has meaning and that the patient feels really understood.

Let us take for example the case of a young man who sought analysis because, in his relationships with women he almost always found himself in two significant relationships simultaneously. Such behavior was inconsistent with his values and ethical standards. He was not promiscuous and always wished that he could settle on one person, but could not make up his mind since each one of the two women with whom he was involved represented the gratification of separate and differing needs. One woman met his sexual and esthetic needs; the other, while not sexually unattractive, nevertheless did not come up to the standards of girlfriend number one, but satisfied his intellectual and cultural needs and provided the pleasures of a companionable enjoyment of everyday life. Was he unable to tolerate frustration? Did he need to have everything? Did all his needs have to be met? These were some of the questions that we asked in the course of his therapy. The answers were generally negative and seemed to lead nowhere.

In the course of our dialogues his profound attachment to his mother became increasingly clear. It would have been easy to interpret his emotional situation as the inability, because of the incest taboo, to fuse the tender and affectionate aspects of his feelings for his mother with his erotic and sexual feelings for her. I did not yield to the temptation of indulging in this stereotype. Instead I literally felt myself into the quality of his paradoxical feeling and began first, with his participation, to put verbal images to the more physical aspects of his feelings—to describe the nature of his satisfaction, the wish to be cosseted and to enjoy being the object of his mother's admiration and affection. As we spoke, the very early childhood quality of these gratifications became evident. I began to describe what I felt were preverbal imprints of a blissful, paradisiacal time of secure oneness with his mother—a satisfaction that in adult life had translated itself into the sexual and erotic gratifications that were being fulfilled in the more erotic and esthetic of his two relationships. It is also important to be aware, as was the patient himself, that his erotic relationship was just that: it was outside the realm of reality, like a perpetual honeymoon, isolated from the realities and difficulties of life. There was in the relationship scarcely any area of realistic compatibility other than the physical and the purely human.

But why the split? Why two women? As I asked myself this question, I suddenly and spontaneously found myself saying, "It is as if you had two mothers." Knowing the unique history of his family life, I had sensed the effects of a very traumatic situation on his mother's life that inevitably redounded on the nature of her relationship to the child. When the patient was between 2 and 3 years of age, his father fell victim to a life-threatening disease. His mother faced the possibility of early widowhood and the full responsibility, both economic and familial, for the survival and upbringing of her son. Inevitably she became a different person. The honeymoon of early childhood was over, and a companionable loving relationship grounded in reality developed between himself and his mother. The present split between two women was indeed a mirror and a concretization of an earlier inner experience in which one individual—his mother—became two. The internalization was not a split between good mother and bad mother, for although the patient was aware and had from time to time experienced certain angry feelings toward his mother, the overriding internal images as well as the relationship in reality were predominantly benign and positive. The patient's primary conflict regarding his relationship to his mother was not rivalry with his father, but the need to recapture the earliest, rapturous relationship to his mother before the trauma that caused the loss of that relationship and put the bond between them on a much more realistic basis.

One might well ask, why was it so difficult, in fact well-nigh impossible, for this man to consolidate his dual experiences with his mother into a love relationship with one woman who would meet both needs? I am not certain of the answer, but the pattern of his life suggests that he is constrained to repeat his bifurcated experience as if the very process itself stood for his mother in both her aspects, and to give it up would mean the anxiety-producing separation from her that he was not yet ready to face. It is significant that in the course of the unraveling of this rather unique destiny of a mother attachment, the patient reacted as if he felt more profoundly understood than ever before. I had respected the uniqueness of his individual biography and had validated my respect by the detailed exploration that I undertook with him. My ability to undertake this exploration grows out of my own uniqueness, a product of constitutional givens and accumulated life experience. Although my capacity to convey such understanding and respect in relation to another's uniqueness is present in interaction with a wide range of individuals, it certainly does not resonate with everyone.

The extent of such a capacity depends on the variety, breadth, and length of life experience, but most especially on the freedom from anxiety that enables one to be creatively self-expressive—to be and to use what one *is* in the interaction with another human being. It is the unique individuality of persons that keeps psychoanalytic treatment from being a technique that can be learned and applied across the board to all people alike. While the accumulated experience of many analysts who have written about their actual clinical work or about their theoretical speculations has given us a body of psychological generalizations (which can scarcely be called knowledge), they merely form useful guideposts in our efforts to comprehend the person with whom we are working. We keep these guideposts in mind in our work with patients; but against this background, in working with a particular and therefore unique patient, we must juggle our thoughts, feelings, and intuitions within an interaction—a dialogue—that begins innocently, naively, as if unknowing (for indeed we do not yet know the person with whom we are working). Together we arrive at a depth of communication that is healing because it is at one and the same time separating and uniting. One individual's acknowledgment of the uniqueness of another is separating because there exists an observer and an observed, an I and a Thou that permits the existence of individuality; yet there is a uniting in the closeness of such understanding that affirms the other's uniqueness, a coming together, a confession of oneness despite difference.

There have been analysts who, without specifically focusing on uniqueness, have conveyed in their therapeutic stance an awareness that help or cure for the patient comes not primarily from a cognitive process of understanding but from a relationship in which the loving atmosphere conveys the feeling of being understood. Sometimes this goes by the name of love; currently it is called empathy.

In 1954 Izette de Forest, a pupil of Sandor Ferenczi's, published a book entitled *The Leaven of Love* in which she defines what she calls "cherishing love"—the love that parents should express toward their children and therapists toward their patients:

> A love that cherishes is a love that seeks empathically to comprehend another's individual temperament and individual needs; one that in essence sufficiently respects the feeling life and passionate nature of the other person to allow him their full expression and development; one that refrains from intruding upon the precious privacy of another's mental and emotional existence. [p. 108]

De Forest (1954) then continues at some length to define the therapist's responsibility, calling it in broad terms the countertransference: "The therapist must cherish his patient, must labor for the recovery of his characteristic nature and for its growth and maturity. He must respect his patient's emotional temperament and its expression" (p. 109). This is an echo of Ferenczi's therapeutic philosophy—a point of view that brought him into conflict with Freud.

At about the same time as Ferenczi was experimenting with varying techniques in his therapeutic endeavors, Otto Rank (1968a) too realized that the uniqueness of personality called for a special and empathic appreciation of the individual patient: "One can really only love the one who accepts our own self as it is, indeed will not have it otherwise than it is, and whose self we accept as it is" (p. 11). Such acceptance, when carried over from its original source in the mother-child relationship to the therapeutic situation, requires that "every case has its own technique, its own analysis, and its own solution. This adjusts itself to the patient's personality and to the situation and ought not to be moulded according to theoretical presuppositions and ideals" (Rank 1968b, p. 39).

Using different, current self psychological terminology, Kohut (1984) concludes a chapter on the role of empathy in psychoanalytic cure with a statement that also makes the importance of empathic understanding clear:

> We must never confuse the deep human response called forth in us vis-a-vis another human being's thoughts and emotions with sentimentality and companionship. Parents and analysts, respectively, will insist on the child's and the analysand's confronting unpleasant realities, including the limits that all of us have to recognize, but they will do so while simultaneously acknowledging the facts that all of us rightfully feel special and unique and that we cannot exist unless we feel that we are affirmed by others, including, and especially, by our parents and those who later come to have a parental selfobject significance for us. [p. 190]

The analysts whom I have quoted represent a point of view that places emphasis on the rehabilitation of personality, not on the reconstruction of the past but on the immediacy of authentic experience in a relationship and an interaction that are is dominated by an empathic attitude. I would add that it is specifically the analyst's empathy with the uniqueness of the patient that carries the potential for the cure, change, growth, or betterment of the individual. In this process, the analyst too has the opportunity for growth and change. Such processes do not take place within a therapeutic model that emphasizes the neutrality of the analyst and the universality of causes for conflict. Change and growth are stimulated by an awareness and affirmation of uniqueness that is always present at the creative edge of the general and the universal.

10

Some Psychosocial Factors in the Development of Ego and Self: Individuation, Identification, and Identity

There are fashions, confusions, and ambiguities in the use of terminology in the field of psychoanalysis. For example, Sigmund Freud used the term *identification* in at least five different ways, according to Robert White (quoted in Yankelovich and Barrett, p. 122). Erik Erikson (1920) used "identity" in three different ways. While such seeming lack of precision makes for difficulties in the study and treatment of personality, it is not necessarily the result of sloppiness on the part of investigators, but rather of the enormous complexity of human psychology. Not only are terms hard to define but also communication among individuals working in the psychoanalytic field is impeded by the fact that each person tends to think and comprehend within the framework of his or her own terminology.

In trying to formulate my own thoughts, I struggled between the terms *ego* and *self*, finding it hard to differentiate them and being uncertain about which to use in the title of this chapter. Finally it occurred to me that they are indeed two separate entities that stand in a developmental relationship to one another. I therefore use the term *ego*, not in Freud's sense of a structural part of the personality, but in the sense of a *developmental process* within the psychological growth of the individual by which he or she achieves a differentiation between himself and the outside world. Margaret Mahler (1975)has observed and described this process with sensitive attention to detail and refers to it as *individuation*. The stimulus that induces this process is conceived in terms of the fate of tension reduction and the shifting of libidinal cathexis within the matrix of the mother-child relationship. Hers is a refinement of the classic Freudian conception of the molding of ego as the product of gratifications and frustrations of reality, on the one hand, and of the instinctual drives, on the other. Mahler's emphasis is on the *reactive* aspect of ego development, rather than on the existence "in potentio" of capacities for ego growth.

However, primacy of ego in the developmental sense exists in the same way that motor development exists in potential, and certain of its functions emerge at a biologically predetermined stage of growth. I am reminded of an experiment done in Vienna at the Psychological Institute under the sponsorship of Charlotte Buehler in which it emerged clearly that at 10 weeks the infant perceives the bottle as a *Ding an Sich*, a thing in itself as such. Thus, there is a developmental process of the perceptual function and in very primitive terms of the cognitive function that enables the infant to differentiate the outside world as having a reality of its own. Notice that I did not write that the infant is able to differentiate the bottle (or breast or mother) from himself. The outer perception comes first; the infant as yet has no awareness of his or her own being as such, and so one cannot yet speak of individuation. The inception of ego thus begins with its *function* of perceiving that which is outside itself, not with an awareness of its own existence. We know the outer world before we know ourselves. For, despite the fact that as a total organism the infant in the first weeks of life is withdrawn into sleep about 90 percent of the time, when he is awake his embryonic ego moves *toward* stimuli, is outer-directed according to the capacities of the developmental level of a particular period. This in no way negates the fact that inner bodily sensations are taking place at the same time and that they are responded to and perhaps leave some imprint.

For those authors who think in energic terms (e.g., Mahler) this phase has been characterized as internal absolute primary autism. Yet, it is the outer-directed, exploratory function of the infant organism that attests to the primacy and innate existence of ego potential.

What I have tried to describe above is the earliest manifestation of ego function. It is innate, primary, and developmental and precedes awareness of the mother as a totality. The awareness of the breast as a separate "thing in itself" is probably the first separately perceived fragment of outer reality to which are then added an awareness and recognition of the mother's voice, her smile, and finally her face, so that a "Gestalt mother" is created by the developing ego. Although Freudian theory attributes such development of ego function to the influence of the pleasure-pain continuum upon the growing organism, I emphasize the unfolding of developmental potential. This does not negate the possibility of the influence of affective states upon ego development; it merely stresses the importance of the primacy of ego potential and its intimate relationship to the maturation of the nervous system.

Once the mother is perceived, we can speak of the mother-child matrix, which I have in other works called the social matrix. Now all the subtleties and nuances of interaction that are so crucial for the proper emergence of ego begin to take place. In the mother's affectional responses lies the secret of the quality of the earliest impressions that the infant receives regarding himself and the outside world—impressions that are then internalized not only contribute to the formation of ego but also lend it its particular coloration. All the writers in the depth psychological field, whatever their theoretical differences, agree that the mother-child matrix is essential for the survival of the human child, that the ego is nourished by the mother's empathic love, especially the early ego, and that the character of what the mother reflects back to the child—of her feelings about him and about herself—will determine the emotional health of the child's personality.

But while ego is being formed in the context of the mother-child relationship, the growing individual is also striving for autonomy. Thus, processes of incorporation are concurrent with processes of separation. Mahler has described in great detail the separation process as it serves individuation: the mutual adaptation of mother and child to cues and selective responses within the context of their interaction.

This description of individuation relates to the ontogenetic development of the individual child. It leaves out the important parallel psychosocial development that is so well described by Erikson (1950) and that deals with the phase-appropriate values, affects, and ego states that are transmitted to the child by the specific quality of mothering that he or she experiences. Certainly, whether the mother is secure or anxious, ambivalent or predominantly loving, rigid or relaxed, accepting or critical will depend on the fate of her own childhood development. But above and beyond the psychosocial influences that derive from individual experience and that impinge upon future development of the individual, both mother and child, there are larger social forces that reflect the particular ethos of a given historical period and that are also communicated from mother to child. How children are regarded, the extent to which they are valued or shunned differs dramatically from culture to culture and from one period to another. For example, in the Middle Ages children were not valued much above domestic animals and shared much of their time with the dogs that played and ate under the table. At a very early age they became part of the labor force so that their value lay in their economic importance rather than in their worth as individuals. Today we value children highly, are profoundly aware of the significance of their individuality for future generations, are self-consciously aware of the importance of child rearing, and sometimes lose perspective on the strength and adaptability of the human being that is reflected in his or her ability to overcome handicaps, deprivations and deficits. But even in our own time there have been changes in social values that are reflected in the nature of the mother-child relationship. The heritage of the puritan ethic and of sexual repression and inhibition is still evident in clinical material that we encounter today, albeit in diminishing quantity. Nevertheless, a mother's attitude toward sexuality, both her own and that of her child (if she can admit the existence of childhood sexuality at all), will be reflected in the process of individuation. For example, at an early age it will determine her respect—or lack of it—for the bodily integrity and autonomy of the child, and this in turn will either facilitate or retard separation-individuation.

Individuation is a process in human development through which, under the influence of psychological and social factors, separation from the mother takes place and the formation of ego is achieved. But occuring at the same time and almost inseparable from individuation is the process of identification. In the course of the internalization that begins with imitation and introjection and eventuates in identification, the consolidation of identity takes place.

I would like to emphasize that individuation and identification are *processes*; identity is a *state of being*. All are influenced by the social and cultural framework in which they transpire, as well as by the psychodynamics of the interactions within the familial situation. The subtle influence of prevailing social attitudes toward childhood as a factor in determining the ease or difficulty or the phase appropriateness or inappropriateness with which individuation is accomplished has already been described. As regards identification, the influence of social values is even more apparent.

We know from the direct observation of children (Mahler, Masterson) as well as from derivative conclusions in analytic work with adults (Kohut,

Menaker) that the child identifies with the mother's mental image of her child, with her feelings and attitudes about him or her, and that these become part of his or her self image and contribute to the presence or absence of appropriate self-esteem. This process has been referred to as "mirroring." As in the case of individuation, the content of identification will also be determined by the mother's attitude and feeling about her child, which will in turn be influenced not only by her individual psychodynamics but also by the existing social attitudes toward such issues as mothering, childhood, sexual identity, career, and a general philosophy of life. As the child continues to grow he internalizes the demands, expectations, prohibitions, as well as the strivings and aspirations of his or her parents. The content of these values will be greatly determined by the prevailing social and cultural values, mores, and convictions of a given time.

As ego develops through processes of individuation and identification, the varied, even disparate, internalized experiences, images, feelings, values, and aspirations will be consolidated into a sense of self. One could call this identity or, according to Erikson, ego-identity. It is an awareness of the uniqueness, the separate and specific character of one's own personality combined with a feeling of belonging to a particular group or category. Thus, one's sexual identity is a very primary aspect of identity formation. But in addition one may also identify oneself as belonging to a social or economic group—as rich or poor, as intellectual or not, as religious or not, as practical or impractical, as ascetic or hedonistic, and so on. There are innumerable facets to one's identity, but one has only to mention a few to realize how many are socially conditioned.

In 1958, a controversial book appeared called the *Quest for Identity*, by Allen Wheelis. The author was profoundly moved to call our attention to the shifting values in a changing society and to relate them to the difficulty for an individual in consolidating an identity. "Identity is not to be found; it is to be created and achieved. . . . [It] is founded on value . . . specifically on those values which are at the top of the hierarchy—the beliefs, faiths and ideals which integrate and determine subordinate values. These organizing values are . . . constitutional in nature, and so are vulnerable to the attrition and, sometimes, to the shock of the instrumental process" (p. 205), (by which Wheelis means the expedient values dictated by pragmatic need). He writes further, "It is becoming increasingly difficult to maintain a firm sense of identity on the basis of these values; for their life expectancy has decreased, and is continuing to decrease with a deceleration that is reciprocal to the acceleration of the instrumental process" (p. 209).

Thus, the development of self, of a consolidated identity for the individual is dependent first upon the processes of individuation and identification, and its success is relative to the outcome of these processes. At this level social values play a part, but it is in the consolidation of identity that they achieve a major role. If, however, in the earlier process of individuation and identification with parental figures there has been insufficient separation or overriding conflict, the maturing individual may look too exclusively to the social scene for the values, beliefs, and meaningfulness out of which to build an identity. Within limits, however, the turning away from the values of the parental heritage to those existing in the larger milieu of the period is a normal aspect of adolescent development. The crisis of adolescence, with its bodily changes, its newly awakened sexual drives, its uncertainties about the future direction of relationships, education, and work, leads to a tendency to consolidate one's personal identity by identifying with the values of one's group. Erikson makes this very clear in his discussion of group identity. And Otto Rank as early as 1914 wrote:

> The detachment of the growing individual from the authority of the parents is one of the most necessary, but also one of the most painful achievements of evolution. It is absolutely necessary for this detachment to take place, and it may be assumed that all normal grown individuals have accomplished it to a certain extent. Social progress is essentially based upon this opposition between the two generations. [pp. 67-68]

The necessary and painful step of separation threatens the stability of a previously arrived at identity, for it is important to bear in mind that, while earlier in this discussion I emphasized the fact that identity was a state of being as differentiated from a process, it is by no means a static state of being. Ego processes may—in fact, usually do—actively change their character or identity in the course of a lifetime. This change occurs partly as a result of the accomplishments of the ego itself—or in less fortunate circumstances, as a result of the lack of achievement—and partly through the impact of social forces and changes. The character of the self is both stable and changing. The dissolution of its integrity is threatened by stressful situations that arise during maturational phases as well as during periods of social change or upheaval.

When in adolescence the individual turns too exclusively to the values of his peers or to current ideologies for a definition of self, to the exclusion of the parental values that formed his or her earliest identifications, there results not only a certain instability of personality but also the potential for disillusionment. The over dependency on the ideology of a group to achieve separation from parental imagoes, and thus an autonomous identity, ironically repeats the original dependency that was insufficiently overcome. Subjectively, therefore, the sense of identity is experienced as somewhat spurious, and the resulting conflict and dissatisfaction are projected as fault finding with the values of the group. The disillusionment and often the depression that follow are characteristic of adolescence. But the synthesis of conflicting or partial identifications in the formation of self-identity can be caused by changing social values, societal mores, and cultural norms. The effect of social transition on the formation of identity thus parallels the effect of maturational changes such as those occurring in adolescence. Adolescents especially today are doubly vulnerable to the forces that tend to disrupt identity formation, since they experience both the instability of their own maturational change and that of a changing society.

Yet, despite the difficulties, obstacles, and dangers that lie in the developmental path of self formation, the human striving to consolidate an identity is overriding. Usually it is a normal process outside the realm of awareness and only surfacing from time to time in the consciousness of one's self-conception. Sometimes, however, the integration of identity is achieved through the ego's capacity to mobilize the will in the service of this process. Perhaps nowhere is this more apparent than in the case of the self-healing efforts of individuals with serious emotional pathology. I am reminded of a young schizophrenic girl—a dancer, about whom I have written elsewhere (Menaker 1979), who suffered severely from feelings of depersonalization. Often when she awoke in the morning she was unable to mobilize herself because she could not achieve a convincing feeling of her own reality or that of her environment. Her artistic imagination came to her rescue in the form of a daydream. She pictured herself as follows: "I am a sprite, running, jumping, dancing on a wide sandy beach. I have on a little petalled cap of moss green velvet and a short tunic. I am slim, gay, and free." Once she had created for herself this identity, however fragile, however isolated, she was able to function within limits.

The primacy and persistence of ego function as it creates the identity that we know as the self are here made poignantly clear. It is also clear that human survival depends on the development of identity and that it takes place under the impact of individual psychodynamic forces as well as of those that derive from an ever-changing and evolving societal framework.

11

Self and Culture–Clinical Implications of Culture in the Treatment of a Japanese-American Woman

Both culture and the self are enormously comprehensive themes, each in its own right, and their relationship to each other is equally broad. The impulse to give such a broad base to this chapter is a reaction to the almost complete lack of concern or understanding for the influence of culture on the nature of conflict and on the structure of personality that characterized the early days of classical psychoanalysis in which I was originally trained. Freud generalized and universalized about the nature and structure of personality and about human motivation with little regard for the influence of cultural, social, or economic factors. Perhaps we would not have had a legacy of some very basic understanding of the metabolism of personality—for example, the influence of the unconscious on human motivation and behavior—were it not for Freud's universalizations. However, we cannot remain with these universalizations alone, for observation has taught us that cultures and subcultures have profound effects on the social institutions through which personality is formed. Culture is the medium in which self grows.

In the early days of psychoanalysis there was little differentiation between ego and self. Freud blurred the distinction between the two, and
although Hartmann (1950) wrote of the importance of differentiating between them it was not until Heinz Kohut developed a psychology of the
self that we gained a deeper understanding of how the total person reacts,
develops, and grows, first within the familial environment and then within
society and within a specific culture as a whole. Kohut (1985) refers to "the
self as the center of initiative" (p. 234) and from his clinical observations
evolves the concepts of selfobject and of transmuting internalizations to
explain development. These two concepts are crucial for an understanding
of the relationship between self and culture. And so the title of this chapter might better be "Some Thoughts on the Influence of Culture on the
Nature of Selfobjects and the Conflicts that they Induce." To illustrate the
influence of culture, I present in this chapter the case of a young woman
who comes from a culture in many ways very different from our own, yet
one somewhat influenced by ours in modern times—namely, the culture of
Japan.

I was fortunate to have the opportunity to supervise a Japanese student who was treating the young Japanese woman whose psychotherapy so
beautifully reflects the influence of culture on the nature of the self-structure and at the same time highlights the nature of conflict both from the
standpoint of the self and from that of drive theory. It was fortunate that
in the supervisory process I had the chance not only to discuss the psychodynamics of the patient but also, in discussion with my supervisee, to learn
about the cultural factors that give rise to certain kinds of attitudes and
behavior.

Naomi was in her late twenties and had been in the United States for
about three years, although she had left Japan a number of years earlier to
travel in other countries before coming here. She grew up in a small vil-
lage in an isolated part of Japan where her father worked as a government
bureaucrat. He was a stern man who was clearly the autocratic head of the
family, brought his children up with strict discipline, and brooked no challenge to his will. He was the prototype of the patriarchal father characteristic for the Japan of that period and, in fact, despite the Westernization
and modernization of Japan, represented a type still quite prevalent in the
Japan of today. The mother was dominated by her husband whom she served
and obeyed; she was also the prototype of the submissive Japanese woman
who knew no life of her own other than that of being her husband's ser-
vant and subordinate. The hierarchical nature of Japanese society is reflected

in the hierarchical nature of the family structure. In fact, family structure and social structure mirror each other.

Certainly, this almost feudal structure of the family and of the society as a whole is not unique to Japan. There are many other cultures in which a hierarchical pattern prevails (Germany, for example) and in which we observe a development of the self differing markedly from self-structuring in a more democratic milieu. I have chosen an example from Japanese culture largely because of the unusual opportunity that I had to observe in detail and in depth the workings of a culture different from our own on the development of the self, and also because these very differences create contrasts that illuminate the nature of self formation as well as the problems that arise when certain conditions for healthy self-development are absent.

Naomi came into treatment because she was hurt and depressed by the recent breakup of a relationship in which she had played a very masochistic role. She also feared the return of a psychosomatic symptom, alopecia (the loss of hair), that had occurred under stressful conditions a few years earlier. At that time, she had left her parental home and gone to a larger town where she had secured a job on the office staff of an industrial company. There she had some difficulties with supervisors as well as with other workers. She was lonely and depressed, and the hair loss had become so marked and extensive that she was forced to give up her job and return home.

Upon her return home, she was not welcomed by her father, who scolded her for her weakness in not being able to adapt to the difficulties of the real, work-a-day world. This scolding reflected his generally denigrating attitude toward her. Naomi had been the older of two children. Her young brother who was about four years her junior had drowned in a boat accident when he was about 8 years of age. The father never recovered from the loss of what had been his favorite child and vented his rage on his daughter and on the mother whom he accused of being responsible for his son's death by not being vigilant enough. Naomi's childhood was dominated by a longing for her father's attention and approval, which she never succeeded in obtaining. There were times, as for example when he would try to help her with her homework, when she pretended to understand his explanations, although in reality she was confused and failed to understand. In this behavior of pretending to understand we see a meeting point between the specific psychology of an individual—Naomi feared her father's anger and also did not wish to appear stupid in his eyes—and the etiquette and psychology of a culture. That is, one concurs with an explanation by one's superior because to do otherwise would not merely be a confession of one's own limitations but would also be offensive to the person above one in the hierarchy.

In the treatment situation Naomi's relationship to the therapist reflected a powerful idealizing transference, especially at the outset. This was to be expected on two counts: first, because of a longing for a good father who would devote his attention to her, and second, the tendency in the Japanese culture as a whole to look up to the person in authority.

Naomi's social life reflected both the nature of her inner conflicts and her self-structure. With her girlfriends she was indeed capable of having close relationships, although she tended to become impatient with their complaints and with their masochistic behavior in interactions with men. This impatience reflected her own tendencies. In relationship to boyfriends she was quite masochistic, consistently accepting a submissive position, yet often becoming demanding and angry when her legitimate needs were not met. She was not promiscuous but her relationships lacked depth because the relatedness to another person, especially to men, was, on the one hand, overshadowed by her need for a good father, and was on the other hand, inhibited by her identification with her mother who represented the traditional submissive role of the Japanese woman.

Let us return for a moment to some theoretical considerations. In describing how the self grows and develops, Kohut advanced the important concepts to which I have already referred—those of the selfobject and of transmuting internalizations. It is important here to emphasize a crucial difference from Freudian theory. For Freud the Ego—and his distinction of Ego from Self was not very clear—developed out of frustration, out of the child's failure to experience complete gratification of instinctual drives. Identification with the love-object who failed to provide the satisfaction was a defense against the experience of the absence of gratification. Thus, the formation of psychic structure is seen as a reaction to deprivation, not as a positive growth process. In Kohut's thinking the world of other individuals—initially, of course, the parents—provides a source of nourishment for the child's growing self. They become the selfobjects to be internalized and are changed within the child by many interacting individual factors and circumstances into some aspect of the child's self-structure.

This important difference between Freud and Kohut leads to a very different philosophy of treatment. Freud sees the patient as neurotic—a victim of unconscious impulses that collide with the strictures of society as these are reflected in the content of the superego. The strictures of society in Freud's view are largely and most importantly of a sexual nature and are dominated by the incest taboo, thus making the unresolved Oedipus complex the very core of human conflict. In self psychological thinking, emotional difficulties are perceived as the result of insufficient psychological nutrition for the normal growth of the self, i.e. initially the parental self-objects are deficient either in their ability to mirror joyful pride in and love for the growing child, or they fail as objects of idealization. These two views are not necessarily mutually exclusive. They become so when they are presented as the sole cause of human maladaptation.

Let us return to the case of Naomi. It is not difficult to perceive in her frequent repetition of masochistic behavior in the face of some sadism on the part of men—sometimes even provoked by her—the sadomasochistic nature of her relationship with her father. But the masochism reveals not only the nature of her gratification but also the hope that someday it might be different, that she might win the love of her father that her brother had enjoyed. In a culture in which the assigned role of women is to be subordinate and submissive to men, it is extremely unlikely that this hope would ever be fulfilled. Naomi's hope, together with her masochistic behavior, is activated in each new relationship with a man. Given the attitudes of men toward women, a change in the position of woman and corresponding changes in women's self-esteem can only occur through changes in attitudes within the culture. This applies not only to Japan but to our own country as well where despite the more democratic basis of our society, historically important changes are occurring in the way women are regarded and in the way they regard themselves.

The damage to Naomi's self-esteem by her father's rejection could not be salvaged by turning to the mother because her mother was not an adequate selfobject. Her own self-esteem had been injured by the same culture that had damaged Naomi's. However, the mother obeyed and accepted the assigned submissive role that her culture had dictated only externally. Emotionally she rejected it and complained to her daughter about how her husband treated her. Implicit in the psychodynamics of the mother's unhappiness with her own life and her place in society lies a great danger to the self-structure of her daughter, for it spells a rejection of womanliness on the part of the mother and therefore a rejecting of the daughter as female. Since gender is a crucial aspect of the self, such rejection constitutes the rejection of the self itself. It is a distorted image that Naomi has seen mirrored in the eyes of her mother—one on which she could scarcely build adequate self-esteem. But the driving force of the self to actualize and to fulfill itself in spite of cultural and familial structures is awesome. Caught in the conflict between her wishes for her father's love and the unmet need for a usable selfobject to replace her mother, Naomi left the familial scene entirely. She moved to a larger city, found work, and hoped to live independently. The struggle must have been too stressful for it resulted in the alopecia symptoms that ultimately brought her to analysis.

The particular dynamics of Naomi's family situation are indeed representative of Japanese culture, but certainly not of Japan alone. We all see patients from our own American culture, as well as from European countries, whose families could be described in much the same way: the autocratic father, the cowed and submissive mother, and the deleterious effect that this imbalance and lack of egalitarianism have on the children. We must conclude therefore, that the broad features of a culture—whether it is primarily hierarchical or egalitarian, for example—do partly explain the outcome in relation to the structure of the self, in the nature of people's relationship to one another, as well as the effect on the upcoming separation. However, they do not fully explain deeper and subtler cultural differences in values, in social etiquette, in emotional expressiveness, in attitudes, in goals, and in expectations. There are many factors that lie at the root of such differences—so many in fact that we cannot find convincing evidence to account for the diversity. How can we explain, for example, the Japanese attitude toward dependency—their so called *amae* feeling? It is a nonjudgmental acceptance of the emotional need of one individual for another—and for the other for the one. The admission and affirmation within Japanese culture of two interacting needs for dependency within a society that is heavily group oriented are certainly very different from our American emphasis on autonomy, on the development of individuation. Alan Roland (1988), referring to the work of Taketomo, writes, "The motivation of the person who gratifies the one who wants gratification is equally central; thus *amae* should be seen as a 'metalanguage,'" as Taketomo (1985) proposes, to connote the interdependent interaction with its complementary motivations, rather than as the motivation of the dependent person alone. One might say that the relatively small land mass that is heavily populated by the Japanese brings people very close together physically and may account for the need of individuals to be oriented toward the group. This need in turn creates the affirmation of dependency as an emotion that serves an adaptive function. Perhaps. Or one could attribute our emphasis on autonomy to the opposite geographic situation. Our great undeveloped open spaces required highly self-reliant individuals to tame and settle new territories. However, it is important to note that the settling of our West also fostered strong community bonds precisely because people needed each other's help in conquering the wilderness. In our rural and small town areas the tradition of neighborliness still persists.

Let us take another example of the subtler aspects of cultural differences. The Japanese language expresses their way of thinking in opposites or of thinking dyadically. Thus, *omote* and *ura* refer "to the two sides of everything," as in outside and inside, or public and private. *Tatemae* and *honne* express the rules or conventions and the underlying motive behind events of the two words, respectively. As Takeo Doi (1985) describes these dyadic concepts, "it is inherent in the relationship between *taternae* and *honne* that they are mutually constitutive. One does not exist without the other" (p. 38). Surely a culture in which individuals think in opposites or in terms of dyadically dependent concepts will differ from one in which linear, causal thinking predominates, as is often the case in our Western culture.

These differences are inevitably reflected in the clinical situation. The Japanese have less difficulty than we do with the concept of ambivalence since they are used to and accept the coexistence of opposites; we might also expect that inconstancies will bother them less since the coexistence and interdependence of two truths are not unfamiliar to them. In the therapeutic situation it is important to bear such subtle nuances in mind, especially in the evaluation of what we are used to call "resistance." After all, psychoanalysis in its original and most classic form is a dyadic theory; there are two opposing systems of the mind: the conscious and the unconscious. The attitudes toward their opposition may differ in different cultures.

The influence of culture on the nature of conflict and on the structure of the self is profound. There are universal human dynamisms and there are those that are specifically induced or reinforced by the culture in which an individual is reared. In the therapeutic interaction we must address them both.

Let us return to the case of Naomi. Her conflict with her father and her wish for his love and respect are universal. However, in that the culture in which she was raised condemns the conflict, it assigns her a role; it is critical of her needs, regarding them as weakness and intransigence. Her culture condones the father's sternness and his autocratic ruling of the family. She is expected to obey. But for whatever reasons—be it envy of her brother whom her father loved so much, be it pity for her mother's unhappy life, be it a congenitally different temperament—Naomi is different.

Her personality challenges the cultural requirement. But she lacks sufficient strength of self to express her individuality. She breaks down in neurotic symptoms or in repeated masochistic behavior.

Two major causes lie at the root of her inability to fulfill her own goals
and to form a stable relationship with a man. The first cause lies in the
area of repressed emotion. It is not only the wish for her father's love,
especially the erotic aspects, that is at least partially repressed but also the
anger, rage, and even hate for his rejection of her that must flood her psychic life that are deeply repressed. Naomi's culture forbids the feeling of
anger and certainly its expression toward an authority figure, thereby reinforcing the normal repression that would occur in the face of such feelings. The second cause lies in the nature of her self-structure. Her self-esteem
was severely damaged by her father's rejection, and this rejection made it
impossible for her to idealize him and to incorporate the idealized image
as part of her own self. Her self-structure was weakened by the failure to
introject an ideal while, at the same time in order not to lose him entirely,
identifying with the rejecting father in his attitude toward her, thus further reducing her self-esteem and giving rise to masochistic behavior. Furthermore, her mother was an inadequate selfobject so that the internalization of her image also failed to provide Naomi with sufficient nourishment
for the formation of a cohesive self.

What are the therapeutic implications for treating an individual burdened by a weakened self-structure that is the result of family dynamics
reinforced by cultural patterns? If we were operating in a strictly orthodox
manner, we would seek to help the patient acquire insight into the unconscious sources of conflict, that is, primarily the repressed unconscious erotic
love as well as the anger toward her father. We would follow Freud's clearly
stated formula: "where id was, there shall ego be." The vehicle for arriving
at this insight would be the analysis of the father transference as well as of
all resistances that the patient might manifest to the uncovering of unconscious impulses. We would then hope that the insight that the patient might
gain from this procedure would dispel the symptom and resolve the conflict.

We know from experience that this is often not the case. Usually the
patient is blamed for this failure and is described as not suitable for analysis. Or, the analysis has not gone deep enough, far enough, has not lasted
long enough. But perhaps we need a new perspective on the situation. Indeed
it was Heinz Kohut who brought a new perspective to the analytic procedure. If we look at the transference not solely as a repetitive process in
which patterns of relatedness are relived in the patient's relationship to

the analyst, but as a developmental process through which the patient attempts to use the relationship to make good the deficits in the growth of the self that occurred in childhood, then we can add a new dimension to the analytic process. By becoming a selfobject for the patient, an opportunity is created for the internalization of a new image—an image that is a nutrient for the self upon which it can grow and become stronger and more cohesive.

In one of the most important footnotes in all of psychoanalytic literature, Freud warned strongly against any such procedure. In *The Ego and the Id*, Freud (1960), writing of the difficulty in analyzing unconscious guilt feelings, suggests that only if the analyst were to offer himself as an ego-ideal for the patient could such freedom from guilt be achieved. But this role for the analyst is forbidden according to all the rules of psychoanalysis. Yet, it is precisely through the idealizing transference that the patient has the opportunity for a new internalization that will strengthen the self.

Naomi showed considerable strength of self and potential for growth by leaving home and striking out on her own. The very searching out of psychotherapeutic help in itself is a wish for growth. She began her therapy with a strong, positive, idealizing transference with her male therapist. She needed a new, idealized father figure to incorporate into her self-structure in order to strengthen it. Her analyst in no way hindered the idealization. He was warm, friendly, and related in line with Kohut's suggestion of the introspective empathic stance as the appropriate analytic method of observation. Had he assumed a distant, completely objective attitude, he would have set the stage for the repetition of Naomi's original relationship to her father. Any insight into the nature of such repetition would not have helped Naomi's growth process, since developmentally growth is predicated on the incorporation of new images based on the acquisition of new selfobjects.

However, we must ask what of resistances? No idealization can hold up indefinitely. There are always flaws to be discovered in every ideal, and surely the greatest flaw and disappointment for the patient lie in the fact that the personal involvement of the therapist can never fully match the need of the patient.

Naomi moved gradually and slightly from the idealizing transference to a mild, negative father transference. It expressed itself in frequent cancellations of appointments and in frequent lateness. Her obligations at work took precedence over her commitment to her analytic session. The question arose: how best to handle this resistance? The therapist is called upon to tread a fine line between interpreting the patient's behavior as a resistance to understanding the unconscious motivation that prompts the behavior and maintaining the empathic and the idealized selfobject position upon which the consolidation of the patient's self depends. Were one to interpret the resistance alone, one might run the risk of losing the patient since in the patient's eyes one would be repeating the autocratic father role from which she had already escaped once. Or the patient might slip into a role of masochistic compliance, as she had done with her boyfriends. Yet if one ignored the resistance and simply accepted the patient's rationalizations for her reluctance to come and her lateness in a friendly accepting way, the analysis might not reach sufficient depth, a true consolidation of the self would not take place, and whatever characterological changes or symptomatic cures occurred might be based on what used to be called a transference cure. Therefore, the therapeutic procedure should include both approaches: the analysis of conflict in the drive theory sense and the analysis of the self in Kohut's sense of growth, cohesion, and consolidation of the self.

If we are to approach therapeutic undertakings from two perspectives, the question naturally arises about the sequence of events: Should one interpret the unconscious impulses first and then work on the growth of the self? On the contrary, working first on the growth of self is indicated. The sequence is of great importance, and the strengthening of the self is primary. Naomi's case illustrates my point. She could not have benefited from the interpretation of her unconscious impulses toward her father and the way in which they currently affect her relationships to men until her self-structure was strong enough to tolerate the interpretation of her unconscious resistances. The necessary strength depends on the incorporation of the image of her therapist as selfobject and the subsequent transmutation of this image into an aspect of the self. Such internalization takes time and depends on the benign empathy of the therapist.

And what of the effect of culture within this process? The functional aspects of the therapeutic process are universal. The colorations, the intensity, the quality of specific relationships, the goals, ideals, and other values will vary from one culture to another and among differing groups within the same culture. It is important in evaluating the meaning of certain behavior and emotions to be aware of these differences and not to listen to a patient with preconceived notions that derive either from our own culture or from our psychoanalytic subculture that often is all too sure of the meaning of things.

12

Culture and Some Limitations of the Psychoanalytic Method (with Siu Ping Ma)

Psychoanalysis evolved both as a psychological theory and as a therapeutic method at the turn of the century, a time of sexual repression, on the one hand, and of philosophical and scientific enlightenment, on the other. These influences played a major role in the substance of its theoretical formulations, in the norms of behavior and health that it set up, and in the values that it propounded and advocated. These facts are well known. However, when psychoanalysis put itself forth as a general psychology of human behavior, thought, and feeling, disregarding its origins in a specific historical era and stemming from observations within a limited socioeconomic group of individuals, its findings could no longer be regarded as universally applicable. The dimension of that which is culturally specific, as it inevitably influences the behavior, thinking, and values of individuals, must be taken into account in evaluating our perception of the communications of our patients in the psychotherapeutic situation. Thus, it is important to distinguish content from form and function in evaluating the universality versus the specificity of psychological events. For example, two of the most important discoveries of psychoanalysis, the dynamic unconscious coupled with repression and the phenomenon of transference, could be said to be universal viewed from the formal standpoint of their function, much as the function of digestion or of breathing is universal for all animal species. Yet, the content of the unconscious and the nature, quality, and intensity of the transference will be culturally specific. In the broadest sense when we speak of individuals, "culturally specific" includes the historical period and the socioeconomic class into which a person is born.

Even in a relatively homogenous culture such as that which we usually refer to as "Western" (i.e., European and American), classic psychoanalysis often fails to understand certain types of individuals—often those who are exceptionally creative or whose so-called narcissism make them less accessible to classic psychoanalytic technique. Such instances point to limitations in classic theory and technique and occur because norms derived from a specific era in history, and from the specific values of a rather affluent upper middle-class strata of Viennese society of the period during which psychoanalysis was being discovered, continue to be applied to individuals who do not fit the mold, who are idiosyncratic perhaps, but who should not be perceived as abnormal. Put simply, such persons are misunderstood. When I was studying psychoanalysis in Vienna in the early 1930s, having come from the United States, I often felt judged and misunderstood (Menaker 1989). Freud himself failed to understand and appreciate cultural differences. This was especially true of his prejudiced attitudes toward America. In a recently published book, *Freud and Judaism* (Megnaghi 1993), Freud, speaking to a B'nai B'rith audience about death, says, "I say that life loses in substance and interest when the highest stake, life itself, is excluded from its struggles. It becomes as hollow and shallow as an American flirtation, in which it is understood from the first that nothing is to happen, as contrasted with a Continental love affair in which both partners must bear in mind its constantly lurking dangers" (p. 11). The remark was unnecessary for conveying his meaning and reflects his misunderstanding of and judgmental attitude toward a culture somewhat different from his own. How much greater is such misunderstanding when the individual being observed comes from a truly different culture—not Western but Eastern! And how much more crucial it is if the person in question is in a psychoanalytic treatment situation!

In a stimulating paper by Jenai Wu (1994) in a recent issue of *Contemporary Psychoanalysis* entitled "Therapy with Asian Patients," the issue of the influence of culture as it virtually collides with psychoanalysis is brought into sharp focus. One approaches the paper with the expectation that inevitable cultural differences in mores and etiquette, for example, would be described, their significance understood, especially since the author is herself Asian, and some changes would be made to accommodate the difference from the usual approach to Western patients. This was far from the case. Dr. Wu adhered to prescribed classical analytic prodedures—an impersonal neutral stance, a waiting, quiescent attitude, a complete lack of self-disclosure, and a failure to convey to the patient that most often the therapeutic goal is best served when an interaction takes place between therapist and patient and a relationship is formed out of this dialogue. It is particularly ironic that Dr. Wu chose not to modify classic analytic proce-dure despite her awareness of the Asian patient's sensitivity to issues of shame and what she calls "verticality," which we prefer to call the hier-archical nature of the classic analytic set-up. The result is that, generally, Asian patients leave the therapeutic situation. And indeed Dr. Wu lost the patients whom she describes.

What, then, is her point? Should we conclude that Asian patients are not suited for analytic therapy? However, if we believe empathic under-standing together with insight into previously unknown and unconscious dynamics, discovered in the context of a relationship, to be the way in which one individual can help another, then perhaps we should think in terms of modifications of the original psychoanalytic techniques. The Asian lack of tolerance for this procedure makes palpably clear how culture-bound the original technique is, although there are also Western individuals who find the rigid technique odious. It used to be said that such persons were unsuit-able for analysis, usually because they were thought to be too narcissistic to form a transference relationship with the analyst. And indeed the analy-sis of the transference, resistance, and defense stands in the center of classical analytic procedure. But why should we fear that if we do not ex-clude ourselves as much as possible from the analytic situation, a transfer-ence will either fail to develop or will be so contaminated by the intrusion of reality factors as to be unanalyzable?

Freud (1915a) himself made it clear that transference phenomena occur throughout life itself and are not peculiar, except in their intensity, to the analytic situation. To be human is to be able to relate to others, to love, and therefore to have transference reactions. Even psychotic patients form transferences (Schwing 1940). And while insight into the patterns that originate in the past is helpful, it is not the ultimate, curative factor in the analytic method. Rather, the curative factor lies in the relationship to the therapist, which offers an opportunity to overcome the inevitable repetitive transference responses, provided the therapist is able to be empathic to the feelings, goals, and values of the patient. Since these grow out of his or her culture to a large extent, the analyst must be open to adapting procedure in the name of creating the relationship.

Dr. Wu understands the Asian culture at least more than most Westerners. But she chooses to identify with the dictates of the orthodox psychoanalytic method, rather than with the cultural needs of the Asian patient. It is this overidentification with the prescribed psychoanalytic method, with its suspicious attitude toward reality in the name of ferreting out resistances and banishing defenses, that leads her to misinterpret certain culturally characteristic postures and expressions of her patients.

For example, let us take the issue of the Asian's so-called inscrutability. As one would expect, Wu (1994) thoroughly understands the Asian's relationship to affect. She writes: "In Asian culture, the inhibition of many strong affects, but particularly the aggressive ones, is inculcated from childhood" (p. 160). Although some control of feelings is taught from early childhood in most cultures, in Chinese culture the value of the "golden mean" as taught by Confucius has profoundly shaped the ego-ideal in this culture. It stresses moderation in all things. Therefore, strong emotions are frowned upon. In addition, the importance of saving face, of avoiding shame and social approbrium is also very central. Thus, the expression of strong affect, since it is not approved of, is experienced as shameful. What Westerners sometimes experience as the stone face of the inscrutable Asian is most often the result of a lifetime of experience in controlling emotion. However, as one becomes more familiar with Asian people one learns to observe nuances in their expressions that one could formerly have readily overlooked. These nuances are also perceptible in some of their works of art, especially in sculpture. The faces are far from inscrutable.

It is a mistake to equate the Asian's indirect and subtle way of expressing emotion with the repression of emotion or of the impulse connected with emotion. It is rather a fulfillment of the ego-ideal of *regulating* emotion. Nor should one speak of "hiding" affect. Regulation of affect is not hiding; nor is "face" (persona) the false self. With the discovery of the unconscious and of repression, there is a false assumption that the only *true* reality is that of the unconscious.

The art of a culture can often express its attitude toward emotions. In Chinese painting one is struck by the repetitive roundness of forms and the prevalence of curves rather than straight lines. These features are not accidental. The culturally stated attitude is against angles, which are felt to be expressive of aggressive feelings. The "roundness" is thus a statement of benignity. For example, meals are best served at round tables so that all the participants can share equally the food that is placed in the center. Psychoanalysis, in its enthusiasm for the discovery of repression and other defenses, especially against unacceptable emotions, would be quick to interpret this cultural style as defensive, rather than to see it as an ancient and successful mode of adaptation. Especially in the therapeutic encounter, in making interpretations, an analyst's tendency to apply psychoanalytic norms of behavior, even of morality, as if these norms were universal, may not only be mistaken but may also be highly destructive to the individual patient. The culturally specific diversity of norms makes all too clear the rigidity of the Western norms adopted by psychoanalysis. The psychoanalytic commitment to the medical model of treatment is also highlighted by the needs of individuals from other cultures. If one is treating a case of pneumonia, the use of antibiotics is indicated irrespective of an individual's cultural heritage. However, if we seek to alter behavior, character structure, or feelings and images of the self that are unacceptable to the patient, our understanding of the problem, our diagnosis of what is pathology will depend heavily on our understanding of the social and psychological norms of the given culture in which the individual has grown up. For in making psychological appraisals we must measure behavior, states of mind, or interpersonal relationships in relation to social norms—always accounting for individual differences, of course—that have their origins in specific cultures. What is acceptable in one culture is frowned upon in another.

For example, let us take the issue of dependency. In Japan as Doi (1981) points out, the *amae* feeling—a loving dependency of one individual on another—is not only acceptable but it is desirable, and the Western ideal, especially in the United States, of inculcating in the child strong ideals of self-reliance and independence from family is frowned upon. In India with its tradition of strong family bonds, the very structure of the self is part of what Roland (1988) refers to as the familial self. Is it not obvious that in evaluating dependency in the therapeutic situation, especially as it is reflected in transference reactions, when we work with individuals from cultures whose ideals and values differ from our own or from those advanced by psychoanalysis, we must empathically enter their cultural world in order to distinguish what *for them is* normal or abnormal? Or to take another example, psychoanalysis, with its emphasis on sexuality and the sexual development of children, placed great emphasis on the avoidence of situations within the family that could be construed as sexually seductive and experienced as such by the growing child. Yet we recently heard of a 3-year-old Asian boy, a child of unusual sensitivity and intelligence, who had been sharing his grandmother's bed on a regular basis. In his culture it is not unusual for small children to share a bed with an adult family member. One day his father, who had been away for some time and had recently returned, asked the child to sleep with him that night. "No," answered the child. "Grandma would be very sad if I did that." Clearly for him sharing a bed signified a warm, affectionate bond—a bond that he had with his grandmother who at this point was his primary caretaker. The sleeping arrangement was natural for everyone because it was accepted as such by his culture.

Let us suppose that this very child came into psychoanalytic treatment as an adult because of some emotional problem, and let us suppose further that in the course of treatment he felt lonely and disappointed and a memory of the sweet security he felt as a small boy sleeping with his grandmother came to him—a longing to experience this again momentarily overwhelmed him. Should the psychoanalytically trained therapist promptly conclude that the early memory was one that carried a sexually seductive valence? Certainly not without a careful inquiry. The general meaning of sharing a bed in Western culture is more inevitably sexual than it is in some parts of the East or in other cultures. One cannot know with what symbolism or implication the routine interaction between peoples is charged in all cultures. Therefore, it is important to approach new interactions with an open mind rather than with preconceived norms that derive from a largely deductive and speculative psychology originating in a highly specific Western middle-class culture.

This leads us to the inevitable conclusion that a psychotherapeutic technique cannot be applied to individuals with emotional problems or even with discrete psychological symptoms in the same objective way in which a medication can be prescribed for the treatment of a disease. The therapist (analyst) is part of the cure, and the nature of his or her interaction with the patient is crucial for the outcome of the undertaking. Just as the patient's difficulty has its origins in the interactions of family members functioning within the larger framework of a specific culture, so an interactional system—that between patient and therapist—is crucial to the cure. But it is not enough to understand a patient's family dynamics; one must become acquainted with the culture that spawned them. Failing this and applying arbitrary norms or inflexible techniques can only lead to a misunderstanding of the patient and often, as in the case of so many Asian patients, to a cessation of therapy.

The failure on the part of psychoanalytic orthodoxy to take the dimension of culture into account is more than a disservice to the therapeutic process. Through the setting up of rigid norms for behavior and subscribing to a belief in their universal validity, the neglect of culture can become a defense against the awareness of the mixture of feelings that the perception of cultural differences may produce. The fear of stereotyping individuals, as Wu (1994) points out, has led us "to shy from investigation along cultural lines" (p. 152). In the United States, ours is a multiethnic, multinational, and multiracial culture in terms of the origins and backgrounds within its diverse population. We constantly perceive difference and are confronted with the task of assimilating and working through our reactions to these differences, to some of which we may have negative reactions. The human reaction to difference, which may have its origins in psychobiological responses, is a subject too vast for the dimensions of this chapter. However, our national conflict around this issue needs to be addressed. As a democratic society with humanitarian aspirations, our cultural ego-ideal requires that we tolerate and accept differences, but in the course of this process our reactions, especially if they contain elements of distaste, cannot always be admitted and are therefore often suppressed. Indeed, they are sometimes repressed and make their appearance in other realms. Thus, a prescribed therapeutic procedure that inhibits free exploration and acceptance of cultural characteristics can serve to rationalize and justify therapeutic failure. The realm of psychological investigation requires a special awareness of the dimension of diversity in the human species—a diversity that is expressed in individual difference as well as in the variety of cultures that groups create.

In formulating theories about behavior and in their practical application in the psychotherapeutic process, we must be wary of imposing preformed interpretations—interpretations that quietly acquire the character of stereotypes—upon individual patients without regard for their individual differences and for the culture in which they were formed. It is the dimension of culture that is most often either totally neglected or grossly misunderstood. This is probably because in the highly subjective "science" of psychoanalysis we came to believe that all people were like ourselves—or almost.

13

Otto Rank and Ego Psychology

It is a reflection of the times we live in that emphasis has shifted in both psychoanalytic literature and practice from the unconscious impulse life to a concern with ego or self. Historically and sociologically this shift is understandable. Freud's discovery of the importance of the instinct life, as it is reflected in the dynamic unconscious, character, behavior, and neurotic symptomatology, had to be exhaustively explored before the psychology of human beings could be viewed from another perspective—development of the ego. Freud speaks of the ego as the instrument of repression, but he devises no actual psychology of the ego until the publication of *The Ego and the Id*, (1960) and then because he has discovered not only that the drives are unconscious and therefore differentiated from the ego but also that parts of the ego are unconscious as well. The model of the mind had to be recast from the early division of conscious and unconscious to a structure consisting of id, ego, and superego, in which ego and superego could be unconscious. Furthermore, the focus on the psychology of the ego is in part a response to the emotional needs of present-day individuals, suffering as they so often do from alienation, loss of meaning, disillusion, and an absence of faith in themselves and others. The mere statement of present-day needs as they differ from those of Freud's time points not only to the need for an ego psychology but also to a psychological relativism that did not characterize early psychoanalytic thought.

There was one early psychoanalyst, however, who viewed human psychology primarily as a phenomenon of ego development and who saw its relationship to the social setting in which it grew. This was Otto Rank. Considering the dimension and uniqueness of his contributions to psychoanalysis, he is little known, rarely read, often misunderstood and misinterpreted, and insufficiently appreciated. It is important to mention some of the events that led to Rank's rift with Freud and his development of an independent line of thought. The rift itself has much to do with ego psychology.

Rank in his early years was largely self-educated. He made his first contact with Freud through extensive reading. He was impressed with psychoanalytic theory and thought it explained the creativity of the artist, a subject that had always interested him. He thereupon set about on a creative effort of his own. Rank (1925) wrote a small treatise called *Der Künstler* (The Artist), using psychoanalytic theory to explain the driving force and the productivity of the artistic personality. It was this work that ultimately brought him in contact with Freud. Rank gave the manuscript to Alfred Adler, whom he had heard lecture, and Adler showed it to Freud. Freud was so impressed with the work that he sent for Rank, took him under his wing, encouraged him to complete his education at the university, and ensured his financial ability to do so by making him the secretary of the Psychoanalytic Society. These events led to a sort of father-son relationship between Freud and Rank, a relationship that met profound needs for both men and that lasted for some 20 years. Rank received his Ph.D degree as a psychologist from the University of Vienna, and throughout his early years in the psychoanalytic movement, his work focused on what was then called applied psychoanalysis. He had a vast knowledge of mythology, religion, and literature, and his interest in art, the artist, and in creativity continued unabated. He wrote extensively in these fields. It was when he began to do clinical work that the soil was prepared for the ultimate break with Freud.

Unfortunately, Rank is most known for the work that initiated the split with Freud—namely, *The Trauma of Birth*, published in 1924. It is a work that can and should be looked upon as the beginning of Rank's concern with separation and individuation, and therefore as the beginning of his psychology of the will and of his understanding of ego processes from a perspective that differed from the then current psychoanalytic one. Instead, the book is misunderstood as Rank's final theory of anxiety, rather than as a phase in the development of his own thinking. Its implications for ego psychology have been utterly disregarded.

The Trauma of Birth itself was born into an unfriendly environment. In a way, it was an illegitimate child. Rank was, at the time, a member of the secret committee of the Seven Rings, a group of loyal followers whom Freud had gathered to preserve the pure gold of psychoanalysis and to protect it from such heresies as those of Adler and Jung. Rank was the youngest member of the committee. Its members had agreed that no one would publish anything without the knowledge and approval of the entire committee. When Rank prepared and published The Trauma of Birth somewhat secretly as a surprise gift to Freud on his birthday, it was misconstrued as a breach of their agreement. This angered the other members of the committee and provided fuel for the fires of their already existing envy and professional rivalry. Rank felt a profound emotional intimacy with Freud. Like Joseph of biblical fame, who exacerbated his brothers' envy through boasts about his father's gift of the coat of many colors, Rank aggravated the tensions among the "brothers" by keeping his creative work a private matter between himself and his so-to-speak adopted father. The older members, like their ancestors, threw the favored brother into a deep well of what they hoped would be extinction.

But Rank did not expire; instead he entered a period of great productivity and independent creativity. The publication of The Trauma of Birth represented his own birth—his emergence as a separate individual.

What has all this to do with ego psychology? Surely it was not merely the rivalry and hostility of his colleagues that separated Freud and Rank and led Rank to regard himself no longer as a psychoanalyst. It was something in the content of that fateful book—or something in the direction toward which it pointed—that was read by other analysts as a threat to psychoanalytic theory.

On the face of it, The Trauma of Birth is a very Freudian work. Rank thought of it as a contribution to the theory of anxiety and therefore as an explanation for neurosis. Its publication was almost concurrent with Freud's Inhibitions, Symptoms and Anxiety (1961b) in which Freud too saw the birth experience as the prototype for anxiety. But Freud's main concern was to modify his theory that anxiety was the discharge of accumulated libido. His new theory introduced the participation of the ego in the origin of anxiety. Instead of automatically converting libido to anxiety, the ego used the libido of the to-be-repressed instinctual impulse for the production of anxiety. This energic view of the psychic life is characteristic for Freud. For him birth represented an accumulation of undischarged and undischargeable—because of the immaturity of the organism—libidinal energy that became the source of anxiety.

Rank's perspective is quite different from Freud's, despite the apparent similarity in the idea of birth as the point of origin for anxiety. For Rank separation from the mother organism is the crucial issue. It is becoming a discrete, autonomous entity, wrested from the oneness of the fetal situation, that is the source of primary anxiety. For Freud the danger precipitating the anxiety lies in the accumulation of forbidden instinctual impulses that must be repressed; for Rank the danger lies in the loss of a completely protective and satisfying environment with which the individual is at one—an environment later to be perceived as "mother." One might say with Rank that the anxiety imprint of birth originates not as an intrapsychic conflict but as an interactional experience with the human environment. The source of anxiety for Rank is interpersonal.

Initially Rank had a literal conception of the relationship between birth and anxiety: the more difficult the birth, the greater the traumatic experience, the greater the quantity of fear to be mastered. Had Rank remained at this level of thinking, he might have continued to be a good Freudian, but he evolved to an understanding of the figurative meaning of birth as individuation. It is in this sense that he is the forerunner of ego psychology, although he did not think of ego in structural terms but more in terms of what today we would call "the self." Individuation, like birth, takes place in relation to another individual and involves differentiation and separation from that "other." Rank refers to this as a "Thou psychology" and states explicitly that it is inseparable from an ego psychology. As life proceeds, all the symbols of separation that evoke the original separation induce anxiety.

The dream of a young woman patient of mine illustrates this concept. The dream followed her family's move into a newly purchased house. She dreamt: "We move into our new house; it is terrible; the backyard, instead of being beautiful, is a graveyard containing the graves of all the previous owners. Also, there is a slum close by." On one level the dream reflects the perfectionism of her extremely obsessive-compulsive character structure. She is always on the lookout for "the best" and is never sure that what she has is that. In a state of doubting and uncertainty she constantly seeks something better, be it a house, a job, furniture, or a dress. Her dream expresses the fear that the house may not be the best and, failing this, may be terrible. The perfectionism and grandiosity represent an identification with her own mother's extremely narcissistic use of their relationship. Her mother's demands expressed the need for a perfect daughter to reflect favorably upon her mothering. My patient has internalized her mother's image of her and has remained in a symbiotic relationship to her. Perhaps this symbiosis is represented by the graveyard in the back of the house. The graveyard may stand for the fact that the patient is haunted by her forebears and fears she cannot break away from her past. Separation from this internalized narcissistic image is the central therapeutic problem. Here Rank's profound insight into the issue of separation from the mother, that is, birth as an individual, is crucial.

But how is this differentiation manifested in the emotional development of the individual, Rank asked himself. He viewed the striving for individuation as primary, resulting in the emergence of ego. The force with which this ego expressed itself he called will—an unpopular concept in the so-called scientific philosophy of psychoanalysis. The ego is mobilized by a "cosmic primal force," by which Rank meant the energy of universal life, not specifically sexual or aggressive energy as with Freud. The strength of this force, expressed as will, varies from one individual to another.

This represents Rank's second fundamental deviation from Freudian theory. I have already mentioned the first: the emphasis on the interpersonal nature of the emergence of the individual ego. Now we see that the motor for personality is not fueled primarily by the instincts and the need for tension reduction, but by the energy of the ego that is vested in expressions of the will.

The will is a creative force, according to Rank, whether it is expressed in the creation of personality itself or in the creative work of the artist. The fact that every individual is endowed with creative will makes for an emphasis on growth, change, and expansion in Rankian psychology and leads to a very different therapeutic approach than one based on the deterministic dominance of instinctual impulses and the life of the unconscious.

But every view of the human situation has its limitation and points to the existence of problems that were not apparent previously. Would one think that the expression of will would be accompanied inevitably by guilt feelings? Rank found this to be the case. Here his understanding of guilt is original and profound: he understands it not in relation to some forbidden impulse, but as a consequence of the striving toward individuation—that is, as a byproduct of the process of separation from the significant other. Guilt originates in the course of development as a byproduct of willing or self-assertion. It begins as counter-will, as negative will. This is a familiar phenomenon to all those who have observed children in the 2- to 4-year-old contrary phase. Rollo May (1969) refers to this expression of will as "protest" (p. 192). Without awareness of any relationship to Rank's psychology, he appreciates the developmental importance of the child's capacity to take a negative stand against parents. The exercise of this capacity inevitably results in feelings of guilt, however, simply because this act of separation contains elements of aggression toward a parent on whom the child is dependent and toward whom he has loving feelings, but also because the child has empathy for the parent, especially the mother. The capacity for empathy, a psychobiological given, is built into what Rank calls the ethical nature of the mother-child relationship. We can empathize with "the other" because once we were one with the other. With the birth of consciousness, both the self and the other are born psychologically, and the capacity to project oneself into the situation of the other person—in fact, the inevitability of so doing—brings self-interest into conflict with the will of the other. Guilt arises because one part of the self, that which is asserting individuality, is not in harmony with another part of the self, the internalized part that originally was identified with the mother and therefore empathizes with her. The conflict between self and other is experienced as separation at the expense of the other and is internalized as a split within the self. It is a conflict that is experienced throughout life in all significant relationships, and it inevitably leads to feelings of guilt.

Let me illustrate this concept with an example from the treatment of a young woman patient whose emotional history manifested an incompletely resolved symbiosis with her mother and who became acutely hypochondriacal some months after the birth of a daughter. Her fear that some misfortune would befall the child or that she herself would die of some dire ailment overwhelmed her. Herself a psychologist and a person of insight, she attributed her anxiety to an evocation of her symbiotic ties to her mother: "I feel as if some part of me [the baby] was outside myself and as if I had no control over it." During her pregnancy, the patient dreamt that she looked in the mirror and saw her mother's face instead of her own. The merger with the mother is obvious. The wish for the protection, security, and freedom from responsibility that such merging implies is clear. Even the fear of separation in the face of this strong wish is not hard to account for. But wherein resides the guilt?

First it is important to realize that in both the wish and the fear there is a duality. The young woman wishes autonomy, but also a loss of self; she fears the individuated role of the grown woman who has become a mother, but she also fears the loss of identity in a merging with her own internalized mother. The duality is not one of drive[1] but of the affective relationship of the self with the mother; if the ego acts upon one side of the split, it fails the other side. In attempting to understand why guilt feelings should arise out of contradictory feelings, it is important to remember that the contradictory duality originally existed within the mother who has been internalized. The mother was narcissistically overattached to her daughter (my patient). Her own wish for maintaining the merged relationship and her wish that her daughter should become an independent person are reproduced in the self-structure of the young woman through processes of identification. My patient's guilt arises because she cannot separate from her internalized, symbiotic mother and at the same time be true to the wish for a merged identity with her mother. In the sense that guilt arises within the context of a relationship, albeit internally, it is a social phenomenon and is therefore ethical in Rank's sense of the word.

The hypochondriacal symptom produced from this conflict is both punishment for infidelity to the symbiosis and fear that the split self will disintegrate totally. The original lack of cohesiveness in the self is reinforced by life circumstances that made my patient a mother before she resolved the separation-autonomy conflict with her own mother.

In the language of psychoanalysis, the problems of separation-individuation lie in the realm of narcissistic phenomena, that is, in the individual's struggle to shift libidinal energy from the cathexis of the ego to investment in love objects. In other words, the issue of the delineation of the individual ego is basically a libidinal one, a problem of the distribution of sexual energy. However, Rank sees it differently. Primal life energy is manifested in the will; the will in turn expresses individuation. But because of the human capacity for relatedness through projection and introjection, which Rank calls the ethical nature of man, willing results in guilt.

It is through a creative act that guilt is to some extent expiated. The individual who has expressed himself at the expense of "the other," gives back, through a loving relationship or a creative product, that which he feels he has taken for the enhancement of his own ego. But the human creature cannot escape guilt; the very act of creative guilt redemption is a

---

[1] Such duality is to be distinguished from ambivalence that is directed *at* the love-object (mother) as love and hate, whereas the duality of which we speak concerns the position of the self vis-a-vis the love-object (mother) within the configuration of the self.

further assertion of his will, which produces additional guilt. The creative artist, in whom Rank was very interested, is constantly driven to creativity, in expiation for having produced his previous work. In Rank's view, guilt is not the product of instinctual impulses conflicting with moral dictates, but rather of autonomous acts of will. It belongs, therefore, in the realm of ego psychology. It is the crucial issue in the the treatment of neurosis, for neurosis is not primarily a disturbance of sexual function, but of ego function. The most important task of therapy is to liberate the patient from excessive feelings of guilt and anxiety. The guilt stems from strivings toward individuation, the anxiety from fear of separation.

The human fear of separation and aloneness is profound, and Rank has some deep insights into the defense mechanism against it. For example, he speaks of denial in a very different sense from that to which we are accustomed in classical psychoanalytic theory. For him denial is not a response to external danger that would threaten the gratification of instinctual need, but to the danger of perceived difference between the self and the "other." To deny this difference is to create the illusion of oneness with the other individual, thereby cancelling out separation. The conflict against which the defense is erected is a conflict within the domain of ego processes, not between ego and instinct.

It is important to bear in mind that Rank's therapeutic goal is liberation of the patient's will rather than acquisition of insight into the patient's symptomatology or character disturbance. This does not mean that Rank eschews insight; it is just that he does not regard it as the curative agent, but rather as a preparation for the real experience of relating to the therapist. Through insight, an individual can be freed of the compulsion to repeat the past; through the actuality of the relationship with the therapist, he can exercise his will for change. Willing is a creation of something new, a freeing oneself from the exclusive influence of the past. The act of will bridges a gap between the present and the future and in this sense institutes a new chain of causality.

But how is the patient's will liberated in the therapeutic situation? Central to success is the therapist's affirmation of the patient's unique individuality and a belief in his or her capacity for growth. This affirmative belief must be conveyed in the real interaction between patient and therapist, and it must be understood as well as experienced. It is here that Rank's *constructive* therapy differs from analytic therapy, for he distinguishes the analysis of transference from an understanding of what takes place in the real present-day relationship.

We can take the issue of the will-to-health (i.e., the will to change) as an example of how the conflict surrounding the act of willing plays itself out in the therapy. Rank accurately perceived the patient's expectations upon beginning therapy. He writes, "For the first thing the patient does when he begins treatment is to project his will-to-health onto the analyst who represents it, as it were, just by virture of his profession" (Rank 1945, p. 17). In psychoanalytic terminology we would speak of the patient's passivity or passive wishes. The patient believes the therapist to be powerful enough to make him well, thereby putting aside his own will in the matter. When I was a student of analysis in Vienna, case discussion often emphasized the importance of the patient's *Krankheits Einsicht* (insight into his or her illness). It was thought that if an individual had no insight into the fact that he was neurotic or if he was not suffering from conflict, then treatment lacked the necessary leverage. But the admission of illness, even the wish to be well, is quite different from the will to change, for both the awareness of neurosis and the wish to be rid of it can be projected onto the therapist as an expectation that he or she will effect the change. Rank felt it was crucial that the therapist not permit the will-to-health to be projected onto himself. Instead he should "function as counter-will in such a way that the will of the patient shall not be broken, but strengthened" (1945, p. 16). The strengthening takes place through acceptance of the patient's will expression, thereby reducing his guilt for willing.

This is not always an easy task, nor is it always successful. I have in mind a patient who had been in analytic treatment for many years with a series of therapists. She was a middle-aged professional woman, married to a man toward whom she had very ambivalent feelings. The ostensible reason for therapy was her inability to make a decision concerning her marriage. She was unhappy staying in it and fearful and unhappy at the thought of breaking it up. No amount of insight, acquired in the course of all her therapies, helped resolve her inability to act. It is important to mention that she was deeply committed to psychoanalytic ideology, of which she had considerable knowledge. She was convinced, despite all her previous therapeutic experiences, that the answer to her difficulty lay in some as yet undiscovered cause of her indecisiveness and anxiety. Any attempt on my part to steer her away from causal thinking, to engage her in the experience of our relationship, met with severe criticism: I failed to understand her, I was not active enough, I was not sufficiently concerned with transference phenomena, I was unable to deal with hostility. At no point did she assume responsibility for implementation of the insight that she had acquired, for squarely facing her anxiety, or for stopping projecting responsibility for her woes onto others, such as her husband, her friends, and her analyst. My attempts to point this out, to deal with her profound passivity, yielded little reward. The psychoanalytic precept that the analyst promotes insight and cure by interpreting the conflict surrounding the instinct life strengthened my patient's neurotic position. It was easy for her to justify her position in analytic terms and to charge that I was not proceeding correctly. The analytic style encourages passivity. Rank wrote that the analytic approach, because it is causal, negates the will principle, which is open ended and creative. When psychoanalysis becomes an ideology, it can be used defensively, as can all other ideologies regardless of the validity of their content. Perhaps this is a clue to the puzzling fact that as therapists we seldom succeed in changing our patient's ego-ideal.

It should be clear now that Rank's focus on the creative will is an ego psychological issue. He saw the human being as burdened with consciousness, that is, with the awareness of his separateness, of his autonomy, which he both wished for and feared. The realization that this hard-earned individuality is finite, that it can cease to exist, is also part of the burden; with the awareness of mortality comes the striving for immortality. Through the works of the creative will, some measure of immortality can be achieved. But the expression of will is always attended with guilt, so the major therapeutic task is to help the patient affirm his or her will without excessive guilt. In the Freudian view, the patient learns to accept his impulse life because the analyst accepts its universality and communicates to the patient that he cannot be held accountable for his instincts. In Rank's view it is the therapist's acceptance of the patient's unique individuality (i.e., of his ego) and its expression through acts of will that enables the person to affirm him- or herself, to make peace with the nature of life and the inevitable fear and guilt that accompany the emergence of a separate self.

14

Interpretation and Ego Function

We pay too little attention to the implications of some of the miracles of life that surround us. One of these miracles is the phenomenon that one individual can influence the behavior, thinking, attitude, and feeling of another. Pragmatically, we make use of this fact in countless aspects of our daily lives—in child rearing, in education, in social encounters, in politics, in business—and certainly in our own field of psychotherapy. In fact, the "influenceability" of human personality is the indispensable condition for any psychotherapeutic intervention.

Yet, perhaps because of the dangers implicit in the misuse of the power to influence, the issues surrounding the factors of influence in human interaction have been side-stepped; even more, they have generally been disparagingly dismissed as "suggestion," and the technique of interpretation has been advanced as an antidote to the possible dominance of any element of suggestion in the therapeutic procedure. In the early days when psychoanalysis was being born out of the techniques of hypnosis, Freud was aware of the inevitable factor of suggestion that played a part in the efficacy of interpretation, as well as in mass psychology and certain ego phenomena. However, because of the transitory and limited effects of hypnosis as a therapeutic method and the discovery of the dynamic unconscious and of the phenomenon of repression, Freud regarded suggestion and interpretation as antithetical therapeutic techniques. Suggestion, whether implemented by the authoritative or lovingly persuasive stance of the therapist, placed the ego of the patient under his domination, whereas the uncovering and consequent interpretation of hitherto repressed impulses made available for the patient new self-knowledge, thus expanding the boundaries of his ego and creating opportunities for new integrations.

The emphasis, therefore, in the classic psychoanalytic technique was on the uncovering of unconscious content, be it of drives or of defenses, and the interpretation of these to the patient. To the extent that this viewpoint seeks to increase the patient's ego autonomy, it is valid in its intention, for it corresponds to the patient's own conscious motivation to alter his behavior, thinking, and feeling. However, it rests on a limited technical definition both of suggestion and of interpretation and on an assumption that they are opposing phenomena relative to the human ego.

I should like to advance a different view: that interpretation involves much more because of the innate tendency of ego to synthesize meaningful wholes, to integrate inner and outer experience at increasingly higher levels of significance. Thus, interpretations—sometimes irrespective of their validity but given a positive, trusting, and viable atmosphere between therapist and patient—may become foci around which the patient structures new meanings that satisfy the ego's need for oneness. These human attributes are the evolutionary product of our neurophysiological history as a species and attest to our plasticity and ego-growth potential as individuals.

The term "suggestibility" is used here in its broadest sense. It appears in infancy in its earliest and most primary form as receptivity to the loving ministrations of the nurturing mother. As we know from the studies of Spitz, Bowlby, Escalona, and others, such loving care, which involves much more than the giving of nourishment, is essential for the development of the nervous system, the emergence of consciousness, and the ultimate structuring of ego. It is important to remember that the interaction system of mother-child, is a crucial communication system in which the child's capacity to receive is as important as the mother's ability to love. One possibility of influencing the development, formation, and direction of human personality rests in this capacity to receive communications—be they tactile, kinesthetic, auditory, visual, or verbal—and first to convert them into neurological structure and subsequently to integrate them into psychic functions. Specifically, the processes of introjection, imitation, and identification, which are innate, primary capacities of the human psyche, are responsible for the efficacy of personal interactions in promoting new and higher levels of ego integration and functioning.

Implied in this juxtaposition of interpretation and ego function is the rather obvious fact that the purpose of interpretation is to improve ego function, whether such function is impaired by anxiety, inhibition, or the formation of neurotic symptoms or character disorders. In the Freudian view the value of interpretation in meeting these ends lies in the fact that, by making conscious what had previously been unconscious, a shift of energy takes place within the psychic systems, making energies previously associated with unconscious processes now available to the ego. Thus, the Freudian conception of change or cure depends on a redistribution of energy within a closed system, and the function of interpretation is to bring about this redistribution.

When one views personality, and ego as its essential psychological core, not as a closed system seeking stabilization through the reduction of tension within its confines, but as an open system striving expansively toward optimal realization of its potentialities, then one's view of the nature and function of communication between individuals changes and a new perspective on the therapeutic interaction appears. Classic psychoanalysis has found major support for a conception of personality as a closed system in the repetitive phenomena of the transference, of the repetition compulsion in the occurrence of neurotic, often self-destructive, life patterns. These phenomena undoubtedly do exist. They must be among the things interpreted appropriately in the psychotherapeutic situation; but they do not necessarily argue for a conception of personality as a closed energy system. There are other phenomena which we observe in the therapeutic situation that bespeak the expanding, evolving nature of the human ego as a part of the total life process, which is an open system. As an example, we can cite the operation of *choice* in the patient's motivation toward therapy as a means of achieving a higher level of ego-integration, optimal expressiveness, and self-realization, thereby striving to achieve a self-conception more consistent with his ethical goals and his conception of and need for love and relatedness. It is important to bear in mind that not only *conflict* can motivate a patient toward therapy, but also *ego-ideal aspiration*. When the therapist has an awareness of this fact, even though it remains unexpressed or even unconscious on the part of the patient, his interpretations are geared toward the support of such strivings and aspirations. He approaches the therapeutic task with a belief in the patient's capacity to transcend himself. Such belief is as crucial for the patient's betterment as the young mother's belief in her infant's capacity to grow is for his actual development. The transmission of this belief—this basic trust in the life process—

be it by implication or explicit statement, is a crucial, curative aspect of interpretation.

Empirically the application of classic forms of interpretation has had only limited effect, that is, in the uncovering of unconscious defenses and the corresponding unconscious impulses that it has been their function to ward off, together with the discharge of affects appropriate to such conflict and the working through of this process on successive levels of libido organization. Such failure has its roots in two main causes. One lies in the Freudian deterministic, mechanistic conception of personality that, when transposed into the act of interpretation, presents to the patient, from a position of authority, a partial truth about himself as if it were a whole truth, thereby doing violence to his ego, restricting its operation within a given system of thought, and inhibiting its expansive potential to new and higher levels of integration. In essence it is a misuse, however benignly motivated, of the suggestive capacities of the ego. Inadvertently, by leaving no room for the human equality of patient and therapist, the authoritative stance perpetuates what is an inevitable, yet it is hoped temporary, dependent, submissive position of the patient in the therapeutic encounter. An interpretation that points up the possibility of true insight to the patient, thus catalyzing his own ego processes, has an entirely different appeal to his ego than a flat statement designed to expose a defense or an unconscious impulse.

A second source of therapeutic failure in the classic psychoanalytic approach was the assumption that change in thought, feeling, or action follows automatically, if not directly, upon the interpretation of the unconscious and then certainly upon the working through of the interpretation and the discharge of appropriate affect. In actuality this rarely happens. Following is an example of the essential and positive contribution of the interpretation of the unconscious, as well as its limitations and what might be added to bring about greater autonomy of the patient's ego.

An attractive and intelligent young man of approximately 25 had been consulting me throughout the past academic year because of feelings of estrangement, fears pertaining to his sexual identity and acceptability to women, and certain inhibitions in his work life. He was a graduate student in one of the arts, was living away from home, but was being supported by his parents. He was in a total state of rebellion; he wished to do almost none of the things that one is supposed to do and did practically all the things that the conventional adult world frowns upon, from smoking marijuana to being irresponsible about his studies. Such negativism obviously presents the therapist with serious problems. An important asset of the patient, however, enabled me to achieve excellent rapport with him. He possessed a high degree of creative psychological imagination and was motivated by a great desire to understand— to uncover the meanings of perplexing emotional experiences and to reintegrate these into a unified account of his life. Despite his estrangement, he tried to reach out to people, and his wish to love and to be loved belonged to his almost explicitly stated aspirations. It was a pleasure to share his joyous sense of wonder when he made a discovery about himself. We made some of the usual discoveries: among them his unexpressed anger, sometimes even rage, toward parents who meant well, but whom he experienced as controlling and dominating and his highly ambivalent attitude toward an older brother whom he loved, was dependent upon, yet hated, and with whom he feared to compete. He saw his insufficiency at work and school as expressions of his anger; he saw his difficulties with peers, both men and women, as in large measure influenced by the unresolved conflicts in his brother relationship, which precipitated passivity, guilt, and powerful feelings of inferiority. At times he expressed hostility toward me, and he was able to understand this expression as a projection of his feelings toward his mother. Yet, none of these insights appreciably influenced his overt behavior.

As we approached his final sessions before the summer holiday, it became clear that he had mismanaged his attempts to get a summer job so successfully that he had nothing lined up for the ensuing months. This young man who complained so bitterly about his dependence on parents was so in the grip of rebellious anger against them that, at the cost of suffering great guilt and feelings of worthlessness, he was impelled to make them pay.

At this point in his treatment, however, I did not reinterpret his inhibition as resulting from the passive, aggressive impulses based on revengeful feelings toward his parents and brother or from defenses against the fear of his own hostilities against them. These connections, which had originally been unconscious, were now known to him, hut they were not operative. Instead I said: "I suggest that you try to get some kind of work for the summer. You will feel much better with money in your pocket that you have earned; you will be your own man. There are so many things you could do with your talents and experience (and I enumerated some of them for him). You know what will happen if you don't work; you will only feed your feelings of worthlessness and guilt, and that doesn't help in any of your relationships, especially with women. I hope I'm not reminding you of your mother when I say these things."

He assured me that I was not reminding him of his mother, that he felt what I described was right, that he did in fact want to get a job and that he appreciated my urgings.

Can these simple, common-sense suggestions and depictions of the consequences of action or inaction be properly called interpretations? Perhaps not in the usual usage of that term. Yet, there is a hierarchy of interpretation, in the course of which having gone the accepted Freudian pathway from unconscious ego defense to deeper unconscious impulse, one again returns to address the ego—not the ego that institutes and executes defenses nor even the inherent conflict-free ego sphere that guarantees the autonomous development of certain ego functions, but rather the ego that is motivated by striving and aspiration to fulfill its optimal potentiality, to achieve a higher, more autonomous degree of integration, to participate more completely in human interaction. In a therapeutic atmosphere in which the therapist conveys his trust in this progressive capacity of ego, as well as an empathic understanding of the patient's conflict and anxiety, and in which the ground has been prepared by making available and meaningful for the ego that which was previously unconscious and unknown, an interpretation that might otherwise be regarded as simple exhortation becomes a catalyst for the self-realization of the patient. Thus applied. the function of interpretation goes beyond its content, to the expression of the capacity of one human being to bring influence to bear upon the expansive ego potential of another.

15

Questioning the Sacred Cow of the Transference

The transference is the sacred cow of the psychoanalytic treatment method. Since I have always been skeptical about sacred cows, I thought it worthwhile to examine this one and to question some of the premises that the psychoanalytic world has taken for granted.

In Freud's work with Breuer (1895/1957) on Anna 0.. he observed that some of her symptoms, dreams, and fantasies were elicited by her feelings toward Dr. Breuer, her therapist. Although they had a life of their own that originated in her own familial experience, they were then—in the course of her "talking cure"—reflected in the mirror of her relationship with Breuer. Anna O.'s feelings were largely of a sexual nature—a fact that was more disturbing to Breuer than to Freud, for whom sexuality was the primary motivating force in human life. The phenomenon of the projection of emotions that originate with the primary love-objects in one's life onto other individuals who are experienced as having similar roles, Freud (1912) called transference. Although he was aware that transferences take place in relationships outside of analysis, he was primarily concerned with making use of this general phenomenon for purposes of psychoanalytic cure. It is important to remember that Freud's great discovery was the dynamic unconscious and its role, because of repression, in the development of neurosis. The major task of treatment was therefore the uncovering of the unconscious through the lifting of repression. Since the expression of emotions in the transference reflected unconscious aspects of the patient's ways of loving, of hating, the transference became an important vehicle for understanding an individual's deeper life. Not that the emotions expressed in the transference were unconscious; on the contrary, they were usually very strongly and consciously experienced, but their origin and significance for understanding an individual's way of relating to others had remained unconscious until they appeared and were analyzed in the transference relationship.

The transference is at one and the same time a phenomenon of memory and an "acting out" in the analysis of these memories in the sense that the feelings toward the analyst—the wishes, longings, fears, angers—are expressed. Thus, if an important goal of analysis is the recovery of repressed memories, and it was that for Freud, then the transference in which the feelings are expressed though not acted upon may be seen as a resistance to this process. Yet, Freud saw the analysis of the transference as an unusually convincing way for the patient to experience, in the flesh as it were, the validity of the repetition of emotions that originated in very early childhood. The interpretation of the transference—the bringing into consciousness of the connection between past and present emotions—freed the individual's ego to choose other ways of reacting. The bond to the past could be altered, the repetition compulsion need not be in command, and balance could exist between the various parts of the personality.

Why should I speak of pitfalls in this well-thought-out, logical conception of the role of the transference in the cure of neuroses and other behavioral and emotional disorders? To answer that question, let me first return to a discussion of the psychoanalytic situation. The analytic relationship between analyst and analysand is set up (and I am speaking of classical psychoanalysis) in such a way as to reproduce in reality and in actuality certain aspects of the childhood situation of the individual under analysis. The inevitable hierarchy of the parent as protector but inevitably as final authority on the one hand and the dependent child on the other is repeated in the authoritative position of the analyst and the inevitably submissive position of the patient.

It might be argued that whenever one person seeks help from another a similar situation exists: the physician and patient, the lawyer and client. To some extent this is true for all transference responses that are apt to occur whenever one individual needs another. There is, however, an important difference between the psychoanalytic situation and other situations in which help is sought. The physician and the lawyer, for example, have something very concrete to offer in response to the expressed need, to the request for help: medical advice, a medical procedure, or legal advice or strategy. The request made of the analyst, on the other hand, is for an emotional response, and this is precisely what the analyst is enjoined not to give in the name of maintaining the powerful transference experience for the patient. The analytic situation recreated the unrequited love, on the sexual level, of the childhood experience. But it does more. In childhood there are normally other aspects of loving that the child experiences, such as affection. tenderness, care, and protection. Except in some cases, there are in the analytic situation only very attenuated forms of caring and protection, especially if the analyst is at pains to maintain a so-called neutral stance. By definition and intent the analytic situation is one of abstinence and rejection in the sexual sense, as indeed it should be. Whether it should be so in regard to other forms of loving and relatedness between two individuals in which one is dependent on the other is a moot point.

Nowhere in the clinical application of psychoanalytic theory do its origins and history become clearer than in an exploration of the transference. As is well known, Freud's (1915b) theory of repression, his knowledge of the unconscious, derived from his experience with hysterical patients, and he concluded that they suffered from repressed memories of sexual experiences or wishes, more specifically of repressed oedipal wishes. This insight then became generalized: repressed memories were the cause of psychic illness, and the memories were sexual in nature—in fact, they were specifically oedipal. To the extent that the rejection of the gratification of these wishes when they surfaced in the transference is therapeutic, their evocation by the analytic situation is appropriate. But is the recovery of memories and the making conscious of sexual wishes the curative factor in psychoanalytic treatment? And is the oedipal complex truly at the root of neurosis?

The word "neurosis" is scarcely appropriate today, for we deal with many different kinds of disturbances and maladjustments of personality that are not primarily the result of repression and very rarely of sexual repression. In this age of sexual expression—at least in the overt behavioral sense—individuals seeking emotional help suffer from a lack of relatedness and from inhibitions in the ability to love, to feel affection or tenderness. This inhibition results from a deficit in early childhood experience, from a lack of the experience of being loved and accepted unconditionally so that there are insufficient internalizations of previous experience to build a cohesive and integrated personality. It becomes quite clear that the Freud-

ian definition of the transference as a projection of unconscious wishes is
inappropriate, or at least limited, in terms of today's patients. What is needed
to effect a cure is not the lifting of repression, not the regression to the
wishes of an earlier time, but rather the opportunity to grow in a better
environment—an environment that can provide through the active participation and relatedness of the analyst a model for how loving, caring, and
affirming are conveyed, so that this positive experience of receiving affirmation can be internalized and can become part of the patient's personality
for future relationships in which he or she can then be the one who actively affirms others.

I am sure that by now you will have recognized Heinz Kohut's (1977)
conception of the transference as a relationship with the analyst that recre-
ates not the original situation of childhood, but rather creates a new parent-
child relationship in which the old deficits in affirmation are not repeated
and the opportunity for new internalizations is provided. Kohut made these
valuable contributions to our understanding of human development on the
basis of his work with narcissistic personality disorders. As his work grew,
he too generalized about the applicability of his concept of the transference to all persons. Transference has two distinct aspects: what Kohut called
the mirroring transference referred to the interaction between analyst and
patient in which the deficits in affirmation during childhood are made good,
and the idealizing transference is one in which the patient idealizes the
analyst's image and internalizes it. This inner representation of the idealized analyst forms a large part of the patient's value system.

It is important to contrast Kohut's concept of the analytic situation
with that of Freud. For Freud the ego is to gain strength through frustration
and rejection in the transference experience; for Kohut the self is to become
cohesive and integrated through the active participation of the analyst in giving
to the patient what he or she either lacked entirely in childhood or experienced in insufficient quantity or inappropriate quality. The first is an experience of deprivation: the second, an experience of fulfillment. In each case
there are transference reactions. Where then are the pitfalls?

In the first instance, in which the premise upon which cure is founded
is the lifting of repression and the stance of the analyst is neutral and
uninvolved, the pitfall has two aspects. The first lies in the dubious authenticity of the patient's emotions vis-à-vis the analyst, for it is the technical
maneuver of unresponsiveness or unrelatedness that artificially induces the
patient's extreme emotions of the transference. It is true, to some extent,
that such emotions are based on expectations that originated in childhood,

but their artificial recreation in the analytic situation takes away from their credibility and furthermore produces anger that is then analyzed as if it were the unjustifiable product of the patient's neurosis. Freud called this the "transference neurosis" and thought that to induce it through the abstinence of the analytic situation was the optimal road to cure.

If an individual is uncertain about the authenticity of his or her feelings, however, the very foundation of reality testing is challenged. The uncertainty is felt not only in relation to one's own emotions but also spreads to include many aspects of reality itself. The patient loses the conviction of the validity of his or her own perception of reality and instead internalizes the analyst's belief in the truth of his (the analyst's) perceived reality. The loss or impairment of this important ego function is scarcely the way to cure.

Furthermore, if a patient's psychic disturbance is not primarily the result of repression but rather of deficits in the emotional nutrients in the course of development, then only the opportunity for positive mirroring and for idealization in the transference can be of help. For such patients—and today they are in the majority—the contrived experience of projection in the transference that is mandated by the technique of classical psychoanalysis can be extremely destructive. These are the patients who used to be referred to pejoratively as unanalyzable. There was no thought of giving up or altering the sacred cow. A second pitfall of the transference is created by the analyst's inability to listen for and perceive the real nature of the patient's needs.

There are in every human interaction or relationship, in varying degrees, both types of transference reactions: the one that offers the opportunity for projection and the one that offers the opportunity for introjection. In the first instance, the premise on which cure is based is the offering of insight to the patient—insight into the ways in which the unconscious heritage of the past has influenced present-day feeling and behavior. To achieve such insight the repetition compulsion is invoked, and the theory contends that the conscious knowledge and experience of repeated and undesirable patterns of behavior and feeling can inhibit their further repetition. We know from experience that this is not necessarily the case; at best, that insight can be partially helpful in altering and integrating personality. In the second type of transference reaction, the premise on which the concept of cure or change is based depends on the analyst's ability to offer him- or herself for new internalizations on the part of the patient—internalizations that will correct the developmental insufficiencies and deficits of the past. The original personality disorder is thought to be the result of an arrest in growth; therefore, the chance to provide an opportunity for growth is essential.

At this point I am reminded of the fact that Freud inveighed precisely against the analyst's offering himself as an object for identification on the part of the patient. This important statement is to be found in a footnote in *The Ego and the Id* within the context of Freud's (1923/1960) discussion of the treatment of masochistic patients. He was aware of the difficulty such patients have in giving up old destructive patterns of behavior, precisely because they have learned to find satisfaction in them. Knowing the extent to which personality is formed on the basis of identifications Freud concluded that the patients' masochism was, at least in part, the product of a masochistic relationship to the internalized parental imagoes, and he saw no way of neutralizing the power of these identifications short of forming new ones based on the relationship to the analyst. To encourage such identifications, however, would, according to Freud, put the analyst in a godlike position. a situation that he strongly opposed.

Freud failed to see that the transference in the analytic situation, as he conceived it, inevitably created precisely that masochistic stance of the patient that he wished to cure. This is the product of the hierarchical relationship between therapist and patient in which the patient must be submissive, must accept the analyst's truth as well as his or her rejection and lack of responsiveness. The classical analytical situation thus becomes a breeding ground for the formation of masochistic character structures. This is certainly a pitfall to be avoided. But in fact the analytic situation need not be so structured.

Kohut's work in self psychology addressed a very different aspect of the transference relationship. While Freud used the transference to address unconscious *libidinal* needs, Kohut addressed developmental needs of the self. Let me use a very simple example. A young female patient wishes to disidentify with her mother and adopts the particular, rather unique dressing style of her female analyst, thus expressing the striving to consolidate a self according to a new, freely chosen model. This is not to say that in doing so the problem is solved. Not at all. Neither the original conflict with the mother nor the imitation of her analyst is understood in any depth. The behavior is only a symbolic expression of the striving to reintegrate and re-create a new cohesive self.

An interesting question arises. Should the analyst interpret the idealizing transference? For in the wish to be like the analyst there is certainly some idealization. Although the answer cannot be an unequivocal "yea" or "nay," for much depends on the particular individual in question, and on the point in treatment at which the issue arises, the key to the answer lies in the fact that a *constructive process* is going on and an interpretation would interrupt that process. The patient would become self-conscious and therefore inhibited. The answer then, in general, is "no." It is best not to interpret these aspects of the transference that pertain to the structuring of the self.

Sometimes an embarrassing situation can arise for the analyst. Recently I experienced this with a very sophisticated, middle-aged female patient whom I shall call Katherine, who suffered from an extreme work inhibition. In former years she had been successful as a consultant in the business world. But when she came to me she could not even mobilize herself to look for a job. She had had many years of analysis at the hands of outstanding classical analysts and had acquired considerable insight into the origins of her conflicts in relation to her family. She was a middle child of three. Not only was there considerable rivalry with an older sister but her parents also had focused all their expectations for success on this sister, expecting practically nothing in the way of achievement from my patient. She understood the connection between her childhood experience and her lack of will to work. Since there were no expectations, there were also no rewards. We established very good rapport in our work together; I shared some of my own experiences with her, especially as they referred to the way in which I worked and my enjoyment of my work. It was also clear that I liked her and enjoyed our interactions. It soon became apparent that she was beginning to idealize me. One day she asked me quite bluntly if the way for her to be helped with her inhibition was to identify with me. It was an awkward moment. One feels immodest in recommending oneself to someone as a person to be emulated. However. I stuck to what I perceived to be true. I confirmed her own statement; it might indeed be helpful to her if she could identify with my way of working and my enjoyment in my work. I never pushed her to work, but I expressed my confidence that she would overcome her inhibition; and at one point I actually put her in touch with an agency that could help her with some vocational counseling.

We have not yet reached our goal. My patient is not yet free to express herself, to make use of her abilities and talents, as well as of her experience. There have been a number of ups and downs in the course of her treatment: there are times when she is able to take action and other times when she is so severely depressed that she can barely get out of bed.

While insights gained in previous therapies as well as those gained in her work with me have been helpful in orienting her within her emotional world, they have not liberated her from her profound inertia. Her "cure" will depend heavily on her ability to make new identifications. It is hoped that she will introject my positive response to her as a person as well as her idealization of me as someone—at least in certain respects—to be emulated.

It is interesting and instructive to observe two aspects of the transference as they have played themselves out in the course of my work with Katherine. The transference based on projection makes its appearance at times. For example, I became the hated and envied older sister. This is especially the case when she is extremely depressed and experiences me as insufficiently helpful. But even when Katherine is feeling these emotions, is in fact quite authentically involved in them, she can spontaneously take some distance from them. She is aware of the projection and knows that what she is feeling toward me is not a reaction to the "real" me. At times she can even laugh at her own distortions of reality.

And then there are the introjective aspects of the transference, when the self of the patient makes use of the analyst in order to grow. The personality of the analyst and his or her own feelings for and relationship to the patient act as nutrient, when they are ingested, for the developing self. It is extremely important that the reality and authenticity of the analyst's personality be expressed in the analytic situation so that the patient can identify with an actual reality.

One of the most important pitfalls of the transference is to confuse those transference reactions of the patient that grow out of libidinal needs, result in distortions, and are induced by the abstinence requirement of the analytic situation with those that strive to nourish and consolidate the self through identification with the analyst and to which the analyst should respond in terms of the reality of one of the profoundest human relationships.

16

Self-Disclosure, Transference, and Countertransference

Very little has been written in the psychoanalytic literature about self-disclosure, that is, self-disclosure by the analyst. In fact there is no such category in the Grinstein *Index of Psychoanalytic Writings* (1956-1975). This is not surprising since the very essence of the philosophy of classical psychoanalytic technique rests on the premise that the "cure" for the patient depends on the creation of a transference neurosis within the context of the psychoanalytic situation, and this in turn depends on the neutrality of the analyst. Neutrality in this case means a minimum of self-revelation: no disclosure of opinions, values, or advice, no sharing of personal experiences or biographical facts. The analyst is to remain a non-person in the name of fostering the development of the transference—that projection onto the person of the analyst of each individual's specific way of loving or hating that is the legacy of constitution and early childhood experience (Freud 1921). In the face of a person's search for psychological help, the therapist, according to classical psychoanalytic theory, is to remain *neutral*, that is, not interact with the patient in any other way than to foster the uncovering of unconscious impulses and to communicate such insights to the patient. This procedure is founded on the premise that help or cure for the patient is based on the lifting of the repression of unwelcome impulses; that is, the making conscious of previously unconscious wishes would effect cure or change in an individual's personality. This premise is in turn based on another preceding premise, namely, that neuroses or disturbances in personality functions are caused by repression of impulses, especially sexual impulses. Neither premise, while describing some truth about personality functioning, has been found empirically to be the exclusive cause of neuroses or of disorders of the personality. It should then follow that, in the name of therapeutic efficacy, the *cultivation* of the transference is unproductive. The emphasis is upon the word "cultivation," for it is indeed impossible to prevent the development of transference phenomena in any human interaction between two people, be it in life or in the therapeutic situation. The way of loving or hating that is so much a product of past experience becomes an intrinsic part of an individual's personality and is bound to express itself in psychoanalysis as well as in life in general. Freud was aware that transference phenomena take place in life as well as in psychoanalysis, but he wanted an intensification of transference feelings for the analytic situation and to this end he advocated the neutrality of the analyst.

Many years ago, a patient, whom I shall call Ruth, came to me because her relationships with men were never consummated in a permanent relationship of any kind. She found herself to be either with married or inappropriate men, or to be unable to find men to whom she might be attracted. She was about 40 years old, not particularly attractive physically, but she had a fine character, was fairly intelligent, and had a lively, outgoing personality that made up for her deficits in the realm of beauty. She described her needs and wishes to me very clearly in our first meeting, realizing fully that her social difficulties with men had to do with inner conflicts of which she was not fully aware. As we concluded our arrangements for her therapeutic work with me, I experienced an impulse to tell her something of my life.

I was about 65 at this juncture. It was a time about a year after the death of my husband when I began to live with an elderly man who had been a mutual friend of ours many years ago in our student days in Vienna. We had met again, were both free, were attracted to each other, and were unusually compatible. We decided to join our lives, and since I had a large apartment, he moved in with me. My office and home were combined, and as patients waited for me in a small anteroom near the front door, they occasionally saw family members coming in or out of the apartment. I knew that sooner or later someone would see my new "roommate" entering or leaving the house. Contrary to classical psychoanalytic policy practiced by most of my colleagues, in order, supposedly, not to interfere with transference reactions, I wanted no unknowns, no mysteries about the major biographical facts and events of my life. I told Ruth about my life arrangements of that time. Her reaction is extremely important. After having listened intently, she turned to me and said, "Then there's hope for me." "Yes, of course," I replied.

As I look back on the fact that I followed my impulse to reveal the nature of my personal life at the time, if only in broad generalities, I wonder what impelled me to follow my inclination—an inclination so opposed to the therapeutic philosophy in which I had originally been trained. Yet even that statement is not entirely accurate, for in my second analysis with Willi Hoffer during my psychoanalytic student days in Vienna, he himself was changing his personal life situation. He had been divorced, and when I began my analysis with him, he was living alone and working in an apartment from which he was about to move. When he gave me his new address, I asked about the reason for the move. He told me that he was to be married soon and that he and his wife were to move into the new apartment. He even told me who his new wife was—Hedwig Schaxel, a nonmedical analyst who was a member of the Vienna Psychoanalytic Society and a person whom I had seen at meetings.

I expressed surprise at this forthright answer to my question, for I had been indoctrinated to believe that any personal revelations on the part of the analyst would interfere with the purity of the transference reactions. "But," said Dr. Hoffer, "I believe that a patient has the right to know the basic biographical facts of his or her analyst's life: whether he or she is married or single, whether he has children and what his educational and psychoanalytic training consisted of." He presented this as if he considered the biographical facts to be in the nature of credentials whose meaning would differ for individual prospective patients, but whose reality would give individuals the opportunity to make choices. The simplicity and honesty of his remarks pleased me and had the therapeutic efficacy of creating trust. I never had the opportunity to discuss with Dr. Hoffer the extent to which his modifications of standard psychoanalytic procedure were a part of a thought-out therapeutic philosophy or derived naturally from his broad empirical experience with human reactions that he was willing to affirm and take at face value. It is significant that he never wrote on this theme and that, in fact, most classical analysts are timid about revealing what they regard as "transgressions" of accepted procedure.

My experience with Willi Hoffer liberated me at that time (described in my memoir [Menaker 1989]) from any tendency toward absolute faith in the validity of psychoanalytic theory and its technical practices. Undoubtedly in my interaction with the patient described before, the nature of my analysis with Dr. Hoffer and his lack of fear of self-disclosure (at therapeutically appropriate times he had told me memories about his childhood and about his warm relationship with his father, a country doctor, whom he often accompanied on home visits to his patients) reinforced my own inclination to share my life situation with my patient. But to what end, one might ask? Not only to create an honest atmosphere in which to conduct her analysis—although I consider this extremely important—but also to make clear to her, who was longing for a relationship with a man, that even at my late age this was possible.

Her answer about hope for herself confirms the effectiveness of my self-disclosure. A number of years later she did indeed meet a man within her professional circle with whom she fell in love and with whom she has established a permanent and compatible relationship. Obviously it was not merely my remarks about myself that enabled her to establish a good relationship with a man. Much analytic work took place in the intervening years. She learned a great deal that had been unknown to her before. Her over-attachment, yet ambivalence, to a father who was inclined to be grandiose, and the way in which this affected her life became clear, and her identification with him diminished. She came to be less critical and more appreciative of a mother whom she had formerly regarded with predominantly hostile feelings. Such insights played a major role in the changes that took place in her character and in her behavior.

However, it seems important to emphasize that the analysis took place in an atmosphere of nonjudgmental dialogue about shared experiences. We had much in common: our values and our familial background were similar. Our parents were professional people of Russian origin. I understood the idiosyncrasies of that culture and could often respond to her anecdotes with similar ones from my own background. This created a powerful bond between us. Some might say that the special circumstances that derived from certain actual similarities in our emotional experiences invalidate the assumption that self-disclosure is of great importance. On the contrary, what is in this case an actual similarity points to the importance—in the interactions with all patients—of finding and expressing those human commonalities that exist for all of us. It is also important to convey in these interchanges an affirmation of our common human heritage and an expression of hopes that the realization of the patient's goals for his or her life, which is the reason the treatment was sought in the first place, will be fulfilled. Does such an exchange of experience and emotion between patient and therapist preclude the development of the transference that is, in the thinking of the classical analyst, the sine qua non of the psychoanalytic undertaking? I think not, for the simple reason that transference reactions occur constantly in all our life situations, as I have already remarked and as Freud himself stated. We carry with us the baggage of our past, which influences all our perceptions. In academic psychological circles, it used to be called our apperceptive background. The imprint of past experience influences our perceptions of present-day events, including the perception of people and their interaction with us. Furthermore, the self-disclosure of the analyst is not, nor should it be, a contrived technique calculated to further the therapeutic process. The analyst unavoidably reveals him- or herself in the course of interacting with the patient through appearance, tone of voice, choice of words, gait, and body stance, to mention only a few of the cues that we all pick up in the course of any human interaction. But self-disclosure of the analyst in the analytic situation is a spontaneous empathic response to the patient's communication by sharing an analogous feeling or experience in the life of the analyst. The purpose of the disclosure is to underscore for the patient the fact that the analyst has understood the import of the communication and that he or she affirms the patient's reality. Sometimes, of course, such an interaction goes awry. The analyst may not have understood or not have understood fully. But no matter; for the very willingness on the part of the analyst to share experiences creates an atmosphere congenial to dialogue, and in the course of the subsequent interchange greater understanding and trust are inevitably achieved and a closer bond between the two participating individuals is created.

The fostering of an understanding bond between patient and therapist in the name of arriving at a mutually acceptable understanding of the patient's reality is, of course, the opposite of the Freudian approach, which seeks to uncover a reality unknown to the patient—the repressed and therefore unconscious unacceptable instinctual impulses that are seen as the cause of neurosis or of neurotic symptoms. A major vehicle for this archaeological task is the analysis of the transference: that projection of the patient's inner emotional life, complete with distortions, upon the relatively non-participating personality of the analyst. Thus, a "truth" is arrived at that supposedly reflects hitherto unknown feelings, wishes, and impulses. Once such previously unconscious impulses are brought into awareness, they exist in the domain of the ego and can be volitionally accepted or rejected, acted upon or not. The possibility of choice has become part of the patient's psychological life. The premise that underlies this approach to therapy is that the curative factor in the analytic situation is the uncovering of the unconscious (largely through free association, the analysis of dreams and fantasies, and the analysis of the transference), making it known to the patient and helping him or her work through and assimilate the newly acquired knowledge. The "real" or "actual" relationship of the patient to the analyst is rarely of any consequence since the analyst is viewed as an outside observer, not as a participant in a relationship. This is the model in broad strokes of the classical Freudian philosophy of therapy. It is based primarily on a theory of conflict in which human development takes place primarily as a struggle between drives that seek pleasure (the release of tension) and superego constraints that represent the demands of society.

A different view of development leads to a very different theory of therapy—one in which the active role of the analyst plays a crucial part and in which the element of self-disclosure may contribute to the outcome. It is in the approach of self psychology, as it was begun by Heinz Kohut, that the patient's relationship to and interaction with the analyst are decisive for change and/or cure. The analyst's way of observing as a self psychologist differs from that of the Freudian analyst. For Kohut advocates what he terms an introspective, empathic stance. The analyst is an active participant in the interchange with the patient, observing the patient not as an object to be comprehended from a distance outside oneself, but as someone whose emotions one can take in even to the extent of momentarily losing oneself and merging with the patient. It is through such empathy that the self psychologist hopes to make good those deficits in the patient's development that are responsible for the maladaptations and unhappiness that brought him or her to seek psychotherapeutic treatment. Self psychology rarely speaks of neurosis or of conflict but rather of arrests or deficits in an individual's development due to familial experiences that failed to provide adequate nourishment for the child's developing self. A major aspect of the analyst's task is to provide that nourishment.

The rudiments of self-structure are given from the beginning of life in the very nature of a child's constitution—in the way of responding to the environment, the sensitivity to stimuli, and the reactivity of the nervous system, for example. There are great individual differences in the basic psychobiological nature of individuals, for each person is unique. This uniqueness is further augmented by the specific nature of the familial experience in the course of which the structure of the self is laid down through processes of internalization. The child takes into him- or herself the parents' very way of being: first the external traits—the way of speaking, of walking, of gesturing; then the more internal—the way of thinking, of relating to others, of feeling about oneself. Thus, the self of the child is structured.

Of course the child is not a duplicate of his or her parents, for the identifications have been added to the initial predispositions, and a new and unique personality has been structured through this amalgamation, as well as through the internalization of experiences and contacts with individuals outside the family. Often identifications are rejected. Particular aspects of a parent's character or behavior are found objectionable. Often as therapists we hear, for example, from young women: "I never wanted to be like my mother" or "I have made up my mind that I would never treat my child as my mother treated me." But all too often the rejected identification is repressed only to appear in some distorted form when the child-rearing situation becomes a reality. Whether identifications are successfully assimilated into the self-structure or are repressed, or are rejected out of hand, or are simply absent, leaving large vacancies in the self, is determined by the nature of the parent-child bond during the phases of development. Successful internalization that leads ultimately to a cohesive self-structure takes place in a familial atmosphere of love, of relatedness, of parental affirmation of the child. It is loving respect for the growing, striving self of the developing child that forms the nourishing soil for the integration of a self in the growing individual—a self that can relate well to others, make emotional commitments in close relationships, and enjoy a secure sense of self-esteem.

One day a psychologically sophisticated middle-aged man whom I shall call Karl, who had been in treatment at various times in his life and with me for more than a year, came to his session in a discouraged mood. He had been looking back on the history of his emotional life and realized that he had never been able to make a commitment to a woman that had any degree of permanency. He had had two unsuccessful marriages, and his current relationship was one to which he felt he could be loyal only in a limited way. He wished very much to be able to love fully enough to commit himself to a marriage. He feared that it would always be this way, for while his various therapies over the years had provided him with considerable insight into the psychodynamics of the emotional interactions among family members, they had not been able to help him toward a full love relationship.

Knowing a little about the emotional limitations in his relationship to his mother and suspecting that there might still be aspects of this relationship of which he was unaware, I began asking him about his mother in greater detail. My patient began to describe a person who was timid, uncertain, and unassertive in her relationship to individuals outside the home and who was unfocused and detached in her relationships within the family. She sounded unformed in her own personality structure and unable to be totally committed to relationships—to her children, to her husband, and to those outside the family.

It suddenly struck me that my patient's inability to commit himself to a relationship signaled a profound and completely unconscious identification with his mother—with her inability to relate to others and with her detachment and isolation. He had incorporated this identification and it became a profound imprint that determined the nature of his relationships to women. I communicated my hypothesis to him. I emphasize the word *hypothesis* because the manner in which an insight is conveyed is of great importance, especially in relation to the issue of self-disclosure. To hand down interpretations as absolute truth is to present oneself as an autocratic therapist, even as an autocratic individual. The authoritarian stance vis-à-vis the patient is, to some degree, the psychoanalytic legacy of its historical origins in hypnosis, although, even in this connection, psychoanalysis distinguishes between the authoritarian and the persuasive maternal type of approach in hypnosis. If, on the other hand, one is engaged as a therapist in a dialogue with a patient—a dialogue that seeks to explore possible explanations for a patient's character structure or behavior—in an egalitarian atmosphere, one wins the patient's trust and reveals oneself as an empathic person capable of precisely that kind of relatedness that the patient lacked in the course of development.

My conjecture about my patient's possible identification with a withdrawn mother made a profound impression upon him. He could scarcely believe that, in the many years of therapy that he had experienced, the possibility of this aspect of his personality development had never been unearthed. He seemed relieved by the insight—by the knowledge that he had been a victim of an unconscious unwelcome introject that was his mother's way of relating to others. He was imbued with some faith that this introject could be exorcised. He could become his own person and discover his own way of loving.

Karl began his treatment with me in the reserved and somewhat distant manner to which he was accustomed from previous therapies. Gradually he began to respond to my somewhat casual manner. In the beginning I noticed his surprise if I shared some of my experiences and reactions with him. For example, we might recently have heard the same concert or have gone to the same art gallery. It would not be unusual for me not only to hear about his reactions with interest but also to share my own with him. I recall clearly an occasion when we spoke about an exhibition of primitive art that he particularly enjoyed. It happened that I had found this art form somewhat uncanny, and I described to him my hypersensitivity to any quality of eeriness in works of art or even sometimes in natural scenes. I told him of a childhood experience when, upon returning from school one afternoon, I had come unexpectedly upon a reproduction of the Mona Lisa. The picture, which had just been given to my mother by a neighbor, was standing against a wall waiting to be hung. I had been frightened by her strange enigmatic smile and ran screaming down the hall to ask my mother, "Who is that Indian down the hall?" Even as an adult and even after having seen the original, I have never succeeded in feeling comfortable with da Vinci's supposed masterpiece.

Such small vignettes out of my own life, particularly out of my childhood, that revealed my own emotions gradually helped Karl experience his own feelings in a less muted form. My disclosures also enabled him to perceive and experience me as a real person with strengths and weaknesses, with tastes and values that sometimes coincided with his own, but were sometimes quite different. What is therapeutically important is that my revealed authenticity helped him delineate and define his own.

But what of the transference, that supposedly therapeutic vehicle through the analysis of which memories are to be recovered, repressions lifted, insight gained? The transference both in life and in the therapeutic situation, since it is an individual's way of relating to others, occurs inevitably. Yet the classic analytic situation. by virtue of the analyst's lack of participation, intensifies and distorts the projection of the patient's emotions onto the person of the analyst. I am reminded in this connection of a film that grew out of Brazelton's infant research that I had the good fortune to have seen in 1977

The researchers were studying mother-infant interaction. One frame showed an infant of about 9 months sitting in his high chair, expectantly awaiting the arrival of his mother. When she entered the room, smiling, cooing, and expressing her pleasure in being with him, the little boy smiled, made gleeful sounds and body movements that he could scarcely contain for sheer joy. The same child on another occasion in which the set-up was the same was confronted by his mother, not with a smiling face but with a "dead" face in which no emotion was expressed. The disappointed and frustrated child tried in every way, by cooing and smiling himself and by physically reaching out toward his mother, to elicit a response from her. It was all to no avail. She remained stony-faced. Finally, in frustration, the child began to cry, and what began as a cry that expressed need, longing, disappointment, and anxiety at being thus abandoned turned into a cry of rage.

In the psychoanalytic situation, a similar scenario is recreated: the childhood situation of the patient in which "the inevitable hierarchy of the parent as protector but inevitably as final authority on the one hand and dependent child on the other is repeated in the authoritative position of the analyst and the inevitably submissive position of the patient" (Menaker 1988, p. 44). Furthermore, the objective neutral stance and noninteracting posture of the analyst that are recommended for classic psychoanalytic procedure are contrived techniques that artificially induce extreme emotions in the transference—usually and ultimately rage—that are then interpreted as products of the patient's neurosis. These extreme emotions are in fact normal reactions to needlessly created frustrations in a situation in which one individual is asking another to be of help.

A patient's reaction of anger to the unempathic, detached behavior of the analyst is not necessarily a regression to the infantile reaction to frustration that I have just cited in my description of the film on the infant research study. The parallel between the "dead" face of the mother and the unresponsive, so-called neutral, stance of the analyst illustrates the normal human need for social interaction.

The issue of self-disclosure on the part of the analyst is ultimately bound up, as we have already seen, with the problem of the transference, which in turn reflects the analyst's theory of neurosis, as well as the very philosophy of cure. We are confronted here with two separate views of neurosis and therefore with two different conceptions of therapy. I would like to emphasize the existence of two distinct vantage points, both of which can play a role in the actual treatment of a particular individual, but that are philosophically separate.

If, with Freud, we view neurosis as the result of the repression of unacceptable sexual impulses that have been banished from consciousness but that, from their existence in the realm of the unconscious, continue to exert a deleterious effect on the personality of the neurotic individual, then the goal of treatment becomes the lifting of repression. It is important in psychoanalytic treatment to bring the repressed impulses into awareness so that they can exist in the domain of the ego and can thus be controlled by the ego. The use of free association and the analysis of an intensified transference to the analyst thus become the essential hallmarks of a classical psychoanalysis.

Freud attributes the intensification of the transference to the factor of abstinence, i.e. the absence of the gratification of impulses. It is precisely the lack of reciprocity in the classical analytic situation that causes the libido to leave the world of reality, to regress to earlier stages of libido development, and thus to reanimate the internalized imagoes of early childhood toward which the impulses were originally directed. To justify or rationalize this regression, the patient in the psychoanalytic situation distorts by a process of projection his or her perception of the analyst to achieve a correspondence between reality and the infantile imagoes that reside in the unconscious. Making this process of distortion conscious for the patient constitutes a major therapeutic goal of the analytic process.

The fact that the analyst is an objective observer, rather than a participant, and that there is no reciprocity in the relationship accounts for the intensification of the patient's need for response—much as the infant's response described above. The regression, the infantile response is induced by the analytic situation and the analyst's technique of nonparticipation. For the classic analyst, the return to the past is considered of primary importance for the patient's cure or betterment. The transference phenomenon becomes a vehicle for unveiling what psychoanalysis considers a convincing return to the infantile past that is supposedly at the core of the patient's neurosis.

However, a different view of the genesis of neurosis would lead of necessity to a modification, if not a complete change, in psychoanalytic procedure. It is to Heinz Kohut that we owe a different perspective on the origins of personality disturbances. For him there was a major line of human development that differed from the development of the libidinal stages that Freud had hypothesized. This was the development of the self. The rudimentary self that is given at birth develops further as the child grows through processes of internalization, namely, through the internalization not only of parental imagoes but also of those parental attitudes toward the child that were experienced in the interaction between the child and the parents. Kohut's emphasis in evaluating emotional disturbances was heavily weighted in the direction of a concern with self-esteem. Self-esteem in turn depends on the nutrients for self-development that the child receives from the parents in the form of mirroring or the opportunity for idealization.

For example, the pleasure that a child perceives in his mother's face as she enjoys his or her activity, his accomplishments, in fact, his very being, is internalized and becomes his own image of himself in which he can take pleasure; his self-esteem is nourished and becomes secure. In addition, if a parent—often the father—furthers the child's idealization of him (or her), the growing self of the child is given another opportunity through an internalization of the ideal to support his growing self and thus to achieve a good sense of self-esteem.

In familial situations that provide only a dearth of the nourishment needed for the growth of a healthy, cohesive, and integrated self, the child suffers emotional damage that is manifest in behavioral and psychological maladaptation. Most often the result of such deficits is a loss of self-esteem. This is true not only for narcissistic personality disorders, as Kohut thought at first, but for all those disturbances of personality that come to the attention of the psychoanalyst. The analyst's therapeutic task then, according to Kohut, is not primarily to uncover unconscious impulses and make them accessible to the conscious personality of the patient in the name of resolving conflict, but rather to strengthen the self by making good those emotional deficits of the patient's childhood that resulted in his or her failure to form a securely consolidated self. This is achieved through the analyst's clear affirmation of the *person* of the patient.

Otto Rank, who can be considered a forerunner of self psychology and who thought that neurotics suffered from an inhibition in the function of *willing*, due to a failure on the part of parents to accept the child's will, also emphasizes the therapeutic effect of affirmation—in his own terms, affirming the patient's will. Above all the analyst must not further damage the patient's already fragile self-esteem. This can easily happen if the analyst presents a cold, distant, authoritarian stance. One of the dangers in the classic approach is precisely that the observing objective (neutral) stance of the analyst can too easily become an attitude of detachment, which inevitably lowers the patient's self-esteem. The empathic stance of the psychoanalytic self psychologist, because it is participatory, lends itself to interaction between patient and therapist in which the therapist becomes the selfobject for the structuring of the patient's self. In the empathic mode, the purity of the transference, be it mirroring or idealizing, need not be threatened, as in the case of traditional analysis, by the active participation of the analyst. It is the fact of participation in the relationship to the patient that opens the way for self-disclosure by the analyst.

When the analyst reveals something about him- or herself—about his life or experience—at a time and in a context that are appropriate relative to the patient's communication, it becomes an echo, or an elaboration on the echo, of the patient's own experience and thus serves to cement a bond between the patient and the analyst, inhibiting processes of projection and fostering identification. The analyst, since he or she functions as a selfobject for the patient, becomes authentic and thereby better serves to sustain and further the structuring of the patient's growing self. I would like to emphasize the factor of the authenticity of the therapist in the treatment situation; for whatever the nature of a particular human interaction—be it between parent and child, teacher and pupil, friend and friend, or analyst and patient—when the "other" is felt as authentic, the delineation of the self is thereby furthered, differences and similarities come into sharper relief, and the self, as well as the capacity for mature relatedness, is enhanced.

Self-disclosure cannot of course be random. It must be sensitively attuned to the needs of the therapy, that is, to the particular needs of the patient's developing self.

The question of countertransference is bound to arise in connection with self-disclosure: does the analyst have an emotional need to reveal him- or herself to the patient; and if the answer is yes, does this invalidate the procedure? Since we are speaking of an intense emotional interaction between two individuals who undoubtedly have an effect on one another, the answer to the first question may be affirmative. But if the need is not quantitatively excessive, there is no reason to fear that it will interfere with the patient's analysis. In an empathic atmosphere, the needs of each individual as they interact with one another can be met within limits. However, the patient's need for self-development in the therapy must be of primary concern, and the therapist must try to judge when self-disclosure is productive and when it could become an obstacle to the goal of treatment. In general, when self-disclosures are honestly motivated by the analyst's desire to be helpful, even if they misfire because of a failure in perfect empathic understanding, they can be used productively in the analysis to demonstrate convincingly for the patient the struggle between expectation and disappointment.

In conclusion, self-disclosure lends itself much more naturally to the empathic introspective stance of psychoanalytic self psychology than to rigidly traditional psychoanalytic procedures. There also remains the important question of the relation between theory and technique. I have sketched the differences between the Freudian and the Kohutian theory: the emphasis upon the repression of libido in the one case, and, in the other, that of the role of the developing self and the deficits that may accrue to it. From these divergent positions concerning the genesis of neurosis emerge the different technical procedures: that of the "neutral' stance in classical psychoanalysis and that of the empathic introspection of the self psychologist. The important issue is whether psychoanalysis will continue to see itself as an already defined system of theory and practice—the practice of which inevitably reinforces the theory (e.g., the neutral stance actually eliciting the extent of the distortions in the transference)—or whether psychoanalysis will come to see itself as a theory open to being modified by clinical experience. The issue of self-disclosure and its efficacy is one such testing ground.

17

The Selfobject as Immortal Self

Then God said, "Let us make humankind in our image, according to our likeness. . . . " So God created humankind. . . . And God blessed them.

Genesis 1: 26-28

New ideas often call for new vocabulary. Sometimes the new terms sound awkward and obscure, and one has to go back to the context in which they originated to understand their meaning. "Selfobject" is such a term. Heinz Kohut invented the word to describe a particular relationship between two people in which the self of one is nourished and supported by the other—the object of his or her attachment, affection, and love. Through processes of internalization of the "other" (the object[1]), the self grows; it forms its own structure out of the building blocks of the goals, ambitions, and ideals of the other, its chosen selfobject, by adding them to its original inherent self. This process goes on throughout life, changing in context and character according to the needs of given developmental phases.

---

1. The term *object*, which originated in psychoanalytic theory, is often objected to because of its nonhuman implications. However, we scarcely have a good term. For example, *significant other* seems self-conscious and is cumbersome. If we think of *object* not as *thing* but in its grammatical sense as related to a *subject*, it becomes the accusative case of a statement about the self and loses some of its onerous, nonhuman aspects.

Under normal circumstances the mother is the first selfobject. As soon as the infant can even dimly distinguish self and other—and that is very early, usually within the first month of life—the child incorporates into his or her own psychic life the feelings and emotions that the mother communicates (Stern 1985). Those of her emotions that pertain to her feelings about and toward her child are incorporated by the infant and become the basis of the child's self-image. The child merges with the mother so that her feelings about the baby become the child's own. These beginning stages of the development of selfobjects Kohut calls *archaic selfobject formations.* The feelings involved are undoubtedly primitive: yet, they form the very basis of our feelings of security or insecurity, our sense of worth or worthlessness. As we move through life the self. just like the body, needs to be nourished, needs to grow and change. To this end we seek out new selfobjects to incorporate, thereby nourishing and supporting the existing self.

Many years ago I was treating the mother of an adolescent boy. One day, she said, "I'm worried about Jim; he has no heroes." She was right to be concerned, for we all need heroes throughout life: people to emulate, to inspire us, to support us. Those who do become our selfobjects. But a selfobject need not be an individual living person. It might be an historic figure. a character out of literature. or a notable contemporary whom we do not know personally. When the selfobject is chosen from among characters whom we encounter in the course of the variety of life's experiences, rather than through a relationship and interaction in the context of attachment. what we have is, of course, emotionally one-sided. Fantasy and imagination are then called upon to elaborate this internalization, thus making it our own—a cohesive part of our self-structure. Often the structure of the self would seem to involve more than the incorporation of a single selfobject, and one might speculate that these varying internalized parts of the self exist in a hierarchy of importance relative to the emotional life and functioning of the individual.

The striving to find and acquire a selfobject is an inherent aspect of the self. This means that the self is not merely a passive recipient of environmental influences, although it is that too, especially in certain phases of life. But like the ego that Fairbairn (1954) accurately describes as object-seeking, the self actively seeks out "objects" upon which to build itself, to define its content, to support its values, and contribute to its integrity and cohesiveness. This is not a neurotic reaction that some might even regard as showing a lack of independence. It is rather a normal part of the growth process.

The choice of selfobject will differ according to the developmental phase of the life cycle of the individual. But whatever the content—from baseball hero to research scientist—the ability to choose a selfobject speaks for the ability to love. The avidity with which individuals strive to seek and find a selfobject will vary greatly from one individual to another and will reflect the vitality of the life force with which the individual self is endowed. In addition, the extent of early deprivation of an adequate selfobject will determine the degree of need for nutrients for the self and will thus become an important factor, especially for certain types of individuals, in the eagerness with which they pursue the search for the selfobject.

The search for the selfobject, this foraging for nourishment for the self, is certainly not a fully conscious process. Much depends on the age in which it takes place. In infancy and early childhood it is unconscious and largely passive, depending almost exclusively on what the environment has to offer. However, in what has generally been called the latency period, age 7 to puberty, there is an observable preference for individuals—usually adults—whom the child admires and wishes to emulate. Here the process is conscious, but it is motivated to some extent by unconscious factors. In adolescence and early adulthood the selfobject plays a major role in the structuring of the self. The "heroes" and "crushes" of adolescence are consciously sought out and often represent a mixture of selfobject and love-object attachment.

The distinction between selfobject and love-object lies in their diverse functions. The selfobject serves to build and sustain the self, the love-object to gratify the libidinal needs and desires of the individual. For Freud, since libido is primary, the self-preservative needs that are secondary in terms of motivation are met by virtue of their dependence on libidinal gratification. Thus, according to classical psychoanalytic theory, the infant loves the mother because of the oral gratification that accompanies the experience of being fed. For Kohut, on the other hand, the growth of the self is primary, and the relationship to a selfobject that furthers this process could become the basis for feelings of love toward "the other."

The sense of self, the feeling of self-esteem or its absence, depends on the inner relationship between the selfobject and the self. Kohut (1984) sums this up in a long but powerful statement:

> Throughout his life a person will experience himself as a cohesive harmonious firm unit in time and space, connected with his past and pointing meaningfully into a creative-productive future, [but] only as long as, at each stage

in his life he experiences certain representatives of his human surroundings as joyfully responding to him, as available to him as sources of idealized strength and calmness, as being silently present but in essence like him, and, at any rate, able to grasp his inner life more or less accurately so that their responses are attuned to his needs and allow him to grasp their inner life when he is in need of such sustenance. [p. 52]

An individual's sense of worth thus depends heavily on the history of his or her relationship to the individual who represents the selfobject for him or her and subsequently on whether having internalized this selfobject it does indeed sustain and support the self. Sometimes the nature of this process of interdependence between one individual and another as it is reflected in the self/selfobject relationship becomes patently clear when it is observed in the negative.

I have in mind a former patient of mine. In 1963, a fact that is relevant to my story, a woman of approximately 45, who I shall call Carol, consulted me for severe depression. Although she was still functional in her work as a writer and radio announcer, her depression was evident in her unhappy mien, her stooped posture, and her halting gait. There were two main themes in her communications to me: one was of her lonely and unhappy childhood, and the other was of her envy of her more successful colleagues in the entertainment world. Both themes were reiterated over and over again, and both played major roles in what became the dramatic ending of her treatment.

Carol was an only child who grew up in a lower middle-class family in a small town in the Midwest. Her parents seemed to have no aspirations of any kind—neither financial, nor cultural, nor social. They eked out a living doing odd jobs, and even the having of a family was not one of their goals, for they resented Carol's birth and told her plainly that she was an unwanted child. In this emotional desert it is not surprising that Carol's self-esteem was so low. There was no selfobject to internalize that would have sustained the "self" and given her a sense of worth. Instead she internalized what was undoubtedly her parents' depression, together with their failure to appreciate and enjoy her as their child and as a person with a potentiality for fulfilling her own goals. ambitions, and aspirations. It is in fact quite remarkable that Carol achieved as much as she did. She acquired a college education and found employment that made use of her literary talents. It was in the area of social relationships that her greatest lacks manifested themselves. She was unmarried and had never succeeded in having a significant, intimate relationship with another person. There were women friends in her life, but the shadow of her envy and her feelings of inferiority fell upon all of them.

We made little progress in the treatment, for although my goal was to support all the positive productive and creative expressions of her personality, her negative, envious transference to me always had the upper hand. I was married, had children and a profession as well. Although at the time of Carol's treatment my psychoanalytic orientation was more classical than it would be today, I was aware of her inability to identity with me, to use me as a role model, to respond positively to my appreciation of her as a person and of her achievements, despite the odds against which she had had to labor. She could not take me in as a selfobject. The early, profound deprivations of emotional nutrients, which she experienced as the absence of any reflections on her parents' part of joy in her existence and as a lack of aspirations and ideals with which she could identify, so damaged the self that Carol was unable to make use of supporting selfobjects that might have presented themselves in her environment.. Nevertheless we continued to struggle and to hope that Carol's depression would become ameliorated. But a tragic national event ended all our efforts. It was the assassination of the president, John F. Kennedy.

The entire nation was in a state of shock. Anguished, bereft, enraged by the horror of the crime. the country was able to look beyond the tragic loss of its leader to the personal tragedy for his wife and children and to identify with their grief. There was also room to admire the courage and fortitude of Jacqueline Kennedy as she prepared for the solemn ritual of her husband's funeral. It was with a reserved expression of these inner feelings that I greeted Carol on the occasion of her first appointment after the assassination. "I hate that woman," was her reply. "She has everything I would have wanted. She is beautiful; she is wealthy; she is married to the President of the United States." It was my turn to be shocked by her response. Her overriding hateful envy so obliterated any suggestion of empathy as to be almost inhuman. I remember pointing out to Carol the tragedy of Jacqueline's loss and her courage in handling it, suggesting that she herself might derive strength from such an example and that in that respect at least she might try to emulate rather than envy Mrs. Kennedy. It was to no avail. Carol could not be inspired, she could have no heroes, she could not relate to a selfobject; in a word, she could not love. Perhaps I might have been some help to her had I been more able to accept her envy. But that is a moot question, for we never know the extent of the possibilities for change in any given individual. As it was, Carol persisted in her rage; she stormed out of my office, never to return again.

This is an extreme example of the inability to relate to another person so that that person can become a selfobject and be taken into the individual's psychic life to become part of the self-structure. But to be able to take in a selfobject one must have known love—both to have received it and to have given it. To love is to create the selfobject, and by creating it and incorporating it into the self, the cohesion, sustenance, and perpetuation of that very self are ensured.

The word "perpetuation" suggests a relationship to the theme of immortalization. Do the transmuting internalizations throughout life of selfobjects as Kohut uses the term—that is, the taking in of selfobjects to make them part of the self-structure—have any bearing on the issue of immortality? It is the thesis of this chapter that the selfobject is the vehicle for the immortalization of the self. The self of one individual in becoming the selfobject of another is not only perpetuated in the personality of that other but also enables the self of that other to grow, to be strengthened, to become cohesive, so that as a consequence he or she may become a selfobject to yet another individual. Thus, it is clear that the selfobject functions so as to create selves in others who are then able to perpetuate themselves by contributing to the self-structure of others. A chain is formed linking the selves of individuals who have internalized aspects of an original selfobject. On a psychic level this process is analogous to the perpetuation of traits through the transmission of genes.

Many years ago I had occasion to make the acquaintance of a simple but very wise woman. She was from Finland and of a peasant character, the kind who functions with great competence and adaptability in the world of reality, but is at the same time aware of the mystery of creation. Such a person is often in tune with the universe and ponders questions of being and non-being. During the time of our acquaintance, her husband died. Her marriage had not been a particularly happy one, yet it was only natural that at times she missed him. One day she spoke of her feelings of loneliness and of the fact that she sometimes ruminated about whether there was some sort of life after death. "But no," she concluded, "there is only memory."

Her remark has stayed with me for many years. It points to the wish for immortality, even for those individuals particularly grounded in the reality of this world and not particularly given to religious or mystical thinking. But perhaps most important, the comment about "only memory" is of great psychological significance. It is such an ambivalent statement! It seems to say that after all, in relation to immortality, there is memory, which is better than nothing, but the word "only" makes it clear that memory is not enough.

Certainly when my friend made the remark she meant that memory was not enough for her, and I am sure that this applies to many others. But perhaps this is due to the fact that for most people to be remembered by others calls up a series of images—the visual image of the deceased individual, the voice, gestures, habits, attitudes—all external to the personality of the person doing the remembering. However, the memory of an individual with whom we have had a close relationship and who is then lost to us in reality can be more than a series of images. The memory can become embedded in our own personality, can in effect become part of us. Memory is more than a photographic plate. It carries an emotional valence from past experience, and it is this affective element of the memory traces that enables us to ingest the memory and make it part of our own personality. The building blocks of personality are the memories of experiences with those individuals to whom we have been attached and with whom we have interacted.

Just as our genetic material, which has been passed on to us through generations and in the immediate sense through our parents, determines the appearance, structure, and nature of our physical being, as well as our intelligence and behavioral and emotional predispositions, so the memories of our experiences and interactions with those toward whom there have been emotional ties determine the nature of our psychic life. Our self-structure depends on a series of memories—memories in which we are the rememberer and can potentially become remembered.

The wish for immortality is universal, taking varying forms in different cultures. The wish is fulfilled for all those who believe in some form of continuing life after death through imagery and conceptions ranging from the literal personal existence of their unique individual soul, to an abstract conception that some sort of spiritual heritage remains in the world after an individual has left it—most likely in the memory of others, as my friend thought.

It is striking that in the literature of depth psychology, beginning with the writings of Freud, there is so little concern with the human wish for immortality. Yet, it is an all-pervasive wish expressed in some form in all the religions of humankind. However, we do owe the beginnings of a "depth" understanding of human personality and behavior to Freud, and since he eschewed a serious interest in religious or spiritual experience, dismissing it as largely infantile fantasy, it is little wonder that psychoanalytic psychology has left us only a limited heritage in the realm of the spiritual. There are, however, two exceptions—one well known, namely in the work of C. G. Jung, and the other, less familiar to most people. in the writings of Otto Rank.

Otto Rank, whose career as a psychoanalyst began as a follower of Freud, soon experienced the limitations of drive theory as the predominant orientation for explaining human behavior, especially for understanding motivation. Whereas Freud saw instinctual impulses, both sexual and aggressive, both conscious and unconscious, as the driving forces that accounted for human action, thought, and feeling, Rank understood the human dilemma as a conflict between the fear of mortality and the wish for immortality. The wish—indeed the need—to perpetuate the self, to eternalize it, is a primary source of motivation for human behavior.

For Rank, the building of the self is a creative act—in fact, the first creative act of the human being. It is a difficult and painful task, for it entails an awareness of separation and differentiation from the matrix of oneness into which the individual was precipitated by the physical act of birth. Paradoxically, after the physical act of birth, experienced as a separation at the very threshold of individuation, we are again plunged into another attachment: a psychological, emotional, oneness with the "other," mother, who becomes our first selfobject. This other is the one whom we must continue to internalize in order to nourish the growing self. but from whom we must also separate to achieve our own distinctive self (Langer 1967). An inevitable human conflict between the wish to remain merged in the matrix of the other and the wish to become a unique, separate, and differentiated self is born out of this paradox. However, the life force, as it has manifested itself throughout evolution, favors movement toward individuation, and the motivation for the structuring of a unique self predominates. It is this dearly bought self that the individual fears to lose and wishes to eternalize. This point of view in Rank may well have stemmed from his profound interest in creativity. His first psychological work was a monograph called *The Artist* (Rank 1925), which attempted to explain the creative activity of the artist as a need to establish continuity for the self through producing a creative work that would outlast the individual. However, since the great mass of individuals are unable to perpetuate themselves through creative works, Rank concluded that for them the human need for immortalization was met in the creation of progeny and through the merging with some ideology, cause. or larger community effort with which to identify—a movement that would outlast their individual lives.

While belief in a personal immortality is a matter of faith and lies beyond the realm of our certain knowledge, there is an aspect of immortality that exists within the province of psychology, is understandable, is connected to the phenomenon of the selfobject, and adds greatly to the creation of meaningfulness in life. As I have tried to show, the individual self is structured by the internalization of emotional experience with significant others—preferably with those whom we have admired and to whom we have been attached. These memory images are transmuted to harmonize with the original, constitutionally given nature of the self to form a cohesive whole. Thus, the "other" lives on—is immortalized—within ourselves.

To this, we must add an important spiritual dimension. For the internalized image to continue to live within the individual, to contribute to the meaningfulness and productivity of life and to the ability to give and receive love, it must be an image that was initially fired in the kiln of love in its broadest sense. Lacking this, as my example of Carol was meant to illustrate, the images resulting from the early experiences of interaction with those who should have served as constructive selfobjects are either rejected and not internalized, or live a destructive life in the psyche of the victimized individual. The parental selfobjects and all those chosen by an individual to follow the original archaic selfobjects, who have mirrored their love for the developing individual and permitted themselves to be idealized by him or her, are immortalized through their continued life as functioning internalized memory images. One can even say, in these terms, that the spiritual dimension in human life is the memory of love.

In addition to the understanding that the psychological life of humankind develops its progeny through the internalization of selfobjects, in analogy to the biological continuity of life through the genes, there is another important perspective in this process that should not be lost. In describing the internalization of the selfobject as a vehicle for a kind of immortalization and the role of this process in forming the self of an individual, it is easy to forget that this very same unique individual can, in turn, become a selfobject for still another person. The importance one gains from this perspective lies in the fact that the human being can look inward to see not only a growing individual who is able to use whatever experience offers in terms of selfobjects for building the self but can also find high self-regard in having been given the opportunity to become a selfobject for others, thus providing them with nourishment for their own self-development. When these processes of selfobject internalization take place in an atmosphere of love, individuals can see more clearly the chain of relatedness that connects them to one another and thus be inspired to perpetuate the best in themselves through the legacy of their selfobject offering.

II

MASOCHISM

The human creature is caught inevitably between self-interest and empathic feelings for "the other" whom he or she needs for building his or her own personality. The conflict can never be resolved completely; at best some acceptable balance between self need and concern for another can be achieved. But the outcome depends heavily on the extent of childhood trauma that an individual has experienced. Should emotional trauma be severe, especially in the early relationship to the mother, the result may be a masochistic personality. The following chapters describe several individuals who survived extremely traumatic childhood situations through the use of a denigrated self-image coupled with an idealized image of the offending parent. In my earlier writings on masochism (Menaker 1953), I perceived this rescue operation of the ego (self) as a way of coping with the anxiety of separation. Although I still hold this to be true, I would now add that the patient's tenacious holding onto the idealization also serves the need to internalize the parent imago in an attempt to secure a cohesive self. The fear of separation is more than fear of the loss of a love-object; it is the fear of the loss of a selfobject—that which nourishes the self. In the face of that danger the moral masochist persists in the idealization of the selfobject at the expense of his or her own self-esteem. Clinical experience seems to confirm the fact that insight into this mechanism alone will not bring about cure or reparation. The patient must find a new selfobject—usually in the person of the analyst.

18

Masochism from a Self Psychological Perspective

At a summer resort I once met an outstanding singer. Our meeting occurred through my own initiative, for without knowing who she was or what she did, I had been observing her in the hotel dining room where she sat alone at a small table. She might have been quite attractive in her younger years, yet she still carried her heavy weight with dignity. She seemed self-possessed, but certainly not joyful, and when she rose to leave the table after the meal, there was something in her bearing as she crossed the room that made me think of a singer coming on stage for a performance. I found an occasion to approach her and was only half-surprised to learn that she actually was a singer. When commenting on her bearing, I revealed my earlier suspicions that she might be a singer. She answered, "One can't be apologetic about one's being if one is going to be a performer." Later, as I reflected on that comment, it seemed to shed light on issues having to do with masochism and the self—the very subject matter with which my mind had been occupied in preparation for writing this chapter.

The singer—let us call her Claire—not only expressed a clear, freely chosen, assertive stance in relation to her "self" but her remark also revealed how well she understood what I was perceiving. I had little to go on, but I reacted to the unmistakable assertion of self in the way she carried herself. A masochist, on the other hand, often conveys an "excuse me for living" attitude, both in body language and in words. As I wrote in 1953 in the paper entitled "Masochism: A Defense Reaction of the Ego," the self-denigrating attitude had a deeply unconscious function and purpose. Ultimately it represented an echo of the qualitative nature of the mother's mirroring response to her child—an attitude both rejecting and critical. The child by identifying with the mother's critical attitude projected a denigrated self-image whose major function was to prevent separation from the mother.

Let me make clear that the subject of this chapter is moral, not sexual masochism, as was also the case in my 1953 paper. Although Freud's conception of moral masochism essentially described a characterological stance, a self-image, an attitude toward oneself in the world, his causal explanation lay in the realm of the drives. Thus, although the very subject matter of moral masochism is a self problem, Freud transposed the causal issues regarding the origins of this extremely self-negating character structure to the area of the instinct life. As primarily a conflict psychology, psychoanalysis explained moral masochism as the result of a punitive attitude toward the self, adopted out of guilt for forbidden unconscious wishes that are in opposition to the dictates of the superego. Furthermore, since classical psychoanalysis conceived of human motivation as dominated primarily by the pleasure principle or its delayed surrogate, the reality principle, a seeming paradox ensued in relation to masochism within the framework of an instinct theory. Wherein lies the gratification is the question that comes to mind. In the case of sexual masochism it is not so difficult to view the ultimate sensual satisfaction (orgasm) as the gratification, albeit at the price of pain and suffering. But in the case of moral masochism the gratification can only come from the superego's need for punishment. This explanation does not fit into Freud's meta-psychology arising out of libido theory and may have been a major cause for his going "Beyond the Pleasure Principle" and positing a death instinct.

The death instinct concept, however, was not congenial to many of Freud's followers, and attempts were made to hold to instinct theory without invoking the death instinct. Reik (1994), for example, in his idea of "victory through defeat," sees masochistic behavior essentially as a victory of the masochist's *will* over that of the person attempting to impose his or her will on another. That the issue of will belongs to the realm of ego or self psychology did not seem to strike Reik nor others who attempted to explain moral masochism. Karen Horney's (1937) explanation of the masochistic character structure comes closest to a self psychological explanation. She perceives moral masochism as a relinquishing of the self in order to avoid anxiety and conflict—in other words, her emphasis is on the defensive function of masochism. It is the ego that is both the defender and the defended, for it is clear that Horney is no longer primarily concerned with the source and nature of gratification (i.e., with drive theory), but rather with how the self-preservative functions of the ego are served by the masochistic stance of the individual. The ego creates, out of the interpersonal experiences of the developing self, an internalized denigrated self-image. Living life in this idiom is the very essence of moral masochism. The ego continues to uphold this image and is in this sense a defender of the self against anxiety. The mechanism thus created, namely the masochistic attitude. is the defensive reaction of the ego.

Although Berliner (1940, 1947) takes explanations for moral masochism out of the exclusive realm of libido theory and understands masochism as a function of the ego in an attempt to wrest love from an unloving, even sadistic love object, he does not focus on the self psychological mechanisms involved in the creation of the denigrated self-image nor on its function as it persists throughout an individual's lifetime.

Nevertheless, the work of these authors attests to the fact that, in the course of the evolution of psychoanalysis, libido theory was found to be insufficient to explain many phenomena fully, and most especially that of moral masochism. If a theory hypothesizes human behavior to be motivated by the wish for gratification—even if gratification is understood attenuatedly to mean the reduction of tension—then it becomes difficult to explain a phenomenon as unpleasureable as moral masochism within the framework of such a theory. This led me among others to look for a broader framework for a plausible explanation.

Before beginning to formulate a theory of moral masochism in self psychological terms, I went back and reread my 1953 paper on this subject. What I found was that, although I used the vocabulary of the 1950s, my argument was essentially a self psychological one. I was at pains to make clear that in the course of the development of the self a masochistic attitude toward the self—a denigrated self-conception—grows out of a profound identification on the child's part with the mother's demeaning conception of the child. For reasons originating in the mother's conflicted and neurotic personality, she, at one and the same time, rejects the child, yet makes him or her dependent in the extreme: failing to support or encourage the development of independent ego functions. In the case of the patient whom I described in my 1953 paper, the mother, fearing to allow the child to walk independently, wheeled her in a stroller until she was 4 or 5 years old. By this time the little girl had acquired such a fear of walking that it was only through the intervention of a sort of witch-woman, who was known in this primitive and superstitious community to have magical powers, that the child was enabled to walk. Similarly the mother, fearing that the child would starve to death, literally spoonfed her until she was 10. Not only are these extreme examples of the inhibition—much less affirmation—caused by the mother of the normal development of age-appropriate ego functions but the developmental lag was also blamed on the child. She was criticized. taunted. deprecated, and made to feel insufficient and inferior. This is the character of the distorted image of the child that the mother conveyed in every word and deed. This image that is a reflection of the mother's hostility to the child and that she attempted to cover over with an overprotective attitude is the child's major source of feeling and knowledge about him- or herself. It is the mirror in which the child sees him- or herself as the mother sees him or her and accepts this as a true picture. In fact, the moral masochist lives his life so as to confirm his mother's image of him.

The reflected image is internalized and becomes part of an individual's self-structure in the form of the self-image. In the case of moral masochism it is a denigrated self-image.

There is an important corollary to the identification mechanisms that participate in the formation of self-structure. The object of identification functions as a selfobject in Kohut's sense of the term: that is, an individual's striving from the beginning of life to structure a cohesive self expresses itself in the use, through internalization, of the significant other. Originally this other was the mother, and in this case we speak of an archaic selfobject. The internalized image becomes part of the developing self. However, in the case of moral masochism we find ourselves dealing with a seeming paradox, for the internalized mother image is highly idealized by the child. Why, we might ask, is an image that holds so denigrated a conception of the child—a conception that the child has internalized—split off so that it is in part idealized? One might expect that if a child suffers unrelenting criticism, denigration, and humiliation from a primary selfobject—the mother— the reaction would be rage. Instead another possible reaction sets in: the rage is turned against the self both in identification with the mother's hostility against the child and as a defense against loss of the mother that would result should the hostility be expressed. To avoid separation from the mother of which the dependent child is so fearful, a powerful idealization of the mother takes place.

It is my impression from my clinical experience that there is a qualitative difference in the tenacity with which the two parts of the internalized mother image—the mirroring part containing the devalued image of the child and the idealized part of the conception of the mother—are lived out and experienced both in the transference in the therapeutic situation and in life itself. The idealization of the mother is not necessarily a projection of "good" qualities onto the mother image on the part of the child. *We* call it idealized by contrast with the image of the child that the mother projects onto the child and that is accepted by the child as valid. It is as if the tenuously formed self of the moral masochist holds on desperately to the devalued, submissive self-image, which constantly seeks as an ever-hungry self to add new idealized images to the selfobject. There is an implication of rejection of the mother as selfobject in this mechanism on the basis of her maternal inadequacy rather than exclusively on the basis of anger for her denigration of the child. Therefore, the moral masochist is often inclined toward idealizations in the search for new images to internalize and incorporate as part of the self, thus filling the gap left by the mother's insufficiency.

The destructive aspect of the internalized denigrated self-image interferes with proper functioning in life and good interactions with others, ultimately leading to depression. When this image is tenaciously held onto or is reworked in given life situations that arise even after some years of freedom from its domination, one witnesses the repetition compulsion and wonders about the etiology of such repetition when it obviously does not serve the life force. Repetition when it is positive serves adaptation; when it is a *compulsion* it is maladaptive and unproductive—operating outside the domain of the individual will.

Let me illustrate the vicissitudes of the formation of a personality structure in the case of a middle-aged man characterized by moral masochism who came to me some years ago seeking relief from depression and anxiety so severe that it can best be described as a chronic state of panic. Mr. G., as I shall call him, had a childhood history no less traumatic than that of the young woman whom I described in my 1953 paper. His mother was overtly psychotic and had to be hospitalized intermittently throughout his childhood. His father, who was almost pathologically dependent on the mother, hated his son and expressed his dislike openly and constantly. Mr. G. mentioned the emotional situation in his home early in his treatment, but it was not until much later that its full impact and meaning, especially of his father's attitude toward him, for the development of his masochism became clear. I will describe this issue later in this chapter.

At the time that Mr. G. began treatment, he was separated from his

wife and was in the midst of divorce proceedings. This situation was not of
his choosing, for as he explained, he would never have left his wife out of
anxiety despite her mistreatment of him. It was she who wished to be rid
of him. In many ways his wife's personality repeated that of his mother.
His mother had humiliated him as he was growing up, saying that he would
never become a man, that no woman would ever love him for he was, according to her, homosexual. Her attempts at humiliating him did not deter
her from the most flagrantly seductive behavior. She was often in a state of
undress around the house, but more, she insisted that Mr. G. sleep in bed
with her. This went on well into adolescence. His wife was equally humiliating. After many years of marriage that were relatively peaceful, she began
to abuse him after his work situation changed. Mr. G. is a chemist. He was
working in private industry and lost his position when certain administrative
changes occurred in the company for which he had been working. He ended
up in the academic world, a situation that suited his temperament much more
than employment in the industrial world. His wife, however, perceived the
inevitable reduction in income as a sign of his lack of manhood and accused
him of this, as well as of not satisfying her sexually—thus humiliating and
degrading him. For him it was as if his mother's prophecy had come true
and as if she had been right all along: he was not an adequate man.

In therapy, since the reality testing function of the masochistic individual is inevitably skewed, I tend at first to emphasize reality and to contrast it with the patient's distorted statement about himself. The exploration of psychodynamics can then follow more convincingly. In the case of
Mr. G. I pointed out that since he was separated from his wife, he had had
very adequate sexual experiences and that furthermore he was very successful in his academic work and was highly respected by his colleagues.
Why then was he so inclined to believe the judgments of his mother and
his wife? Gradually the rational perception of reality prevailed, and Mr. G.
was able to see that his masochistic acceptance of the denigrated image of
himself that had been thrust upon him was due to his fear of separation,
first from his mother and then from his wife. We worked on his fear of
separation for many months—in fact for many years. Slowly, and with much
support and encouragement from me, as well as with his awareness and
experience of the fact that I admired his active vigorous struggle against
his own self-defeating attitudes, Mr. G. gradually began to think better of
himself. During a period reasonably free of anxiety and depression, he
formed a solid relationship with a young woman. They had much in common in terms of interests and values; their sexual relationship was predomi-

nantly amicable. Soon the young woman began to express wishes for marriage, which were met with anxiety, doubt, and reluctance on Mr. G.'s part. He said he was not ready for marriage. At first his anxiety was mild and manageable, but another event augmented it, causing a return of his denigrated self-image, severe anxiety, and some depression. The event was the death of his ex-wife. He realized that he was not entirely free of his attachment to her. Despite her mistreatment of him and of her virulently expressed hatred of him, he could scarcely feel anger toward her, much less express it. In fact, it was the same when he reminisced about his childhood. Whenever he spoke of his mother's humiliating attitudes toward him or of his father's hatred toward him, there was hardly any evidence of anger. Yet there was emotion—feelings of sadness and sorrow.

Mr. G. was naturally disturbed by the reappearance of his depression and anxiety, although they certainly did not return with their initial intensity. Under these circumstances he tried very hard to understand, through mobilizing what he already knew of his own mechanisms, the reasons for this setback. We agreed that the precipitating causes were his girlfriend's pressure for marriage and the death of his ex-wife. Both situations involve loss or the threat of loss in the case of his girlfriend should he fail to comply with her wishes. And we both agreed that for him every separation represented the powerful symbol of separation from his mother—a separation that, despite the reality of her death, he had never fully accomplished psychologically.

Yet despite Mr. G.'s conviction that the fear of separation, re-evoked in part by actual loss, might be the cause of the return of his acute anxiety, he did not feel that it was a sufficient explanation. As was his wont when a problem had to be solved, he sought out causes in the traumatic experiences of his childhood. Could the seductive incestuous behavior of his mother be the cause? Although this was certainly a traumatic experience, I failed to see its connection with the precipitating causes of the reappearance of his acute anxiety and of the return of his low self-esteem. In addition, I explained, I did not think there could be a single cause dramatized by a single trauma that would account for his profound anxiety.

Mr. G. began to reminisce about the relationship with his father who had died some years ago. He remembered the abuse he suffered at his father's hands—frequent unprovoked beatings, but worst of all his father's overt expressions of hatred and his almost complete verbal withdrawal. He said he could probably count on the fingers of one hand the times during his growing-up years when he had actually talked to his father.

During this period in the treatment, Mr. G. complained not only about the reappearance of acute anxiety but also about the specific nature of his low self-esteem, namely, the strong feeling that he was not man enough. As he remembered his relationship with his father, he said, "How could I possibly have identified with him?" How, indeed! The ingredients for the structuring of a strong cohesive self were clearly absent. Lacking adequate male models almost completely, Mr. G.'s development, both as a man and as a highly ethical personality, considerate of others, and actively interested in the world around him, is something of a miracle. But the deficits of his childhood point clearly to the inevitability of weakness in his self-structure. The curve of his life shows a repetitive oscillation between a healthy, active movement into the world—in work, in relationships with women, and in aesthetic enjoyment—and then, after some adverse experience, a retreat to a masochistic position of self-denigration accompanied by anxiety and depression.

In the case of Mr. G., the idea of marriage, which for him carries the dangers of being trapped and demeaned again as he had been by his mother and his ex-wife, is the adverse circumstance in the current situation that is responsible for the reappearance of his anxiety. This trigger, which incidentally is not yet a reality, is effective on two counts: the first is the *nature* of the memories of his early experiences within his family. These memories might well have the character of imprints that can be likened to the imprinting function in the animal world. As described by Konrad Lorenz (1952), inherited behavior patterns are released by specific environmental experiences and then remain imprinted as memory traces within the organism, dictating future behavior. The function of imprinting is to ensure survival—first of the individual and thus of the species.

In the case of humans, we have insufficient evidence to speak of inherited behavior patterns on the level of complex behavior involving feelings and attitudes like the masochism described here. But in view of the unyielding repetitiveness of the masochistic behavior and of feelings of worthlessness and inadequacy as in the case of Mr. G., we are justified in speculating that memories of denigrating experiences occurred so early—most likely at a preverbal period—that they can be likened to imprints. Being nonverbal they have never reached consciousness, but are not unconscious in the sense of being repressed. Therefore, they are not readily amenable to change by becoming conscious. Perhaps that is why the analysis of mechanisms associated with such memories—and they always concern feelings about the self—is not very therapeutically effective.

Second, because of the deprivations and deficits associated with Mr. G.'s early family environment, especially the absence of adequate selfobjects, the structure of the self could not become reliably integrated and sufficiently cohesive. Therefore, any situation that threatens to become traumatic exceeds the threshold of the adaptive capacity of the self and precipitates excessive anxiety.

In my paper on masochism (1953) I viewed the major function of the submissive, masochistic self-image that an individual tenaciously holds on to as a defensive operation to avoid separation from an unloving mother. The mother image must be maintained as good and loving to avoid the expression of hostility that would mean separation, while all the frustration experienced in the mother relationship is attributed to the worthlessness of the self. During the many years of analytic work that have passed since that paper was published, my theory has often been confirmed by the favorable response of masochistic patients to this insight. Most often such patients were able to overcome the fear of separation from the mother, to see the mother in a more realistic light, and consequently to view themselves more favorably. They became more independent and healthily self-assertive. I still believe that the psychodynamics of this defensive function of the masochistic stance and the denigrated self-image is valid. But today I do not view it as the sole explanation, and perhaps not even as the primary one. The insights of self psychology, as well as the experience of my work with Mr. G. and the repetitiveness of his feelings of worthlessness, accompanied by acute anxiety and depression, necessitate an expansion of the theory of moral masochism.

Let me return to the analogy to the imprinting mechanism as it is understood in lower organisms. In the case of Mr. G. his mother's negative mirroring (i.e., her relentless rejection and denigration of her child) resulted in his incorporation and retention of the image of his worthlessness that she projected. Whenever situations arise that the self is not cohesive enough to master, acute anxiety results—an anxiety that must have been present in the earliest encounters with the rejecting mother. Such repetitions were certainly the case for Mr. G. In part, therefore, the masochistic position of the self as it forms under the burden of negative mirroring can be attributed to the imprinting of early preverbal memories. This is the *psychobiological* explanation for the masochistic response. In addition, in the course of the child's growth as the rejection by the mother continues, the struggling self develops the defensive posture of the masochistic self-image that, however poorly, still serves the survival of the self by avoiding the overwhelming anxiety of separation. This is the *psychodynamic* explanation for moral masochism as a defensive operation.

An understanding of the development and persistence of the denigrated self-image that characterizes moral masochism requires two systems of causality: a psychobiological one involving the nature of memory and a psychodynamic one involving the interplay of forces within the personality. It is the impact of these two sources of causality and their mutual reinforcement that describes the tenacity with which the self-image of worthlessness appears and reappears. The self in the course of its growth never had the opportunity to gain sufficient strength to resist the combined power of negative memory traces and the dynamic conflict of contradictory feelings. The result is a greatly weakened self suffering feelings of worthlessness as well as a greatly diminished ability to be self-assertive, self-expressive, and self-creative.

What is the therapeutic outlook for individuals suffering from low self-esteem and chronic feelings of worthlessness of an intensity that would justify the use of the term "moral masochism" to describe their character structure? From my experience, to the extent that the origin of the masochism lies in the use of the expression of the denigrated self-image to defend against the expression of hostility, out of fear of the resulting separation from the mother, the analysis of this mechanism would meet with good results. However, it is not only the analysis of the patient's psychodynamic interactions that is important but also the use that the patient can make of the therapist as a new and affirming selfobject that can help strengthen the self and restore more normal self-esteem. If the origins of the masochistic self-image lie in an early preverbal period, interpretations will be much less effective, and the internalization of the analyst as a selfobject will be a slower, more prolonged process. Nevertheless, the patient can ultimately structure a stronger self, and the masochistic stance toward the self can be alleviated.

19

Self Psychological
Perspectives on
Moral Masochism

Some years ago in a discussion, a colleague who had been practicing some 10 or 15 years asked, "Why is it that after a certain time in the analysis of a patient we give up the analytic stance and tend to exhort our patients to give up their neurotic behavior?" Obviously the analyst in this case was disturbed by the fact that analysis in itself did not seem to work—analysis in this sense meaning primarily the acquiring of insight. But the fact that insight alone is not curative has been known for a long time. Freud himself spoke of the need for "working through" the insights, for experiencing the emotions that accompany them, especially as these appear in the transference. Yet often all these procedures do not effect change. We might well ask why. It is time to examine the premises upon which our therapeutic expectations are based.

The empirical method of science with which the *Weltanschauung* of our modern civilization is imbued sometimes leads us to be unaware of the broad premises that form the framework within which our observations are made. Whether psychoanalysis and psychotherapy are sciences is a debatable issue. Yet within their operation, observations about human behavior, thoughts, and feelings are being made, and some positive therapeutic results are being achieved. However, the fundamental premises upon which observations and procedures are based are rarely challenged; they are indeed rarely perceived at all. They are taken for granted as the psychological air we breathe. Even when new advances in understanding are arrived at, the attempt is usually made to fit them into the framework of the original premises or to disregard their implications entirely. Still, the recent interest in a psychology of the self, especially as it is reflected in the work of Heinz Kohut, represents an attempt to systematize new observations and theoretical conclusions, and to institute new therapeutic procedures, thereby inevitably changing and broadening the premises upon which an understanding of human behavior, both normal and pathological, might be based.

But before going into a discussion of these premises,, let me outline briefly those upon which classical psychoanalysis is based. The differences will put both points of view in clearer perspective.

The soil out of which Freudian psychoanalysis grew derived its character from the scientific ethos of the late nineteenth century. This was mechanistic according to the model laid down by Newtonian physics. Psychology, in an attempt to create a measurable relationship between the mental and the physical, became psychophysics, a close relative of experimental physiology. While psychoanalysis escaped the narrowness of a psychophysical approach to a study of human personality, it nevertheless absorbed its materialism, its reductionism, and its determinism. While contributing to an understanding of mental processes in depth, it adhered to a hydraulic model of psychic energy of an instinctual nature, operating within a closed system. The resultant theoretical system thus contained a paradox: on the one hand, our understanding of mental and emotional processes was deepened by the discovery of the operation of the unconscious; on the other hand, the conception of personality as a historically determined closed system of forces in which the ego was not primary but derivative left little room for the idea of growth or creativity, much less for the ongoing influence of the social environment or of experience.

Furthermore, the insights of psychoanalysis originated from a study of pathology—initially, hysteria—which makes it difficult to distill what is generally applicable to human personality and what must be reserved for an understanding of its abnormalities. As we all know, its procedure was initially and primarily archeological—digging for derivatives of the unconscious through the method of free association. The use of the couch and the relative passivity of the analyst in the human exchange facilitated this process, and the psychoanalytic situation was so structured as to encourage regression and to produce the flowering of the transference. Through the analysis of the transference, of resistances, and of defenses, and through establishing connections between these derivatives and an individual's historical past, repressions were to be lifted, some defenses given up, and a realignment of the relationship between the instinct life—the id—and the ego and superego was to take place. It was such a rearrangement of energies within the closed system of the personality that led to the well-known dictum, "where id was there ego shall be" (Freud 1933, p. 112). Such was the conception of cure or personality change.

The object relations theorists started from different premises. For them—Fairbairn, Guntrip, Winnicott—not instinct but the primacy of the object-seeking ego was dominant. Emphasis shifted from the vicissitudes of drives as they developed in the oedipal triangle, to the fate of the self in the early mother-child relationship. They paved the way for a self psychology within the framework of a depth psychological approach to the understanding and treatment of personality.

It would be a mistake to imply that a psychology of the self begins with Kohut, or indeed with psychoanalysis itself, or that there were not others in the psychoanalytic field who were concerned with the self: Rank, Horney, Fromm, and Erikson, only to name a few. Philosophers and psychologists of various persuasions have long been concerned with the self. For example, William James has much to say about the self. Yet it is Kohut's attempt to go beyond the descriptive level of observation, or the dynamic level of *intrapsychic* interaction, and to systematize a developmental theory of the self that creates an entirely *new premise* for psychotherapeutic procedure. This premise is based on the *primacy of the self* and its development within the familial matrix; its character being determined by the *qualitative* nature of the familial relationships and interactions. It is an open-ended model of personality, which emphasizes growth, as did, for example, those of Rank and Horney. The analyst's belief in the patient's capacity for growth therefore becomes the premise that informs the therapeutic undertaking. No longer is the regressive posture of the classic analytic situation stressed, although regressions are certainly analyzed when they occur; but the patient's opportunity for growth in a new and real relationship with the analyst is emphasized.

I would like to describe the treatment of a young woman with a masochistic character in the light of a growth theory of the self. An exploration of the treatment of moral masochism is particularly illustrative, I believe, for the application of a self psychology, because it is essentially a problem

in low self-esteem, a conflict in the realm of the self-conception and calls
for a reconstruction of the self. However. I would like to remind you that
Freud viewed moral masochism as a product of unconscious guilt feeling
and considered the masochist's stubborn holding on to his neurotic illness
as an unconscious need for punishment which gratified the sense of guilt
(Freud 1924, p. 262-263). The use of the term *gratification* attests to the
embeddedness in drive theory of the psychoanalytic conception of neurosis
and is the very premise that made Freud so pessimistic about the therapeutic outcome of neuroses in which guilt and the unconscious need for
punishment were, as he thought. central factors in their dynamics. In this
connection, he wrote:

> Perhaps it may depend, too, [namely, the possibility of cure] on whether the
> personality of the analyst allows of the patient's putting him in the place of
> his ego-ideal, and this involves a temptation for the analyst to play the part
> of prophet. saviour and redeemer to the patient. Since the rules of analysis
> are diametrically opposed to the physician's making use of his personality in
> any such manner it must he honestly confessed that here we have another
> limitation to the effectiveness of analysis. [Freud 1960, p. 69]

Were we to abide by such rules we should have to give up the treatment of
all those disturbances in which deficits in the development of the self play
a major role, and in the treatment of which the opportunity to "redo" childhood through a new relationship with the therapist is a crucial, if not a
sole, issue.

Let me return to a discussion of my patient and let me say parenthetically that for reasons of confidentiality, there are details regarding the case
that I must omit, but this will not detract from the central theme of my
discussion. Evelyn, as I shall call her, was a married woman in her early
thirties when she came to me complaining of extreme anxiety, some depressive states, inability to make decisions about important issues in her life, a
sense of fragmentation, and low self-esteem. She was somewhat overweight
and had been unsuccessful in her attempts to control her eating. She had
been in psychotherapeutic treatment for a few years before coming to me.
Unfortunately, her analyst had died. It had been a very traumatic experience for her, as she had been benefiting from the treatment and had very
warm feelings toward her therapist.

Evelyn was a person of unusual intelligence, competence, and integrity of character, who, in a state of severe anxiety could regress to a condition of infantile helplessness, disorientation, and pseudostupidity. She had

a successful educational career and was active in professional work for which she received considerable recognition and affirmation from colleagues and supervisors.

However, her self-feeling in no way reflected her performance in the world of her social and professional activities. In a somewhat panicky state she generally brought a debased and querulous self-conception into the treatment situation. This feeling about herself, which she acted out in her family as well as in her therapy, had a long developmental history. It began when she was about 4 1/2 years of age and her brother—her only sibling—was born. Until that time she felt much loved by her parents, especially by her father. Subsequently her brother became the good and beloved child, although important residues of the closeness with her father remained and served to see her through some difficult crises in her life. After the birth of her brother, Evelyn became obese. sullen, difficult to manage, and was in frequent hostile confrontations with her mother. The hostile rivalry and competitiveness with her brother persisted and was reflected in other relationships in her adult life. It was a competitiveness in which she never felt that she could win; quite the contrary, in her mind it always served to reinforce her bad self-image. Much time was spent, both in her first analysis as well as in her work with me, on her hostile feelings toward her brother and her endless measuring of herself against him, in an attempt to help her toward a realistic appraisal of her own worth. The harvest of these endeavors was meager indeed. Evelyn persisted in her self-denigration. It is this constant and stubborn devaluation of self in the service of the avoidance of separation that I call moral masochism and that defines the major pathology in Evelyn's case.

Although her analysis brought to light oedipal rivalry and hostility toward her mother, wishes to be a boy like her brother, and the guilt attendant on these feelings, none of the conventional interpretations of these conflicts had much of an impact on her self-conception. Nor was her extreme anxiety reduced through insight into how these early conflicts of her childhood were reflected in her current interactions with others, either in her family or in her social and professional life. Yet during approximately the first year and a half of her work with me, in the course of which she mourned the loss of her former analyst, she developed a more trusting relationship to me, albeit with accompanying overdependency.

It took two important events in her life—as well as my own frustration with her lack of progress, which resulted in my changing certain procedures—to bring about the accessibility to analysis of the deficits in her self-structure that were responsible for her masochistic character. The first event was her pregnancy. Evelyn had wanted a child for some time. Her husband, however, had misgivings about parenthood, although his feelings were not in any obvious way connected with uncertainty about the marriage, which, considering my patient's personality disorder, was remarkably stable. As one might have expected, the pregnancy was accompanied by great anxiety. My summer vacation came in the middle of it, and I felt it imperative to keep in touch with Evelyn through weekly phone calls. She ventilated her anxieties and her rages against her doctors, of which there were several. since her pregnancy was complicated by metabolic dysfunctions that had to be monitored. I reassured her, informed her, and gave her some psychological insight and perspective when I could. At the end of the summer she gave birth to a normal, healthy boy by Caesarean section.

The second event in Evelyn's life that I believe facilitated a change in the efficacy of her analytic treatment was her family's move from the homestead in which she had grown up a great distance from New York, to a geographic location within easy reach of the city. This meant that after many years of separation. characterized by rebelliousness and alienation on her part, her parents actually reentered Evelyn's life through their frequent visits. Her brother, too, had moved into the New York area. The reappearance of her family, especially within the context of her newly acquired motherhood, activated the conflicts around her introjects and precipitated some repetition of childhood reactions. At the same time it gave us an opportunity to explore the early dynamics of the development of her self-structure and to test her reactions vis-à-vis the reality of her parents' behavior.

During the first months after the birth of her child, Evelyn was happy and in better psychological equilibrium than I had ever seen her She was nursing the baby and was at one with him and the world. This situation began to change in the second half of the child's first year of life. Evelyn became increasingly anxious and severely hypochondriacal. She had thoughts of death, of what would become of the baby should she die, and, on the other hand, of the fact that she was so worthless that she could never be a good mother so she might as well die. In session after session she repeated this litany, until even she became impatient, realizing that she was making no progress in her treatment.

Up to this point, because of her extreme anxiety, I had conducted her treatment face to face. I now felt that we would never get beyond the reiteration of complaints unless she lay on the couch—a situation which for her would mean separation from me. She did so, but was terrified and actually said, "I feel so alone." However, her complaints and hypochondria persisted and her expressions of worthlessness and low self-esteem continued in a way that became increasingly provocative, especially since her functioning in life situations in no way confirmed her devalued self-conception. On one occasion when I was trying to probe the sources of guilt that might have led her to think so ill of herself, she simply stated categorically, "I was born rotten."

In the face of this dead end in the therapeutic road, I stepped out of my usual role, which had never been one of traditional objective detachment, but rather one that Kohut would define as the empathic introspective stance. I sternly exhorted Evelyn to attend to her psychological responsibilities as a mother, and to stop railing against herself and thus perhaps eventually communicating her bad self-image to her son. The rage that followed my admonition was a measure of her narcissistic merging with her child, and of the threat to this oneness that my definition of separate roles had posed. I had also risked the disruption of treatment. But I had based the risk on my knowledge of the good rapport and trust that had been built up between us over a long period. The gamble paid off. After several sessions in which she railed against me, Evelyn confessed—and indeed it had the character of a confession—that she wanted to escape all responsibility, that she wished to merge with her father, to be completely dependent on him, to be completely cared for by him. Such wishes produced strong guilt feelings in her because they represented a betrayal of the opposite, normal developmental wishes to be a person in her own right—autonomous, independent, individuated, and well related to others. Yet these latter wishes were also sources of the most powerful feelings of guilt. This had to do with her father's perfectionistic expectations. Certainly until the birth of her brother, she was expected to be the brightest, most intelligent, best behaved, loveliest child in the community. Early in life she incorporated her father's expectations for outstanding performance, uniqueness, and originality, and this internationalization persisted into her adult life. She had introjected the grandiose, narcissistic needs of her father. These had become her ego-ideal. and led to unrealistic and unrealizable perfectionistic aims in Horney's sense of "self-idealization." As we spoke of these issues, and as she insisted on emphasizing her deficits. she commented about her relationship to her father. She said, "I look into his face and see the disappointment." There was little wonder why she was filled with self-loathing.

It seems to me that this is a clear example of the dependence of the self-image on the introjection of that image that a parent mirrors back to the child. In this case it was the father, although I would venture the guess that there were insufficiencies in affirmative mirroring on the part of Evelyn's mother in early childhood and that the father's demanding perfectionism provided both a reinforcement of those deficiencies and an opportunity to confirm the statement about herself that she originally saw in her mother's face.

In my 1953 paper on moral masochism, I described a patient whose denigrated self-image served to uphold a symbiotic bond with her mother by repressing all hostile feelings toward the mother and taking guilt and hate upon herself. Thus separation was avoided at the cost of self-devaluation and the loss of certain autonomous ego functions. While I knew then that I was working in an area of self psychology and wrote that the potentiality for the psychological development of the ego and its functioning is inherent, and while I emphasized that the issues of separation and ego autonomy were crucial to the development of a devalued self-image, I saw the deprivations that gave rise to this masochistic defense in libidinal terms: "[T]he normal development of the ego is as directly dependent on getting love from the mother at the earliest infantile level as is the physical development on getting milk. If mother love on the oral level is absent or insufficient, the individual suffers a psychic trauma which must eventuate in a malfunction of the ego. The masochistic reaction is one form of an attempt on the part of the ego to deal with this trauma. The ego sacrifices itself, that is, its own worth, to sustain the illusion of mother love—an idealized mother image—without which life itself is impossible" (p. 66).

Although today I would still hold with this statement, I find it incomplete. It does not sufficiently emphasize the introjective, self-building processes by which parental love is conveyed through images, attitudes, ideals, and aspirations and is absorbed by the growing child, determining the character of his or her self-conception. It also does not define this process as an aspect of narcissistic development, a fact that would place the defensive operation of masochism in the area of narcissistic phenomena.

In the case of Evelyn, her wish to merge with her father, to be passive and completely cared for, is a masochistic, narcissistic abnegation of self-autonomy which was precipitated by an identification with her infant son.

If we view Evelyn's malfunctioning personality as the result of deficits in the development of the self originating in a lack of empathic mirroring and the internalization of an overidealized, grandiose, narcissistic father figure, and resulting in a narcissistic self-image, what are the implications for a therapeutic procedure that would help her to develop mature relationships with others and to achieve a realistic and respectful evaluation of her self? My patient of the 1953 paper said to me after some years of analysis:

> "You are the first and only adult toward whom I feel equal." . . . Although she was adult in years, her world was divided into two antagonistic camps: children and adults. She, of course, always regarded herself as one of the children, "put upon" and rendered helpless by the powerful adults. Through an attitude of respect for her personality, an avoidance of any hint of authoritarianism in the analytic procedure, an expressed belief in her potentialities for growth as an independent person, a genuine sympathy for her plight, and a conscious presentation of myself as definitely human and fallible, I was able to create this atmosphere of equality. Thus the analytic relationship had a measure of reality sufficient to *prevent* the repetition in the transference of the masochistic defense and not to provide fertile soil *in* which the masochistic ego could take root, thus making a new type of identification with the analyst possible. Such identification with the analyst strengthened the ego, making possible a discontinuance of the old, symbiotic relationship to the mother out of which the masochistic position of the ego had grown. [p. 65]

From time to time through the ensuing years, I have had contact with this patient and I have witnessed the benefits of her therapy. Many good things have occurred in her life; there were also some serious blows that she was able to weather. But the most positive testimony to the success of her treatment and to her maturation was her ability to successfully raise two unusually lovely children, one of them a daughter. She broke the narcissistic chain of her own mother-daughter relationship through the respect and *value-enhancing love* (Edith Weigert's [1962] term) that she communicated to her children. I think that this derived from her therapeutic experience with me.

I would not change my therapeutic stance today. I would only feel more clearly its necessity and would be more certain of its justification. The strengthening of the patient's ego, which Freud (1933) identified as the therapeutic aim of psychoanalysis, cannot be accomplished *solely* through expanding the ego's capacity to "appropriate fresh portions of the id," so to speak, for in every psychic conflict the ego's strength or weakness relative to the adaptational task at hand reflects its developmental history not only in libidinal terms. but in terms of what the self has ingested as total experience—experience of itself vis-à-vis the significant others of early childhood, experience that has become part of the self and of the self-feeling. This is true, in my opinion, not only for the narcissistic personality disorder of which the narcissistic character defense is an illustration, but for *all* individuals who seek psychotherapeutic help. They, as we, are most vulnerable in those areas that touch upon narcissistic development. It is for this reason that early deficits in the development of healthy narcissism cannot be corrected by insight into these processes alone, but require actual support from the therapist in the form of affirmation and acceptance of the patient's total personality. Such a posture in the therapeutic situation is not to be confused with the gratification of instinctual drives; it is supportive in the name of a reconstruction of the patient's self. The active sympathy of the psychotherapist "is a part of this value-enhancing love, capable of envisioning the personality of the patient in his potential wholeness, even though this wholeness may at present be adumbrated by a preponderance of destructive processes from which the patient seeks liberation" (Weigert 1962).

The therapeutic alliance must mean not only the patient's identification with our therapeutic aims, but our full sympathy for and acknowledgment of him or her in totality. Knowing that the primary genesis of the self-feeling resides in the early mother-child interaction dictates that we must correct such deficits in self-esteem that are the legacy of inadequacies in this relationship by conveying a respect and esteem that is sensitive to the patient's narcissistic vulnerability. This is a major clinical implication of working within the added dimension of a self psychology.

20

Illusion,
Idealization,
and Masochism

As clinicians we are accustomed to think in terms of those factors in personality development that we have been taught are responsible for pathology as well as for the form and destiny of the particular source of so-called normal lives. These factors are purported to have caused repression and to have created a vast reservoir of unconscious impulses and feelings that influence behavior, shape attitudes, and color perceptions. Yet, no matter how great is the effect of such repressed unconscious factors, we dare not lose sight of the importance of consciousness in the life of mankind. The enthusiasm for the discovery of the unconscious in reaction to the extreme rationalism of the pre-Freudian and Freudian eras led to an overevaluation of the unconscious as the determining agent in shaping our lives. Although the theory of the unconscious itself as it is developed in Freudian psychology is highly rational in form, it neglects consciousness, the most rational aspect of human psychology, as a determinant in behavior. Actually it is consciousness that is the miracle of human life, for it is only man in the entire world of living things who possesses the special kind of awareness and especially self-awareness that we associate with the term consciousness.

Self-awareness develops gradually; yet it begins early as the small child differentiates him- or herself from the "other" by referring to himself first by name and later by the pronoun "I." It is consciousness that is ultimately responsible for the development of the "I" and that creates the awareness of self-consciousness.

We know empirically from developmental studies and from clinical work. as well as from theoretical speculation, that the self is formed in large measure through processes of internalization. Superimposed upon an individual's constitutionally given nature and temperament are all the experiences—personal and interpersonal—that are taken into the psychic life, largely through the mediating power of memory, to become aspects of the self. Although the initial experience is conscious, its inevitable accompanying emotion is not always known to consciousness. Yet, both the experience and the feeling are taken into the personality and constitute the building blocks of the self. It is interesting that the content, form, and feeling of what is internalized is not a mirror image of the outside world. The memory image is changed by the nature of the already existing self. It includes previous experience, the sensitivity of perception, specific needs and anxieties, and the anticipations of the future. Such images determine the character of the self.

It is clear that experiences with the earliest significant others—mother, father, siblings—as they are taken into the self to become what we refer to as identifications form the basic structure of the self. Although identifications take place for the most part without the participation of consciousness, there is within the personality a half-conscious driving force that seeks out objects for identification—objects with which to build and nourish the self. The psychic structure needs to be fed as much as the body needs nutrition, and various personalities display differing degrees of initiative in seeking out others with whom to identify.

It is a combination of the subjectivity of perception, the availability of objects for identification in an individual's environment, and the strength of the need and of the drive that seeks out such objects, that plays a large part in determining the extent of the role of illusion in the building of the self-structure. In discussing the early development of the infant, Winnicott (1965) seems to indicate that before the creation of illusion can take place, there must be at least the beginnings of a rudimentary true self when instinct needs can be experienced as internal and their satisfaction can add to the further strengthening of the ego or true self. It is the constant interplay of maturational processes with the experience of the outer world that readies the small child's ego for the enjoyment of the creation of illusion in play and imagination. And it is this capacity for illusion coupled with the mechanisms of internalization that serves to build the self.

The creative ability to change and modify what has been experienced in the outer world of reality and subsequently incorporated into the self, only to be projected outward again in a new form, is the exclusively human capacity to fashion illusion. The needs of the self dictate the nature of illusion. These needs take several important forms: first there exists the fundamental need to internalize the very substance of identification in order to structure the self, second is the need to avoid anxiety and to create a worthy, pleasing, and competent self-image; and finally there is the need to find purpose and meaningfulness in life itself, in one's very existence. It is the latter need that is responsible for the creation of what Rank calls ideologies, be they religious, social, or political. It is to these ideologies that individuals cling so tenaciously because they provide the motivation for the continuation of existence in the face of the disappointments, frustrations, and tragedies that are the inevitable accompaniment of living and dying as a creature burdened with consciousness. It is this fact that led Rank to say that man cannot live without illusion—the illusion, whether self-created or not, that there is some transcendent reason for one's existence. Thus, there are two types of illusion: those that arise out of a human need to define one's place in the cosmos and those that are the product of dynamic intrafamilial and social interactions that serve the very formation of the self. It is these latter illusions that this chapter examines in an attempt to understand their relationship to idealization and to masochism.

Idealization can be said to be a way of loving; it is, in fact, the very nature of being "in love." Yet it is also an essential ingredient in the structuring of the self. Kohut (1977) has demonstrated in his clinical examples the importance of the idealization of love-objects with whom an individual identifies—an identification that, through internal transformations, becomes part of the self. It is as if the maturing and functioning personality senses, in the course of growth, the psychological need not just for nourishment for the structuring of the self but also for optimal nourishment. What is ingested as an image to be emulated must be modified through the creation of illusion into more than reality suggests that it is. Expressed another way, what is to become part of oneself, either in the sense of becoming self-structure or of uniting with a loved person or else what has at one time been part of oneself, is idealized through illusion so as optimally to nourish the self. A mother idealizes her newborn or very young child, and it is interesting to note that her perceptions become more realistic as the child becomes more of a person in his or her own right, that is, more of a separate self. The bride idealizes her husband to be, an adolescent idealizes the hero whom he hopes to emulate, and the child idealizes the parent whom he or she hopes to be like. The creation of illusion ebbs and flows throughout life, assuming varying forms, and intensifies at different periods of development. This mechanism that is at the heart of psychological survival could be referred to as narcissistic; yet, because of the almost inevitable pejorative connotation of that term, I prefer not to use it, but rather to regard idealization through illusion as an aspect of normal emotional development. Certainly through exaggeration or intensification, it can reach pathological proportions.

It seems clear that idealization supports the consolidation of the self through the creation of an illusion concerning the internalized "significant other" whose positive image becomes part of the self-structure. When the illusion is negative and hostile, we usually speak of distortion, and the effect on the self is to render it fragmented. The subjective experience for the individual is one of depression, even despair. The image that has been internalized poisons rather than nourishes the self.

This brings us to the issue of disillusionment, for idealization can suffer disappointment since we are dealing with human imperfections. If experienced by a personality whose self-structure is too dependent for its cohesion on internalized idealized images, disillusion produces a feeling of the loss of an important part of the self with consequent depression. One can observe this manifestation clinically when, in the course of analytic treatment a denial mechanism that has served to maintain an illusion breaks down and can no longer function in the face of reality, then disillusionment takes place and is often followed by depression. For example, one of my patients, a young woman, had strongly idealized her father throughout her life. He had left the family when she was a young child of about 5, and although he had kept in touch with his children, the contact in a somewhat diluted form had been just enough to whet her appetite for more attention from him, but not enough for her to form a realistic image of him. The idealization persisted throughout her life and well into the treatment process, fed, in spite of frequent disappointing behavior on her father's part, by an unhappy home situation with her mother. As the relationship to her mother improved during her analysis, she began to see her father more realistically. The idealization paled.

During her treatment her mother died and it was after this event, when she naturally looked to her father for emotional support and found it not forthcoming, that she realized the full extent of her father's narcissism, of his self-absorption, and of his limited interest in her. Great disappointment and depression ensued. She had not only lost her mother in actuality but lost to her also was the internalized and idealized image of her father on which that part of her self-structure containing her goals and ideals had depended. She reacted with depression, but also with rage.

At first the rage was generalized. The inevitable impingement of people in daily life irritated and angered her. She was touchy, oversensitive, almost paranoid. But soon her extreme and long-suppressed anger and disappointment were focused more appropriately where they belonged—on her father.

The reaction of rage against the former object of one's idealization and ultimately against oneself is not uncommon. We see it in microcosm in our clinical practice, but history and observation of events on the larger social scene reveal it repeatedly in macrocosm; for example, when a previously idealized leader is despised and reviled after some disappointment that threatens the maintenance of the initial illusion. This has happened recently in our own profession of psychoanalysis—at least this is one possible interpretation of the stir and the storm surrounding the figure of Jeffrey Masson.

I do not know Jeffrey Masson. My interpretation of the dynamics of his inner life that led him to uncover previously hidden material in the archives of psychoanalysis, and thus to the conclusions that he drew about Freud's life and personality, derives solely from the recently published material about him and his own book, *The Assault on Truth* (1984), plus my own conjecture about the mechanisms that surround the human need for idealization.

There is reason to assume that a man of Masson's brilliance who began as a Sanskrit scholar and then turned to a study of psychoanalysis has a historical interest in origins, be it of language or the human mind or the very psychoanalytic movement with which he felt himself aligned. In this interest he is closely identified with Freud whose archeological interests are well known and whose theory of the mind and his method for the treatment of its disorders are profoundly historical. This affinity between the mindset of the two men created fertile ground for the idealization of Freud by Masson—an idealization that most likely expresses his own need to internalize a father image that is at one and the same time grounded in reality, yet embellished by the work of illusion. There is a curious parallel in the course and destiny of relationships between Masson's relationship to Freud and Freud's own relationship to Fliess and later to Ferenczi.

Freud's relationship to Fliess is well documented by Ernest Jones in his biography of Freud. Jones (1953) describes Freud's extreme dependence on Fliess and likens it to a delayed adolescence (p. 295). Despite Freud's tendency to self-deprecation in this relationship, Jones perceives this not as a sign of weakness, but rather as the product of "a terrifying strength" that he felt unable to cope with alone. Out of the feeling of aloneness grew an idealization of Fliess, so that his mentor, his teacher, might be strong enough, great enough to be his protector. In describing Freud's creation of an illusion in this idealization of Fliess, especially after Freud's disappointment with and ultimate break with Breuer, Jones refers to the image of Fliess as "Freud's idealization of Breuer." He "overestimated Fliess's capacity at the expense of his own" (p. 303). This is the masochistic aspect of idealization to be discussed shortly.

Such idealizations are second editions of earlier thwarted or unresolved idealizations. For Freud it was not only Breuer who preceded Fliess, but most probably Freud's own father. We know from various anecdotes that Jones relates in the biography that Freud loved his father, yet suffered some of the inevitable disappointments and disillusionments in his character and personality that are the lot of human beings. Through his self-analysis Freud discovered a deeply buried hostility to his father, which left him with the need to find a substitute father. Jones (1953) writes, in an attempt to account for Freud's idealization of Fliess within this context:

> And what more inviting protection against the dark terror [here he is refer-
> ring to the fear of being overcome by the murderous impulses against the
> father] can there be than to find a father-substitute to whom one can display
> the utmost affection, admiration, and even subservience, doubtless a repeti-
> tion of an early attitude to his own father. Only, unfortunately, such false
> cures never succeed for long. Always the latent hostility gets transferred also,
> and the relationship ends, as here, in dissension and estrangement. [p. 307]

In this passage Jones's interpretation of Freud's idealization of Fliess is based on his need for protection from his hostile impulses—originally toward his father. In other words, this interpretation is based on drive theory. However, there is another way of looking at the same phenomenon, a way that early on was explored by Otto Rank. It concerns the issues of *aloneness*, the fear of separation and of autonomy. Freud's genius and creativity in the exploration of the mind, regardless of whether his conclusions were true or not, burdened him with a separateness from the prevailing thinking of his colleagues of the time and symbolized the original separation from his father; for in development, in the course of becoming individuated, a child must not only master overdependency on a mother figure but must also outgrow the dependency on the idealized father figure for continuous affirmation of the self (Kohut 1977). It was precisely such affirmation and confirmation of himself and his work that Freud sought from Fliess and others before and after him. The outstanding creative individual, whose work is an innovative expression of him- or herself, feels particularly alone and, according to Rank, also guilty for the separation from others that such autonomy implies. The need for the support implicit in affirmation is thus especially strong. Freud expressed this need throughout his life, first in the idealization of father figures and later, through a reversal of roles, in the idealization and attachment to son-figures as in the case of Rank.

To return to the case of Jeffrey Masson: I would speculate that Masson, like Freud, had a need for an idealized father figure both as an affirmation of himself and as someone with whom to identify. That figure was Freud. His correspondence of ten years with Anna Freud and his long relationship with Kurt Eissler were not necessarily, as some are inclined to believe, a way of worming himself into high places in the psychoanalytic movement for his own aggrandizement and ultimately to destroy the movement. They can be viewed more positively as a result of his profound identification with Freud: a need for a father, a search for the truth. Anna Freud's complete trust in Masson is revealed in the fact that she made all the most important documents and papers in her possession, as well as in the Freud archives, available to him. Why such excessive trust, especially in face of the fact that she herself had withheld certain materials from the public eye? We can assume that unconsciously, perhaps even consciously, she perceived Masson's profound identification with her father.

Like Freud, Masson became disillusioned with his idealized father figure on the basis of what he perceived as a flaw in his "scientific" theory, based on Freud's failure to face the truth. He accused Freud of a failure of courage. It is interesting that Freud's disillusionment with his father is connected with an often-related incident in which the son felt a failure in courage on the part of the father. It concerns the expression of anti-Semitism that was prevalent in the Austria of that time. Jones (1953) tells the story as follows:

His father never regained the place he had held in his esteem after the painful occasion when he told his 12-year-old boy how a Gentile had knocked off his new fur cap into the mud and shouted at him: "Jew, get off the pavement." To the indignant boy's question: "And what did you do?," he calmly replied: "I stepped into the gutter and picked up my cap." This lack of heroism on the part of his model man shocked the youngster who at once contrasted it in his mind with the behavior of Hamilcar when he made his son Hannibal swear on the household altar to take vengeance on the Romans. Freud evidently identified himself with Hannibal, for he said that ever since then Hannibal had a place in his phantasies. "Submission was not in his nature." [pp, 22-23]

In the case of the previously idealized Breuer, Freud perceived a failure in courage in Breuer's unwillingness to deal with sexual etiology in hysteria; in the case of Fliess, too, the break occurred over so-called scientific differences.

Masson attributes Freud's failure in courage to his abandonment of the seduction theory, which occurred because of Freud's reluctance to challenge the psychiatric community in its belief that the reports of seduction by disturbed patients was pure fantasy. Since Masson makes a case for the seduction theory as the cornerstone of psychoanalysis, Freud's abandonment of the theory represents, in his mind, a major lack of courage indeed. Herein resides the disillusionment in the idealized father to be followed by the expected rage reaction.

It is irrelevant to the issue of the fate of idealization whether the seduction theory is central to psychoanalytic theory or not, although from a theoretical and technical viewpoint it touches on the larger issue of the extent to which, in dealing with patients, one should address reality at all or concern oneself exclusively with fantasy. That issue would require a chapter of its own, especially since it is not always clear what is reality and what fantasy. From the standpoint of this chapter, however, the phenomena of illusion, idealization, and disillusion are in a general sense observable human reactions. Yet, as they appear in individual cases they are highly subjective, and the interpretation of their genesis and individual meanings is not verifiable. This, then, often makes for the use of theory as an instrument of attack when rage against a formerly idealized figure is to be expressed. The many hostile reactions to Masson's uncovering of important omissions in the history of the psychoanalytic movement, which amounted to a tampering with scientific truth, especially when such anger occurs among individuals committed to psychoanalysis as an ideology, can be understood as a fear of losing the idealized image of Freud. The intactness of the self-structure depends too heavily for many individuals on keeping an idealization, even if it means the maintenance of an illusion at the expense of a clear perception of reality.

This brings us to the issue of masochism as it relates to the phenomena of illusion and idealization. I regret the fact that we are saddled with the term "masochism," since in the sense in which I use it it is not a "drive" phenomenon, but rather refers to a denigrated self-conception that derives from an interpersonal interaction. In classical psychoanalytic theory the term "moral masochism" as distinguished from "sexual masochism" comes closest to my meaning.

In Jones's descriptions of the interaction between Freud and Fliess, we read many passages in which Freud expresses an overestimation of Fliess coupled with an underestimation of his own capacities. Paradoxically in the story about his father's encounter with anti-Semitism, Freud is disillusioned by his father's submissiveness and, in his own mind, identifies with Hannibal, an aggressive hero. There is thus a mixture of self-aggrandizement and self-diminution in Freud's character, and I would hazard the guess that this combination occurs frequently in creative personalities. It is not surprising that this duality in the self-image manifests itself so clearly in creative individuals. Otto Rank, who understood the conflict around separation so well, has an interesting and plausible explanation for this duality. For the creative person, the product, which is the result of the creative activity, is an announcement of his or her uniqueness and autonomy. It is a statement of separation that exceeds that of most individuals, and therefore, since separation from "the other" (originally the mother) is inevitably experienced with some guilt, the creative individual who is "more separate" is also more guilty. The artist expiates this guilt by offering further creative work, but his or her self-image is burdened by the guilt, making it denigrated, on the one hand, and aggrandized as a result of the creative product, on the other. When the denigrated self-image gains dominance over healthy self-esteem, a masochistic character structure results.

Let me describe the case of a young woman whose adaptation to the world of reality and to her interaction with others, especially in her closer and more intimate relationships, is distinctively masochistic. Jean is a bright young research scientist of considerable talent and originality. She grew up in a professional family with parents whose relationship to each other and to their children was reserved, to say the least. There were four sisters, and as might be expected, there were often conflicts and difficulties among them. Whenever Jean complained to her mother about some mistreatment at the hands of a sister—or anyone else for that matter—her mother invariably replied, "And what did *you* do?" The onus was always on her. She grew up with the feeling that she was always in the wrong. This feeling applied not only to interactions that were contentious but even to simple things like the clothes she might choose to wear to school on a particular day. There was no pleasing her mother. If she wore one thing, why was it not another, and vice versa. Nevertheless, unlike her sister who rebelled against the mother, Jean never gave up the attempt to please her mother, to win her love and approval. Yet, she was aware of her anger toward her mother. The nature of the illusion in her case is not that the mother is idealized, although she failed to perceive her realistically, but that there is some flaw in herself that if found and remedied would make everything right—would please her mother, heal the relationship, and avoid separation.

Jean's self-feeling was that of a guilty self, always submitting to what she regarded as the better judgment and reality perception of "the other." In her treatment she complained that in the presence of another person she could never be herself, that is, adequate, competent, and autonomous. Her efforts were always focused on pleasing "the other." This was clearly a legacy of her relationship to her mother to whom she was tied in a masochistic bond in which she was always in the wrong. Yet, the wish for separation was great indeed. It would mean a release from the projection of "fault" upon herself and an acceptance and affirmation of the reality of her true worth. The masochistic illusion of her own unworthiness and her attitude of compliance brought her, she felt, the affection of others, but at the price of the inhibition of her assertiveness and her creativity. As a research worker she was functioning in a field that called for creativity, so that her inhibition was a distinct handicap. It also led her into dependent relationships with others whose support she needed to pursue and fulfill her own original and creative ideas.

Even in a personality as insecure as Jean's, however, there is an admixture of heightened self-esteem coupled with the dependent, guilty, and diminished self-conception. It is not all of a piece. In her treatment I have strongly supported her creative efforts and her good self-feeling, as well as her very active attempts to find heroes in the scientific world whom she could idealize and with whom she could identify. Such idealizations provide an antidote to the masochistic tendency to denigrate herself.

If we look back in summary at the three psychological processes discussed in this chapter—illusion, idealization, and masochism—we must conclude that they are all involved in the structuring or adaptation of the self. They depend primarily on the human ability first to internalize the outer world of reality as it is represented by images of emotionally significant individuals and second to alter those images through illusions so that the self is nourished by idealizations. Even if these illusions ultimately succumb to disillusionment, they were among the first essential building blocks of the self, which in the best case has been rendered strong enough to deal with the failure of the illusion. And even if the fear of becoming a separate, autonomous self is so strong as to necessitate a defensive masochistic self-image as a protection against separation, there is still the possibility and the hope that new internalizations may liberate an individual from the bondage of the old illusions that kept him or her insecure and dependent.

It is amazing that the self, which is made up so largely of illusions, should be strong enough to love and share with others, to create, and to be the chief carrier and transmitter of our culture.

21

More on Masochism

In a lecture to a lay audience on love and sexuality, one of my main points was that, for Freud, sexuality was the primary motivating force in human life, and love in its nonsexual expressions—tenderness, affection, altruism, empathy, and creativity—was a derivative of the sexual drives. I expressed my disagreement with Freud and described love as a primary, innate human capacity to relate to others in a positive way, as well as to sense a oneness with the cosmos and to feel its energy and striving within us. This is akin to a religious feeling—a spiritual awareness of a love of life. It was my description of the human appreciation for participation in the life of the universe and my calling it religious that evoked an unexpected response from a man in the audience, when the meeting was opened to questions or remarks from the floor. "Religion is not about love," he said. "It is about suffering. This is the whole meaning of Christ on the cross." He hoped I would comment on this statement. Not being a theologian, I was somewhat at a loss, but I answered him in terms of my own true feelings: namely, that although there is without doubt much suffering in life, Christ's major message is to me a message of love.

Yet, the man's remark stuck in my craw, not from the standpoint of theology, but from that of psychology and especially in connection with the problem of masochism. I began thinking and writing about masochism many years ago, long before the advent of a self psychological viewpoint in psychoanalysis, and it is only recently that I have realized that my paper (Menaker 1953), "Masochism: A Defense Reaction of the Ego," despite the use of the word "ego" in the title (in the early literature, ego and self were not clearly distinguished) is indeed a self psychological study. It is essentially a description, based on case materials, of the use of a denigrated self-image as a defense against the anxiety of separation. The denigrated self-image that signals a massive loss of self-esteem does not arise unbidden, spontaneously, but is the product of the internalization, in the course of development, of the bad, unloved, and unlovable image of the child that the parent, initially the mother, projects onto the child. It is in her eyes that the mother's lack of love is expressed. The image persists and through transmuting internalizations, as Kohut states, becomes part of the individual's self-structure, and is the source of the sense of worthlessness. This sense of undeservedness is expressed in the demeaning nature of an individual's relationship to others or to him- or herself; it is often reflected in the need to stay in, or place oneself in, a disadvantaged position or for example to display incompetence or an inhibition of creativity. This stance in life is called moral masochism.

Moral masochism is an unfortunate term, although I cannot think of a substitute for it. It derives in Freudian theory from a description of sadomasochistic sexual behavior in which sadism is seen as sexual pleasure stemming from the controlling power of anal impulses, and masochism as the pleasure resulting from the erotization of the inflicted pain. Moral masochism, as the term implies, is not sexual and in my view does not involve pleasure. It might be described as an obsessional holding onto a denigrated conception of the self, and in behavioral terms, as hesitation to be self-assertive or to express a feeling of entitlement that would permit the growth and fulfillment of the potential of the self. It inevitably involves suffering, but it does not seek suffering. Suffering is the byproduct of the profound imprint of badness left upon the individual in the course of the development of the self when the absence or insufficiency of love and affirmation on the part of parents resulted in the incorporation of bad images of the self.

However, our sense of worthiness as we live within the human situation is never very *secure*, even if the experiences of childhood giving rise to the coloration of the self were not particularly traumatic. This is because we are social creatures with the ability to empathize with others—to identify with their needs and purposes. When we put our own needs before those of others we experience guilt. Otto Rank, that much-neglected psychoanalytic figure who understood so profoundly this inevitable human source of guilt, attributed it to the empathic mother-child relationship: not only the mother's empathy for the infant but also the child's empathy for the mother. Very early on, the child experiences guilt, not just for wrongdoing, but for putting needs of the self, his or her own, before those of the mother for whom he feels love, attachment, and empathic attunement. In the attempt to assuage guilt of this kind, the child might behave in ways that would disadvantage his or her own self-development. We would be inclined to describe this as masochistic behavior. Yet, to sacrifice the self for the other characterizes the human capacity to love and is as essential for the survival of the species as is love for the development of the self. Thus, it is the human lot to bear a certain amount of guilt for our self-interest and a degree of masochism for our concern for others. All this is to say, when we deal with moral masochism in our patients, we must not be misled into immediately thinking that every disadvantage to the self points to pathological masochism.

A British professor of English and Gifford Lecturer at the University of Glasgow, W. MacNeile Dixon (1958), in a profoundly philosophical work, describes this human dilemma accurately:

> How . . . is the individual to secure his own ends, how exist, expand, realize his innermost, his profoundest needs, without interference with lives and purposes no less justifiable than his own, without injury to them, without the destruction or subjugation of the rest, the vast concourse of other living creatures? Each and all, you and I, have their moral rights to what existence offers. Every man has his case and his claims as undeniable as those of his neighbors. They have not been answered, these questions, not one of them. [p. 225]

I do not propose to answer these questions. But to understand them as an inescapable human dilemma and to perceive moral masochism as an inevitable human reaction should help us to distinguish between normal and pathological degrees of masochism and clarify and accept our responsibility in life with others, from parenthood to psychotherapist, to make sure that the soil for furthering the growth of this inevitable human masochism is not fertile.

We are accustomed to think of the opposite of masochism as sadism. This is true in the sexual sphere and in sadomasochistic behavior that is a derivative of the sexual drive. But in the realm of the moral masochism of the self, its opposite is not a sexualized drive expressing itself as sadism, but rather indulgence in the expression of power. At times the two opposites—sadism and power—come very close together, sometimes coincide, and sometimes overlap, but it is worth noting their differences. Although a sadistic act is motivated by an individual drive to derive pleasure from humiliating and demeaning another person, the exercise of power need not be individually motivated, need not be pleasure driven, nor have as its aim the placing of another person in a masochistic position. Functioning in terms of power may be purely circumstantial. Because of the inevitability of some inequalities in human familial and social structure, of some built-in hierarchies and injustices in interpersonal relationships, there are countless life situations in which one individual is in a dominant position vis-à-vis another person by virtue of the roles they each have under certain circumstances. Let us take the earliest, simplest, and most inevitable circumstance of all—that of the relationship between parent and child. Clearly, the parent is in a position of power; the child is relatively helpless and dependent. Of course this dimension does not characterize all aspects of the parent–child relationship. But power versus helplessness and dependency characterize those dimensions that are relevant to an understanding of moral masochism. In the course of life many situations in which one individual needs another repeat the dichotomy of the parent-child relationship and therefore carry the potential for the development of a masochistic stance on the part of the dependent, that is, the needy individual. This issue is certainly critical in the psychotherapeutic situation. In 1943 I published a paper, "The Masochistic Factor in the Psychoanalytic Situation," in which I described the circumstantial inevitability of the power hierarchy in the analytic situation: the dominant analyst versus the subordinate, dependent patient.

I recall a personal conversation, in those years, with Edith Jacobson in which she failed to understand why I regarded the juxtaposition of the dominance of one individual and the subordinate position of the other as conducive to the development of masochism. I was not successful in explaining it at that time. But since the advent of self psychology the psychological tools for making the dynamics of that human interaction much clearer have become available. The self depends in varying degrees for the regulation of self-esteem on the responses of the thou, the significant "other." This need is present from the beginning of life. For the normal development of the self-structure an individual needs to be affirmed and to have someone to idealize, and it is the powerful parents who fill this need. If parents either fail or are inadequate in meeting this need, the child's self-structure suffers from lack of strength and cohesiveness and above all from an uncertain regulation of self-esteem. If parents abuse the power of their position in relation to the dependency of the child by being overcritical, abusive, or even sadistic, a masochistic reaction on the child's part may result; this is a defensive reaction as I have described it in "Masochism: A Defense Reaction of the Ego" (Menaker 1953). The child gives up his or her self-esteem, at least in part, to hold on to the idealized image of the parent. In that paper I considered the function of this psychological maneuver, in which the individual regards him- or herself as unworthy and views the parent as all good, to be an attempt to avoid separation from the parent imago. I still believe that to be an important aspect of the psychodynamics of moral masochism. Today I would add that holding on to the good parental imago is not motivated only by the fear of separation and consequent aloneness but also by the continual need for nourishment for the self-structure.

The word *continual* is crucial here. For it is not only in the parent-child relationship that the self of the developing child needs nutrients in the form of affirmation from parents. In all relationships throughout life, especially those that repeat in structure the parent-child hierarchy, the self-esteem of an individual depends to some degree on affirmation and respect from the person in the dominant position. Lacking this affirmation, a masochistic reaction, a sense of worthlessness, and loss of self-esteem may result. This is especially the case for individuals who developed a masochistic self-image during childhood as a result of a traumatic situation that denied them love, acceptance, and affirmation and/or subjected them to a constant barrage of criticism, a constant chiseling away at a sense of worth.

It is not hard to see that the power structure in the family could be misused to invite a masochistic response on the part of the growing child and that many life situations—the teacher and student, the husband and wife, the doctor and patient, the psychotherapist and patient—could lend themselves, through the abuse of power on the part of the dominant individual, to a similar loss of self-esteem, a feeling of being undeserving, and perhaps even of being incompetent. It is certainly the moral and ethical obligation of parents and of psychotherapists, not to mention others involved in analogous human interactions, to practice the restraint of power.

Let me describe now the case of a young professional woman whose basically masochistic character structure emerged in the course of her therapy when she found herself in a critical life situation. Lisa had been married for fifteen years, most of them very unhappy years. Her husband had withdrawn from her sexually and was constantly critical of her; he accused her of incompetence, of being emotionally unstable, of unfriendliness, and of being too stern and demanding in bringing up their two children. He was verbally abusive, uncooperative, and unhelpful in the management of the affairs of their daily lives. At times he would have violent outbursts of rage, cursing, throwing, and breaking things in the house. After the first year or two of their marriage had passed, she was extremely unhappy, but rationalized her staying in the marriage as being best for the children. She was competent and successful in her work, which afforded her some satisfaction and security. The discrepancy between her level of functioning as the highly intelligent person that she was and the portrait of herself that her husband held up to her on an almost daily basis was enormous. Finally, when he began to refer to her as "crazy" and challenged her perception of reality with the result that she herself became uncertain about her judgment and the accuracy of her perceptions, she decided that she needed help. She consulted me, and we decided to meet on a regular twice-a-week basis in an attempt to evaluate the situation and plan a course of action.

My first task was to question her masochistic acceptance, not only of his hostility and abuse but also of the picture of her that he mirrored to her. "Perhaps he was right," she would say. "There must be something wrong with me, for why would anyone treat me in this way if I did not deserve it?" Gradually she acknowledged that her husband was abusive and that perhaps she did not deserve to be treated the way that he treated her. Occasionally she would allow herself to feel anger, but usually she dissolved into tears in a "woe is me" attitude.

Finally she decided that she could no longer live in the denigrating situation that her marriage represented. In a bitter confrontation with her husband she asked him to leave. The separation and divorce proceedings began. As is often the case, as discussions about settlement of their respective assets and possessions ensued, the tensions between them grew, and her husband became meaner, greedier, and more verbally abusive. Lisa's masochistic attitude also grew. It was an ugly situation.

My major role continued to be one in which I supported her perception of her husband's meanness and unfairness, for she continued to doubt her perceptions of reality, to blame herself, and to feel misunderstood and abandoned—even by me at times when she felt that I was too hard on her when I pointed to her failure to look at reality. As we continued her therapy, the connections between the events and attitudes of the present and her childhood experiences became even clearer. The imprint of the masochism began early, was deep, and continued throughout her growing-up years. She grew up in the upper-middle-class home of professional parents. Her father was a stern. demanding man who intimidated both his wife and daughter, who was an only child. Often he would interact with the little girl in a way that was a mixture of sadism and playfulness, with more emphasis on the sadism. For example, he would tie her up with strings and ropes in intricate knots and loops and then leave her alone just to see, he would say, if she could get out of the mess. She did always manage to untangle herself, but it was interesting to me that when she reported these episodes it was not with appropriate anger, although she knew that this was not the way to treat children nor did she treat her own children in a similar manner. Her mother, who was often ill, was a somewhat withdrawn, unhappy woman who must have communicated some loving feelings to her daughter if we are to judge retrospectively from Lisa's motherly treatment of her own children.

It was after the death of her mother when she was in the early years of puberty that the deep anger toward her father really took root. Much of it was repressed, and the expression of those aspects of it that were conscious was rarely in evidence. Her father, who had promised her that he would not remarry without her approval, did indeed marry very soon after his wife's death. He married a woman of limited education who came from a lower socioeconomic class and who was constantly rivalrous with my patient, resenting the slightest expression of interest in his daughter on the part of the father. The stepmother's jealousy became quite paranoid, and at times she would tell lies about my patient in order to discredit her with her father. In this difficult situation there was no support for Lisa from the father. Quite the contrary; he admonished her never to cause trouble or difficulty in the home, never to complain, voice protest, or challenge the truth of her stepmother's remarks. If she disobeyed she would be threatened with being sent away from home to live with a relative in another part of the country. Her father bought peace and quiet in the house at the price of his daughter's mental health.

Lisa tried to absorb her father's betrayal, his lack of support and understanding, and the complete lack of empathy by blaming herself for the situation. She must have done something to deserve this kind of treatment. Otherwise why would her father be so mean to her? The defense of the father image at the expense of her own caused the imprint of a masochistic stance in her life and in her interaction with others, a masochism that emerged strongly during the divorce proceedings.

"Why is my husband being so mean and vengeful? I only want a fair settlement," she would say. "I must be worthless; otherwise why would anyone treat me this way? I don't understand it." This highly intelligent, psychologically sophisticated woman could not accept the simple reality that often people are self-serving to an extent that results in meanness toward others. In her therapy she enumerated several situations throughout her life when others had been unfair and mean to her, had taken advantage of her, and had betrayed her. "There must be something about me that brings this about," she would say.

In classical psychoanalytic treatment there is often an overemphasis on interpreting the patient's role in bringing down on him- or herself mean, unfair, or denigrating treatment. This overemphasis is usually done in the name of pointing out some aspect of unconscious guilt feeling for which the individual seeks punishment. Sometimes this is the case, but one must be careful. For sometimes the unfair or demeaning action originates in the need of the individual in a stronger or superior position to exert power over another person who is in a weaker, more vulnerable position. If then the victim says, it must by my fault, I am unworthy, this is a masochistic reaction designed to protect the image of the strong superior. This was Lisa's reaction to her father, which continued in her relationship to her husband. When she reiterated over and over again, "I don't understand it; why should he be so mean and why should this happen to me?," she continued to deny the reality of several facts: that sometimes people *are* mean and unfair to each other, that all people experience a certain amount of disappointing and unfair treatment at the hands of others in the course of life, and that she was not necessarily the cause of either her father's or her husband's behavior.

The denial of these aspects of reality suggests an additional dimension for our understanding of masochism, namely its narcissistic aspects. For Lisa to conclude that she is the first cause of the behavior of other individuals is a narcissistic phenomenon, be it of a masochistic nature. The conclusion that she has been singled out to be demeaned and humiliated by some unfriendly fate makes her *special*, despite the negative nature of the distinction. It is a failure to perceive and accept the reality that she is part of the human race.

Whether we regard this focus on herself as narcissistic by virtue of the excessive libido invested in her ego or regard the narcissism as a way of safeguarding the defensive function of her masochism—that is, the denial of her father's (husband's) mean and unloving attitude—the fact remains that the masochistic stance vis-à-vis her self-image, the feeling of unworthiness, has a narcissistic coloration despite its negative character.

In the treatment of masochistic patients it is of primary importance not to repeat in the analyst-analysand relationship the hierarchical power structure that determined the nature of the interactions characterizing the patient's original family situation. That is the soil in which masochism thrives. The deprivations in empathic understanding that the patient suffered in childhood must be made up by the therapist through strong expressions of affirmation, and finally the patient needs help in the perception of reality and the kind of encouragement that will ultimately result in confidence in his or her own independent perceptions.

In summary, moral masochism, like religion, is not about suffering, but about love—that is, the lack of love that inevitably entails suffering. The love that is needed by the growing individual in a family situation to minimize the masochistic response is the empathic wish on the part of parents to further the self-development, growth, and self-esteem of the child. Freud thought that the human creature was predisposed to neurotic conflict because of the long period of childhood during which the sexual drives experienced many vicissitudes before reaching maturity. In my view moral masochism is not a product of conflict, but a human response during the long period of childhood to the development of a self in a setting in which there is an inevitable inequality between the child's dependency and the parents' power. Under good and normal circumstances we all come away with some insecurity about ourselves and a small piece of masochism. But if there is an abuse of power on the part of a parent, the result for the emerging self of the child will most likely be a deep sense of unworthiness.

I still hold to the notion that the defensive function of moral masochism in which the self sacrifices self-esteem in order to preserve an idealized image of the offending parent as a way of avoiding separation is crucial. I would add, however, that separation from the parental selfobject is particularly threatening since the developing self needs to internalize the parental imago for its own growth. Above all, moral masochism is an exquisitely human attempt to solve the dilemma between the self-interest necessary for survival and the empathic love for others that is equally necessary for our psychological survival.

III

WOMEN'S ISSUES

The point of view expressed in the following chapters on the psychology of women is consistent with my previous writings on women's issues (Alpert 1986, Franks and Burtle 1974, Roland and Harris 1979). Always present is a stern critique of Freud's views on the universality of penis envy and the inferior superego of women. Most important is an emphasis on a psychosocial perspective as it affects the identity of women. Our society with its changing values and rapid transitions in so many dimensions has given women more socioeconomic freedom, but most importantly it has liberated them from a socially assigned role. Although such progress is to be welcomed, it has often left individual women in conflict. The internalization of old values as they are the inevitable heritage of the relationship to previous generations collides with new values and sometimes makes for an uncertain and unstable identity in specific individuals. This is an inevitable but impermanent byproduct of social evolution.

22

Female Identity in Psychosocial Perspective

In Woody Allen's film, *Manhattan*, there is an inimitable scene in which his character meets a vacuous young lady at a party, and in the studied casual conversation that ensues, she says in an offhand manner, "I told my analyst I had an orgasm last night, but he told me it was the wrong kind!" There is as much truth as humor in this remark, for this small satiric vignette depicts incisively and truthfully much of the history of the role that psychoanalysis has played in the setting up of mythical social and sexual norms. Under the aegis of a scientific psychology, psychoanalysis sought to define normal sexual development and normal sexual response, and in so doing it derived its own norm for female as well as for male identity.

But can one rightfully speak of a norm for sexual identity, even of sexual response, without qualifying it in terms of the social, cultural, and historical framework within which it develops? I think not, for identity is itself a social as well as an individual psychological phenomenon. Erikson (1959) has ably expressed this as follows: "The term 'identity' expresses such a mutual relation in that it connotes a persistent sameness within oneself (selfsameness) and a persistent sharing in some kind of essential character with others" (pp. 22-23). The awareness of one's self-image that is basic to one's identity derives its sense of continuity and constancy as well as its content from the vicissitudes of the emotional interactions within the family and from the values that are current in the social milieu. Those societal values, of course, impinge upon the family itself, so that the growing child's identity formation is doubly influenced by society—first through the family and then through direct contact with the mores, conventions, and values of the culture at large.

One can witness the emergence of a sense of identity in the language development of the small child. First, the child refers to him-self or herself by name—in other words, as others call him or her—thus attesting to the *social origins* of one's self-definition. Then the pronoun "I" appears, bearing witness to a greater separation from others and to a keener sense of uniqueness. This sense of uniqueness, combined with an awareness of belonging to a given category of beings, defines identity.

The focus of this chapter is on the development and consolidation of female identity: how does the little girl achieve a conception of herself as belonging to the category "woman" and "female," what is the content of the resultant self-image, and what emotions and self-feelings accompany this image?

In the psychoanalytic world the comment was made—I believe by Helene Deutsch—that one is born a man, but must become a woman. It is ironic that psychoanalysis, so often charged with being too biologically oriented (although to my mind it is a pseudobiology), should have so little understanding of and faith in nature, as to derive "woman" from the primacy of maleness in the manner of the ancient Hebrews whose God created Eve from Adam. It would be more accurate to say that one is born "female" and that one becomes "feminine" in terms of the social and cultural conceptions that define that category during a given historical period.

There have of course been dissenting opinions in the psychoanalytic community. Even in the 1920s, Jones and Horney (in Chasseguet-Smirgel 1970) spoke of the primacy of femininity in the development of the little girl and relegated penis envy in its dynamic effect on female development to a secondary position. But even for Horney, penis envy was inevitable in the psychosexual stages of female development, deriving from the fear of vaginal injury in connection with oedipal wishes that made the little girl adopt a defensive male identity. Yet, it is to her credit that she looked beyond psychosexual development to a view of the total personality and emphasized the importance of social factors in shaping woman's attitudes toward herself. According to Horney, our whole civilization is a masculine civilization; women have adapted themselves to the wishes of men and have felt their adaptation to be their true nature. This was written over fifty years ago, and the social changes that have occurred since then, although not confirming the content of this statement, have validated the fact that the specific character of female identity depends on the social and cultural values that prevail.

Even from the standpoint of instinct theory it is important to note that, although the Freudians view satisfactions in the female functions associated with motherhood as compensatory—second best to being a man—Horney (1967) emphasized the primary gratifications inherent in the woman's biological role. She wrote:

> The conclusion that half the human race is discontented with the sex assigned to it and can overcome this discontent only in favorable circumstances is decidedly unsatisfying, not only to feminine narcissism but also to biological science. What about motherhood? And the blissful consciousness of bearing a new life within oneself? And the joy when it finally makes its appearance and one holds it for the first time in one's arms? And the deep pleasurable feeling of satisfaction in suckling it and the happiness of the whole period when the infant needs her care!

There are also inherent gratifications in femaleness that precede motherhood and that illustrate how beautifully the body can speak to the mind when there are no interfering conflicts, no social strictures, no deprecating cultural values. With profound understanding of every individual's wish to affirm and be affirmed in what he or she is, Otto Rank, speaking of feminine psychology writes, "She has always wanted and still wants first and foremost to be a woman, because this and this alone is her fundamental self and expresses her personality no matter what else she may do or achieve." In a sensitive passage from a novel by R. F. Delderfield (1966), the writer shows a profound understanding of a young girl's pleasure in the discovery of her womanliness. The description concerns a veritable child of nature, a half-gypsy girl who dwelt largely alone in the forest, sharing her life with the wild creatures who surrounded her. She was not burdened by prevailing social values or conventions:

> Sometimes, if the mood came on her, she could forget all else in a long, self-satisfying appraisal of herself, contemplating her golden-brown legs, her flat belly, and her high breasts that were a source of special wonder to her for she could not recall anything more regularly formed unless it was the spread of the lower branches of her favorite oak in the meadow a mile south of her eyrie. She would sit cross-legged and study herself minutely, beginning with her flower-decked hair that reached to her waist and ending with a dedicated scrutiny of her supple toes. usually coated with the fine red dust of the rocks.

Then she would leap down from the slab and fetch the burnished lid of one of her tins to use as a mirror, holding it up at an angle and glancing sideways at her shoulders, then moving it in a slow, tilted sweep, until she could catch a distorted glimpse of her rounded buttocks and the deep dimples above them. Usually she was pleased and would shake out her hair, raise her arms, and wriggle like a savage beginning a ritual dance, exclaiming with the deepest satisfaction. "Youm bootiful, Hazel! Bootiful, do 'ee yer, now? Youm the most bootiful of all, for youm smooth an' white an' goldy and you baint much fur about 'ee, neither!" . . . She was, moreover, probably the happiest woman in the Valley, or any other valley in the West. for her isolated way of life was accepted by her mother Meg. [p. 551]

Here anatomy had a different destiny. Such frank and direct pleasure in and affirmation of what one is as a woman are rarely encountered in our society, for even if we disagree with Freud's view that gratifications for women are chiefly compensatory for basic penis envy, women have been saddled for so long with the imprint of assigned social, intellectual, and even moral inferiority as to make a change in self-image difficult. And it is out of this socially imprinted sense of inferiority that penis envy, to the extent that it exists, arises. For envy itself is inevitably a social phenomenon, whether it makes its appearance in the earliest development of the individual within the familial framework or continues later in life as the spoiler of social relationships. In either case it grows out of feelings of insufficiency, and although such feelings are a normal aspect of human development because of the long period of helplessness and dependency of the child, the further reinforcement of insufficiency through social attitudes as they impinge upon the female child has played a large part in woman's sense of inferiority.

Freud assumed that the sex difference inevitably gave rise to envy of the boy on the little girl's part, for as soon as the girl saw the penis she would wish to possess it. Although such may be the case in specific instances, since the capacity for envy varies among individuals, this reaction is by no means inevitable. For example, the ethologists might provide us with a very different model of the girl's response upon seeing the penis. Assuming that she is a normal, natural girl like the half-gypsy girl I have just described, it is possible that the sight of the penis might function as a release for sexual desire of a receptive nature—in the manner in which the mating behavior of one sexual partner in the animal world may be released by the perception of specific gestures, stances, or sounds on the part of the other partner.

However, I can already hear the argument against such a view. At the time that a little girl is likely to see the male genitals for the first time—which is usually thought to be very early in her development and, incidentally, even this time will vary in different countries—the awareness of her own genitals is at best extremely vague because of their hidden nature. It is therefore very unlikely that her response would be a sexually positive one. So runs the argument. And indeed when we speak of the sexuality of young children we must not think in adult terms, but rather in terms of deeply felt, intuitive, unarticulated modes of responding to the complementarity that the other sex represents. On this instinctive feeling level, if she affirms her body image, it is quite possible that the little girl will feel a receptive longing for the penis. Indeed, is this so different from the existence of oedipal wishes in early childhood that we have come to accept as given?

What makes this view so hard to accept is that the full and unconditional affirmation of her body is rare among women. Yet, I see this rarity as a social, not a biological phenomenon. The self-image—and especially its core, the body image—is formed through internalizations of how we are perceived, what we are told, and what feelings and attitudes are conveyed by those who are our primary caretaker, who is almost always the mother. For the little girl, her mother's attitude toward her child's femaleness is especially crucial, since mother and daughter are of the same sex. But the mother herself is not only the product of her own mother's attitudes—that is, of the psychodynamics of her personal history—but also of the existing social attitudes, conventions, and mores to which she is exposed. The mother then, through what she mirrors of her feelings about herself and her child, becomes a primary carrier of social tradition.

However, in emphasizing the importance of the mother's role in the formation of female identity—of identity in general, for that matter—we should not overlook the role of the father. In my clinical experience I have found that women who have felt unappreciated as little girls by fathers, who either withdrew defensively because of their own fears of sexual feelings, or were truly contemptuous of women, or were absent through death or overcommitment to work and career, have great difficulty in adult life in relationships with men. Fathers, after all, were once little boys whose attitudes toward women grew in large measure out of their relationships to their own mothers. Their daughters very much need their affirmation—affirmation of their worth as individuals—as well as affirmation of their female identity.

It would be hard to overemphasize the fact that all the complex familial interactions that play a major role in the nature of female identity are conditioned by and are relative to the values existing in the social milieu in which they take place. In *Career and Motherhood,* Alan Roland and Barbara Harris (1979) make quite explicit that "crucial to any identity synthesis are the particular prevailing ideologies or value systems of a given historical era" (p. 87). What society thinks of women and the role it assigns to them have a tremendous effect not only on the nature and content of the female self-conception but, more important, also on the affective aspect of the self-image, namely self-esteem. A woman's feeling of inferiority, in many instances even her acceptance of inferiority as if it were a fact, nurtured by our masculine civilization and rationalized by classic psychoanalytic theory, has been passed on through the generations. For if a mother is discontent with her own being, if she regards her body, her mind, her competence, her role in life, even her superego as less than that of a man, then these feelings will be communicated to her daughter and will form the nucleus of her female identity. Inevitably a mother's narcissistic investment in her children is influenced not only by her personal psychodynamics but also by the social values that predominate. Thus, if boys are valued above girls— and this is generally the case—the male child will be overcathected, while the female child will be the recipient of the mother's injured narcissism. I am aware that these statements represent only the broadest outline of very complex and individually colored interactions. Yet, I have been working in this field long enough to recall that some years ago a woman colleague, to whom I had referred the wife of a patient of mine, reported to me that the analysis was going well since the young woman had finally accepted the idea of having a child as a substitute for a penis (see Chapter 23)! Both the therapist and the patient had accepted female inferiority as a given.

However, times are changing. On the wave of great social changes that have called for the active and positive implementation of democratic principles affecting all groups that have been discriminated against, women are becoming liberated: liberated from rigidly assigned roles of wife and mother; freer than ever before to participate in the social, economic, and political life of our society; and freer to choose careers and professions and to combine these with the satisfactions of domesticity if they so choose. They have the opportunity to be freer and more expressive sexually, since moral codes are less inhibiting and are no longer based on the Victorian double standard of morality that granted men sexual freedom—even license—while denying women the gratifications of the sexual experience even within the confines of the conventional marital situation. (Parenthetically, it is to Freud's credit that, seeing the harm done to women by the absence of sexual gratification, he helped liberate them from the strictures of conventional morality, at least within the limits of the marital situation, by opening up the entire subject of sex as a legitimate area for the observation and understanding of human psychology.) It is inevitable that these social changes, which constitute fundamental changes in values, have altered woman's self-image and therefore her identity. She now has more responsibility for shaping her identity, and there are fewer social and psychological rationalizations for feeling inferior.

However, as we know, neither the external manifestations of social change nor their internalization and subsequent transformation into psychic entities take place suddenly. There is a long period of transition, and as in all progress there is a price to be paid, both social and psychological. Currently we are actively in a transitional phase. Our society is groping with efforts to stabilize social institutions that have been temporarily disrupted by the attempt to implement rationally thought-out democratic values that were ahead of our emotional and practical ability to realize them. A most notable example is in the field of education, where, at least for the time being, standards have suffered for the sake of egalitarian values. Psychologically the transitional nature of values has created, if not crisis, then at least conflict for many individuals, men and women alike. On the positive side, women have the opportunity to break the chain of identification with their mothers within a socially sanctioned framework. The ubiquity of the wish not to repeat the mother's life is due not solely to hostile feelings toward the mother in the framework of oedipal rivalry as psychoanalysis has taught us, but also to the communication of chronic dissatisfaction with her lot on the mother's part—in other words, with the disparagement of her own female identity and thus implicitly with a denigration of her female child.

But now it is not only more possible but also more acceptable for women to become more autonomous, more fulfilled, less dependent upon men, and more accepting of their sexuality. However, there is anxiety associated with this step toward greater self-realization, for it means separation from the internalized mother. The departure from her particular feminine identity, which is the historical precipitate of the customs and values of her time, leaves women with a feeling of uncertainty about whether they will be able to synthesize their own independent identity. Ideally such synthesis would include a blending of certain positive aspects of the original mother identification with new values that grow both out of social change and out of the unique autonomy of a particular, individual woman. However, most processes of change are not ideal, and the transition is far from smooth. The fear of not being different, of being mired in a merger with the mother and thus failing to individuate, leads many women to disavow almost totally identification with the mother. This overthrow of what must inevitably be some part of herself makes the integration of female identity difficult and precarious for many women. It can lead to feelings of emptiness and depression. Whether the outcome of the struggle with the mother introject will be positive or not depends on the degree of health of the original loving bond to the mother, on the daughter's innate ego strength, and on the existence of opportunities for corrective experiences and social support for her individuality in the wider world outside the family.

Through the creation of possibilities for new introjects, among other things, psychotherapy can be helpful in the consolidation of a new female identity for those women whose familial and social conflicts have made this difficult heretofore. In this connection, it is important to keep in mind not only the content and the affects that surround the internalizations of which identity is made, but above all the fact that the human personality is "object-seeking." From earliest infancy it is engaged in a continuous process of searching for relationships to others, not solely for the gratification of drive needs, but for the opportunity to build, through its capacity for identification, an integrated identity. Although it is important in the therapeutic situation to analyze the obstacles that stand in the way of such integration—for example the ambivalent relationship to the mother—this is only one aspect of the therapeutic experience.

The therapist must have an empathic understanding of the pivotal position of this generation of young women who are living in a transitional phase of psychosocial evolution, who are struggling to consolidate a feminine identity different from that of their predecessors, and whose personalities will form the basis upon which the next generation will make identifications. Such empathic understanding should enable the therapist to address the growth potential of the female patient, thus respecting her individuality, affirming the struggle itself, and trusting in its positive outcome rather than setting up static norms for what is a healthy sexual and social female identity that have little bearing either on individual differences or on the fluidity of social change.

23

Gender and the
Complementarity
of Viewpoints

In the title of this chapter on gender is the term *complementarity*, which is taken from the world of physics. This term describes the duality, indeed the opposition, between drive theory and attachment theory as possible divergent metaphors for ways of viewing the world—the rational male way and the feeling female way. Such dichotomies bother me, not because they do not exist but because they do not describe a fundamental reality: biologically based differences between males and females in the ways in which they relate to reality—for certainly, some of their realities are different—both are capable of rational thinking and both can be influenced by feelings and attachments. The preponderance of one mental-emotional orientation over the other is largely a cultural byproduct. It was at this point in my thinking that the word "complementarity" came to mind.

Complementarity is a term introduced to modern atomic physics by Niels Bohr, the great Danish physicist and Nobel prize winner whose work, together with that of Werner Heisenberg, has revolutionized not only physics but also the very philosophy of science itself. In the scientific search for the ultimate nature of the reality of the material world, Bohr found that the electron, one of the smallest units of matter, can be defined both as a

particle and as a wave. There were therefore two truths, not just one, and
the exploration and theorizing about each give a fuller and clearer picture
of the nature of atomic reality than could a one-sided theory. The explanations required for two truths *complement* each other. Furthermore, the very
process of observation in the atomic world involves the introduction of
factors—a light beam, for example—that disturb the object of observation,
the electron, so as to render its behavior unpredictable. Thus, an element
of uncertainty was discovered that came to be known as Heisenberg's
Principle of Indeterminacy or Uncertainty. The fundamental reality of the
physical world could be understood only up to a certain point; it was not
absolutely predictable, an element of chance existed, and absolute causality
and determinism were challenged. In describing a mechanical system, quan-
tum mechanics introduced the concept of probability. With it also came
the knowledge that potentiality exists in all things. If this is true of the physical world at the atomic level, how much truer must it be of the psychological world with its myriad variables.

It is clear that, whatever the psychological innovations that Freudian
theory contributed to an understanding of human psychology, the model
for creating this coherent theory was dictated by the scientific ethos that
permeated Western culture for more than 300 years and is still a paradigm
for such scientific thought today. To call this sort of thinking that emphasizes objectivity and rationality "male" says no more than that we of Western society have lived for centuries in male-dominated societies, so that
inevitably the creative expressions and products of the culture—and this
includes ways of thinking, theorizing, or viewing the world—will be predominantly reflections of the major culture-creators, namely men. This in no
way a value judgment; it neither confirms nor invalidates the truth of the
cultural product—in this case psychological theory, specifically drive theory.
It does, however, point to its limitations, to the fact that there are at least
two truths (and probably many more) that will reveal themselves when the
same psychological phenomena are observed from a different perspective—
namely, from a female perspective—and theories concerning them are formulated by a female observer.

Attachment theory, of which Bowlby and Winnicott are representative without themselves being female, is thus a female way of viewing child
development, and subsequently, human conflict. For example, one could
ask: is the child's attachment to the mother anaclitic—one might almost
say "opportunistic"—an attachment that depends on the fact that the mother
feeds the child, thus providing oral gratification as well as nourishment, as

Freud would have it? Or is there a primary, unconditional love of the child for the mother, an instinct for attachment that is independent of the feeding situation? Perhaps both formulations are true: they complement each other as do particle and wave in atomic theory. The so-called reality of the psychological observation and the theory derived from it is compromised in an absolute sense by the nature of the observer.

Gender, therefore, for socio-psychological theory, is akin to the specific light that is thrown upon the electron in the field of physics.

Behind the theory of complementarity lies an important premise that by analogy has implications for psychoanalytic theory. Niels Bohr made it clear that the atomic world is not like the visible world, which is explicable and predictable in terms of causality. In the atomic world, in contrast, predictability is limited by the process of observation that changes the nature of the system. In a parallel sense the psychic world is not like the material world. The material world, as the visible world of physics, is subject to the laws of causality that, when explored and understood, lead to predictability, Freud, in theorizing about human psychology and under the influence of the prevailing rationalistic mode of thought of his time, dealt with the psychic world as if it were the material world. In fact in his writings, informed as they are by a reductionist viewpoint, he expresses the conviction that, some day given sufficient knowledge, the psychological world will be reduced to its physical, chemical elements. This is perhaps true for certain levels of psychological phenomena that are amenable to the laws of causality, just as in the physical world macrophenomena can be understood, explained, and predicted in terms of Newtonian physics. The atomic world, however, in order to be understood requires what Bohr referred to as a *renunciation* of absolute certainty and predictability and an acceptance of approximation and probability. In psychology, and especially in psychoanalysis. the *renunciation of certainty* is particularly important. Psychological forces—both internal and external—as well as sociological and cultural factors constantly change the nature of what is observed. This is certainly true of gender, so that to understand the many facets of its psychology, the principle of complementarity is applicable.

Gender has many aspects. Obviously it is a biological reality with anatomical and physiological characteristics that differentiate male and female. But it is also a sociological and psychological reality, and as such it is in flux, with changing imagery about behavior and values from generation to generation, from epoch to epoch. Anatomy is not destiny—certainly not all of destiny—as Freud would have us believe; nor is one half of the human

race dissatisfied with its destiny and envious of the other half, as Karen
Horney pointed out long ago.

For each individual the sense of self, the feeling of personhood evolves
within the framework of familial experience. Through processes of identification and differentiation the person becomes him- or herself with characteristically specific behavior, ways of thinking, goals, ideals, and values.
Yet, the family is embedded in a given society and either assimilates, rejects, or modifies the cultural influences that are offered. Thus, the individual is affected by the culture indirectly as well as through direct contact
with social institutions. The psychological aspect of gender—that is, gender
identity—is extremely sensitive to influence.

Freud, in the nature of his thinking—and most likely unbeknownst to
him—was profoundly influenced by the "scientific" mechanistic philosophy
of his epoch. It led him to universalize all his theoretical formulations, but
most specifically in relation to sexual development and the formation of
gender identity. He did not take the cultural dimension into account at all.
This had a particularly distorting influence on his conception of the sexual
identity of women—in fact, on his entire misunderstanding of women. As
Helene Deutsch, an early follower of Freud and a supposed authority on
female psychology expressed it, "One is born a man, but becomes a woman."
I recently read a similar statement attributed to Simone de Beauvoir. It is
interesting and culturally significant for the period in which they lived and
from which they tried to emerge, that these two talented and relatively independent women accepted the patro- and phallocentric notions of gender
formation promulgated by Freud.

I am reminded of the tragic outcome of the clinical application of the
classical theory of female gender development—not a theory of what *is*, but
of what *ought* to be—that occurred many years ago. I unfortunately had
referred the wife of a male patient of mine to a woman colleague whose
therapeutic orientation on the issue of female development was much more
literally Freudian than I had anticipated (see Chapter 22). Both my patient
and his wife were successful research scientists. They were in their early
thirties and were planning to have children in the near future.

One day in the course of my patient's treatment I was having a tele-
phone conversation with my colleague, and I asked how my patient's wife
was getting along. "She's progressing very well," replied my colleague. "She
has given up the wish for a penis and has accepted the having of a child as
a substitute. She plans to devote her life to being a mother." I was appalled
at the synthetic molding of personality according to theory, and a very

dubious theory at that. I was not in a position to comment. This analysis took place thirty years ago; the tragedy occurred some fifteen years later, in other words at least fifteen years after the termination of the wife's analysis.

The young couple did indeed have children, and the wife gave up her scientific career and became a full-time mother. When one of her daughters reached adolescence, she became seriously depressed and ultimately took her own life.

I had had no contact with the family in all the intervening years, but when this terrible tragedy occurred the father, my former patient, called me and arranged to see me for a limited time in an endeavor to deal with his own grief and that of his wife and other family members. At the time I felt there was a second tragedy in addition to the loss of a child and the inevitable guilt that parents must experience—the fact that my patient's wife had lost her entire anchorage. Her sense of self that was by then totally dependent on her gender identity as a mother was greatly threatened if not entirely destroyed. She had "learned" too well in her analysis to accept a theoretically arrived at and imposed female identity. In view of her previous interest and activity in creative aspects of science, the imposed self was only in part a true self. However, she had lived with it for many years and had come to think of motherhood as her complete and authentic self. Her depression that inevitably followed the loss of her daughter was therefore augmented by a loss of sense of self.

The biological reality of being born male or female cannot be contradicted by a psychological or sociological reality. How can one possibly be born a man, although one is female, and then through various psychological acrobatics or renunciation become a woman? The wish on the part of women to be male—the well-known theory of penis envy—is a psychosocial artifact, not an inherent aspect of normal development. Both male and female are born as children with the potentiality to become psychologically, as well as physically, mature men and women, and this development would take place normally were it not for the fact that until very recently society has placed special value on being male. So far, the equality of the sexes within the social and economic framework of our culture has barely begun to be recognized, and the psychological residue of the inequality is still very much our legacy. Equality does not imply the absence of difference, but rather the affirmation of difference as existing on parallel planes of human existence.

Have we wandered too far from our initial concern, namely, with the complementarity of viewpoint? The clinical example presented in this chapter illustrates so clearly not only the fallacy but also the possible tragedy of imposing personality theories on individuals as well. Above all, such procedure interferes with the normal growth of an individual to become him- or herself. In addition, the theories may be false, and at best they are formulated from but one perspective—in this case from a masculine perspective. As Otto Rank wrote almost fifty years ago, the psychology of woman has been understood exclusively from the viewpoint of a masculine ideology. A psychology of woman, observed by women, is bound to introduce another dimension to our understanding. Indeed all of psychology would profit and be deepened by the complementary viewpoints that the gender difference makes possible.

The theory of complementarity about which we have learned from the atomic physicists should enable us to do away with the monism of reductionist theories and to understand that varying beams of light can illuminate divergent but reconcilable truths. This is especially true of gender, whose psychological character is so strongly influenced by historical, social, and cultural factors.

24

Conflicts of Women in a Changing Society

It is a truism that what we become psychologically—how we think of ourselves, how we function with others, how fulfilled or frustrated we are—depends to some extent on the social, economic, and historical circumstances in which we find ourselves and to some extent on what we, as unique individuals, bring to the situation. Yet, this acknowledgment that both nature and nurture influence our lives, upon closer examination, reveals an intricately woven fabric of interacting psychological processes. Because we are children of the past, striving in the present either to detach ourselves from it or to integrate it with our ideals for the future, we are to some extent in constant psychological movement and therefore inevitably, to some degree, in conflict. This is especially true at a time of social change when new opportunities and responsibilities, new expectations and pressures give rise to the need for new adaptations—adaptations not only in the overt sense of daily functioning but also inner adaptations of a psychological nature. It is these inner processes in relation to women that this chapter addresses.

The social changes that have affected women and that, in fact, women have to a large extent helped create are part of a worldwide movement for liberation by peoples who have been historically discriminated against either because of race, color, sex, religion, or economic position. One meaning of liberation is obvious; it is liberation from economic and social disadvantage, from squalor, poverty, degradation, and despair. But there is an additional, psychological meaning of the term "liberation"—it is freedom from a socially assigned role that had inhibited the optimum fulfillment of an individual's capabilities. It is in this latter sense that social change is of special importance to women. The traditionally assigned role of wife and mother, which had previously been limited to the domestic functions associated with these roles, has given way to a broader conception of woman as person. As a "person" a woman might fulfill herself in many ways; these ways might include being a wife and mother, but would also encompass participation in the work world outside the home. Sometimes work means a serious commitment to a career; sometimes it means either economic independence or the ability to contribute to the economic well-being of a family; sometimes it means gratification in the actual function of the work as well as the social satisfaction that contact with others can bring. Whatever its meaning, the opportunities that have been created for women through social change for work and participation in the life of the community have changed not only her actual functioning but also her image of herself. And it is the changed self-conception, the new hopes and expectations of life, that come into conflict with that part of the self-image that derives from an identification with the mother, who generally stands for the traditional role of woman.

We are all tied to the past, to tradition, through an identification with our parents. Every small child first begins to be a person in his own right, by imitating the behavior, attitudes, feelings, and thoughts of those closest to him—usually his parents. Gradually these imitations become internalized, and the child is to some extent like his parents, or, as is sometimes the case, just the opposite of a particular parent. This tendency to counter-identification, to a sometimes almost conscious decision not to repeat the lifestyle or personality of a parent, is particularly common among little girls who have repudiated the traditional feminine role as their mothers have lived it. Clinical experience with young women in recent years has made it clear that a major factor in this repudiation is the little girl's experience of her mother's unhappiness, her lack of fulfillment, her bitter feeling that life has cheated her, and, above all, her low opinion of herself. In this deprecated self-image, the mother has accepted the male-oriented social attitude toward woman as an inferior, as a second-class citizen. Thus, she not only thinks poorly of herself but also looks upon her daughter with a mixture of pity and condescension, of disappointment and yet hope that her daughter's lot may be better than her own. And should it indeed prove to be better, the mother's feelings are inevitably tinged with envy. This mixture of conflicting feelings on the mother's part and the daughter's need to detach herself from the mother generally results in strife between mother and daughter in their daily lives and in confusion, tension, and burdensome guilt in the inner psychological life of the daughter.

If, on the other hand, the mother's attitude toward her daughter's aspirations is predominantly positive and affirmative, she inspires much less of the rebellious, counteridentificatory response; the daughter therefore can much more contentedly identify with the feminine role of woman and mother as represented by the personality of her mother, as well as pursue her vocational or career interests at the same time.

For many women, fulfillment of self involves satisfaction on two fronts: the biologically creative front that seeks gratification in a sexual relationship and its ultimate outcome in motherhood, and the ego-creative front in which the individual's unique personality is expressed in work efforts of some sort. The second front is in no way a repudiation of femininity nor an expression of masculine wishes as Freudian theory would have us believe. It is a natural manifestation of individuation that until recently has had little chance for expression because women were subjected by society to an assigned role. In an article that is still timely but that was written many years ago, Otto Rank understood the basic wish of all human beings to be that which they are. He (Rank 1958) therefore disagreed with Freud's theory regarding woman's "masculinity complex" and wrote of woman that she "has always wanted and still wants first and foremost to be a woman, because this and this alone is her fundamental self and expresses her personality, *no matter what she may do or achieve*" (p. 254). It is the last part of this quotation that is of extreme importance, because it emphasizes the fact that it is not the nature of the activity that defines an individual in terms of his or her psychobiological role. Our conception of what is feminine or masculine is socially conditioned, but does not reflect the inner feeling of an individual about him- or herself except as he or she is conditioned by social stereotypes. For example, because of custom and tradition we have tended to think of engineering as a masculine occupation and therefore unfeminine, or of the artist as effeminate and therefore not masculine. These are social stereotypes that are passed down from parents to children and that influence an individual's self-conception to the extent that he or she is emotionally bound to parents or to the social community. But the more autonomous (or sometimes rebellious) an individual is, the less will the socially stereotypic role definition be reflected in his or her self-image.

Historically, a change in social values, which generally means the loss of old values, whether it results from dislocation of populations, a change in political or economic structure, or the opening up of new opportunities for social and economic improvement or for greater self-expression, inevitably results in conflict for the individual. The individual is caught in the paradox of the discrepancy between the wished-for liberation and advancement and the resultant loss of security. This is not to say that we should eschew social progress or the opening up of new opportunities for individuals; we could not even if we would, for social processes are in constant movement and flux. Yet, we must be clear that the benefits of positive social change bring with them certain psychological problems.

For women the opening up of new opportunities for work away from home can represent, at one and the same time, the realization of a longed for ego-ideal of liberation and fulfillment, as well as a loss of continuity with the traditions of the past. However, this loss is far from abstract since the traditional ego-ideal is embodied in the other and becomes, in the course of maturation, incorporated into the personality of the daughter. It is therefore a psychological reality—an actual part of the daughter even though, in the name of new goals, it lies dormant and unexpressed in the daily life of the individual. The young woman, therefore, who has synthesized a new and independent ego-ideal out of the social influences that impinge upon her has separated from her mother as well as from a part of herself. There is always in such separation the implication of rejection, and for this rejection there is always guilt. It need not be an overriding guilt; unless it reaches neurotic proportions it need not seriously inhibit a woman's functioning either in her work or emotional life. But it must be carried as a part of one's emotional baggage. (It should be pointed out that a similar burden of guilt falls upon the man who has rejected his father as an ego-ideal. For both men and women it is the parent of the same sex who represents the primary role model and whose rejection is therefore most crucial in the creation of guilt feelings—not only for deviation from the parent figure but also for disloyalty to a part of oneself.)

The awareness of guilt feelings by a woman who is committed to a career as well as to being a wife and mother often surfaces in relation to her children. She is oversensitive to echoes of the socially prescribed role of the traditional mother as they might be heard in some implications that she does not spend sufficient time with her children. She begins to measure her devotion in terms of time spent, losing the certainty of her emotional attachment to her children as it is experienced in spontaneous feeling. She is a ready victim of the latest psychological nostrums on child rearing, often replacing common sense with the illusion that there is some perfect and correct way to raise children. Could she but follow the proper prescription she would produce the perfectly happy and well-adjusted child—a tribute to her maternal devotion and an expiation of her guilt.

Let me not be misunderstood. The issue of guilt does not arise out of the dual role of women—career and motherhood. The task of coordinating these two facets of life may indeed provide an opportunity for attaching guilt to specific logistical problems in the working out of the two roles, but guilt does not arise from the duality itself. Rather, guilt is an inner psychological phenomenon that takes place within a social context and is socially conditioned only to the extent that societal values correspond to internalized values that the individual has taken over from parents. Clearly, if the social attitude toward the dual role of women is affirmative, her conflict will be lessened and her ability to act upon her aspirations will be heightened. This is the positive outcome of the changes in the social and economic position of women that we are witnessing today.

However, the psychological source of feelings of guilt that so many women experience is primarily in the relationship to the mother. A woman's resolve to be different from her mother, to choose a different lifestyle, to be both wife and mother and to have a career and to challenge her mother's values, her social attitudes, and even her child-rearing practices helps create feelings of uncertainty and of guilt.

The psychological separation from the mother need not necessarily take place in the overt choice of a "dual-role" lifestyle; it may come about in a woman's determination to be a better wife and mother than she felt her own mother to be. This is especially the case when a woman's memory of her own childhood is one of emotional deprivation, or if she perceived the relationship between her parents to have been a stressful and unhappy one. When such conditions obtain and the mother is rejected as a role model, there is hostility in the rejection above and beyond that which accompanies every separation. It is hostility for lack of love, for deprivation; yet, despite the fact that consciously the young woman feels justified in her anger toward her mother, she often experiences guilt—a guilt that arises from the fact that as a small, dependent child she incorporated her mother's values, her mother's ways, and these feelings are now her own. Perhaps her mother was right; perhaps she is really the selfish, disobedient, inconsiderate, and incompetent individual at whom her mother had pointed a finger when she was a child. A repressed self-hatred unconsciously resides within her, and it emerges when she herself becomes a mother. She finds that she cannot easily, nor always, be the "corrected" mother that she so consciously determined to be. The stresses of the maternal experience, the frustrations and disappointments that are inevitable in all human relationships evoke the old, original identification with her mother. She finds herself critical of and impatient with her children, and she hates herself with the same vigor with which she hated her mother for her lack of love and attention and for her belittlement of herself and of her daughter.

This psychological pattern that I have just described is very common; it is practically an inevitable aspect of the struggle between generations. For except in the most rigidly structured and traditional societies, each new generation seeks to separate from its antecedents by placing the stamp of its own individual ethos upon its behavior, its values, its commitment to social change, and its special view of progress. The opportunity to do just this is obviously greater in times of social change and in societies whose structure is open ended. It follows therefore that today women who are able to take advantage of opportunities for the fulfillment of new, self-chosen roles and individual ego-ideals, particularly if they have chosen a dual role, may find the inner psychological conflict with the imprint left upon them by their mothers especially poignant.

To illustrate this point, the case of a young woman I treated some years ago (Menaker 1965) is presented here. Since I treated her, the unhappy crises that developed in her life serve to bring into even more dramatic relief than before her struggle to separate psychologically from her mother and to consolidate a new identity. Her life, viewed now over a longer period in which she became a mother and experienced separation from her husband and the threat of serious illness, illustrates the "return of the repressed" as well, for the old identifications with her mother came to the surface at times of crisis and caused her great conflict, depression, and loss of self-esteem.

Jeanne grew up in a tradition-bound home of immigrant parents in a community in which her family belonged to a minority group. Her parents had rigid ideas about the role of a young woman. She was expected to marry at an early age and raise a family. Higher education or a career of any kind for a young lady was frowned upon. To Jeanne, however, the opportunities of the larger world beckoned. She had literary talent and was determined to make a career for herself as a writer. That she might have to repeat her mother's limited life terrified her. It was in some measure this anxiety that, added to the normal impulse toward greater self-realization and was responsible for the great efforts that she made to obtain an education and training for her chosen field.

The social environment in which she grew up, as distinguished from the environment of her immediate family, offered Jeanne these opportunities for education and training. She broke out of the traditional, assigned role of her familial culture, acquired a good education, and ultimately found work in the field of journalism. There was a price to be paid, as there inevitably is, for this piece of psychosocial progress. Jeanne suffered from acute anxiety and a tendency toward depression. These were her reasons for seeking psychotherapeutic help. It is not surprising that the difficulty in synthesizing conflicting identifications within her ego structure—those stemming from her early relationship to her mother and those arising from the social milieu that offered her the opportunity to choose her own individual pathway—should have led to anxiety. The subjective feeling was always one of uncertainty. "Will I make it? Will I succeed?" thought Jeanne. It is such uncertainty that unavoidably accompanies social change. It is not that social change causes anxiety in a primary sense, but that when it supports the inner processes of separation and individuation it augments the initial conflicts with parental figures.

Jeanne's therapy, by implicitly granting permission for a new definition of self and a new role as a woman, largely through the establishment of an identification with her therapist, enabled her to overcome much of her anxiety. She did succeed in her work, which offered her the chance for some creative expression, and she was no longer depressed. In addition, she overcame her sexual prudery—a heritage of her childhood upbringing, and at an appropriate age married a man for whom she felt genuine love and affection. Her family had scarcely outgrown the contractual conception of arranged marriages, so that Jeanne's choice of a mate in terms of individual expressiveness represented a great advance both in social and psychological terms over the expressive capacities of her parents.

For approximately eight years her marriage was a good one. Then certain specific stresses impinged on inner, more unconscious emotions and aroused conflicts in herself and her husband that the marriage could not withstand. Her first child was a daughter, much loved by both parents and posing no threat to their relationship. However, a second pregnancy eventuated in a stillbirth, and for Jeanne the ensuing unhappiness and depression that this loss precipitated caused a regression to early identifications with her mother. In her marriage she began to repeat her mother's pattern of interaction with her husband—carping, complaining, denigrating, and belittling. A hostile dissatisfaction, an aggressive frustration cast a pall over her marital relationship. She was conscious of the repetition of her mother's pattern of behavior and of her mother's angry feeling toward men, and she was filled with self-loathing for having regressed to an emotional position that she had struggled so hard to overcome.

It was in this atmosphere of marital tension, belittled self-image, and depression that she again became pregnant and in due time gave birth to a son. The birth of a boy, for reasons that are irrelevant to this discussion, threatened her husband's emotional security. He was unprepared to be father to a son, at least within the framework of a marriage that was souring under the impact of Jeanne's querulousness and ready hostility. Within less than a year after the boy's birth, he left the family. It was the circumstance of her having been deserted that caused Jeanne to consult me again, and it was in this second installment of her treatment that the mechanism of regression to her earliest identifications became increasingly apparent. When the realization that her marriage was over was finally accepted, Jeanne began to go out with other men. In these relationships she showed a tendency to be childish and demanding like her mother. With her children she became increasingly irritable and impatient and experienced them as an interference with her social life. Here again was a repetition of her mother's attitude toward her own children, toward whom she was at once possessive yet disinterested. Needless to say, the pull back into her mother's ways filled Jeanne with self-hatred, criticality, and depression. Unfortunately, life dealt her still another blow in the form of a serious illness, in the course of which the old patterns were still further reinforced.

It is not my purpose in this chapter to present the details either of Jeanne's various relationships or of her interaction with her children. Her awareness of the regression to an identification with her mother and her self-criticism of this regression kept her from becoming a duplicate of her mother. Economic necessity, to some extent, dictated her lifestyle. She was fortunate in finding a position in her own field of writing, which enabled her to continue work and motherhood, kept her in touch with the larger world outside her home, and gave her satisfaction in the realization of her independence and competence. She would not be caught in a permanent regression to old identifications largely because she had tasted the satisfactions of a freely chosen lifestyle. The superimposed new identifications, although not completely or securely synthesized with other aspects of her ego. nevertheless left enough of a mark to ensure the functioning of her personality in the name of different ego-ideals and a different value system than that which had dominated her mother's life and personality. It was social change and the opportunity that it created for the adoption of a new self-definition that provided the soil in which new identifications could develop; it was psychotherapy that gave form and substance to these identifications.

The significance of Jeanne's life story lies in the fact that it points up the struggle to consolidate a new identity in the face of the impact of two opposing tendencies: one, the pull of early identifications with a mother who offered, as a model, the traditional mother-wife role, and the other, the opportunity for a new role combining the satisfactions of marriage and motherhood with those of career. In general, the intensity of this conflict for the individual young woman depends on several factors: the initial strength of her own ego and the vitality of her will to be separate and individuated and to resist unwelcome social pressures; her relationship to her father and siblings; the availability of persons in the environment who might offer ego-ideals to be emulated that differ from those of her family; and perhaps above all the nature of her relationship to her mother. If the mother affirms the dual-role aspirations of her daughter either because she herself has lived her life in this way or because she would have wished to have done so, the conflict of identifications for the young woman is much reduced. She is able to identify with her mother's positive expectations, which are in harmony with her own wishes for self-realization and therefore to avail herself freely of the opportunities for work, profession, or career that a changing society offers her.

I emphasize the role of the mother in the formation of a young woman's identity mainly because identification with her is the child's earliest primary identification—one that grows out of the child's first relationship. For the daughter who must consolidate a sexual identity as a woman, as well as one involving her social, intellectual, and professional functioning, this primary identification with her mother is crucial because she is of the same sex as her mother. However, this is not to minimize the role of the father in the young girl's development. What he is as a person, what he represents as an ego-ideal, how he relates to his daughter all have a great impact on the development of her personality. It is important for her sexual identity that her father love and admire her as a little girl with the potential for becoming an attractive woman, and for her ego development it is important that he affirm her goals and aspirations. Often these goals derive from the daughter's identification with her father's vocation, with his achievements, and with his code of behavior in relation to others. To the extent that the father encourages such identifications, especially if they are consistent with her striving for autonomous expressiveness and are realizable in action in the outside world, the daughter's synthesis of a secure identity will be made easier. Indeed, it is the affirming love of a father that makes possible for the daughter the choosing of a husband who will in his turn support the dual-role identity of his wife, should such be her aspiration.

In a period of social change in which the position and psychology of women are changing, the role of men must also change. What is noticeable today on the part of men of the current generation of marriageable age is paradoxically either a flight and withdrawal from any significant or permanent commitment to a relationship with a woman, or, having entered marriage, an increased involvement and participation in the life of the family. It is this latter supportive attitude that obviously frees the woman to choose and achieve a dual-role identity with much less conflict. In this way man participates, not only in the liberation of woman, but in a progressive process of social change.

Although this chapter is specifically concerned with the kind of inner conflict in women that is sometimes augmented by a society in transition, what is herein described is a general phenomenon of which the psychology of women is but one example. Whenever identifications representing traditional values, ego-ideals, or self-conceptions of individuals or groups, are impinged upon by differing values, a conflict arises between the impulse to adhere to the early identifications and the striving to absorb the new values, especially if these promise greater fulfillment in the realm of self-realization. This conflict has been observed by anthropologists and sociologists when studying such phenomena as cross-cultural influences, the migrations of peoples, immigration to new countries, the loss of or change in religious belief, or changes in sexual mores or in moral values. The exposure to what is in essence a new environmental influence in the form of some sort of social change and the need to adapt to it are reflected in the inner psychological life of individuals as a conflict in the area of those identifications that regulate the values and self-conceptions that determine the nature of behavior. Sometimes the conflict is so profound and so unbalancing that it may result in personality disturbances so extreme as to produce severe neurosis, psychosis, or even criminal behavior. This social change may all too readily become social upheaval, and that which inaugurated the constructive development of greater freedom and self-expressiveness for individuals may herald a destructive imbalance in their psychic lives. We can only guard against this latter outcome through the awareness of the pressures of internalized conflict and the knowledge that these pressures can be eased by the establishment early in life of loving and flexible identifications that can withstand the onslaught of new ways and new values. In the development of a woman for whom the structuring of personality is particularly complex because of her dual role—her need to be true to her self as well as to her biological role—the quality of the early identifications with both parents is crucial. Therefore, not only for her own sake but also for the well-being of society is it important that parents deviate from historical precedent and express a special love and affirmation of their daughters.

25

Comments on Freud's "The Psychogenesis of a Case of Homosexuality in a Woman"

"The Psychogenesis of a Case of Homosexuality in a Woman" (Freud 1920) is a period piece highly relevant for our psychological understanding. It depicts upper-middle-class society in Vienna at the turn of the century, reflecting what were considered psychological problems at the time as well as, by omission, pointing up issues that were disregarded as unimportant in the development and growth of personality. Freud's paper also tells us much about the history of psychoanalytic thought. In 1920, Freud was profoundly anchored in libido theory and in the conviction that the Oedipus complex is equally at the root of psychic conflict and of aberrations in the realm of feelings and behavior.

From our current perspective we note the fact that the young girl of 18 has no name. She is neither Dora, nor Anna O., nor Fraulein Elizabeth von R . She is nameless, referred to as "the girl." This namelessness, together with her so-called masculine traits—"her intellectual attributes . . . for instance her acuteness of comprehension and her lucid objectivity, insofar as she was not dominated by her passion"—confirms for us what we already know of Freud's attitude toward women. They are not only inevitably afflicted by penis envy but also have inferior superegos and lack intelligence equivalent to that of men. It is not surprising therefore to find in a letter to his close friend, Wilhelm Fliess, announcing Anna's birth, the following sentences: "If it had been a son, I would have sent you the news by telegram, because he would have carried your name. Since it turned out to be a little daughter by the name of Anna, she is being introduced to you belatedly."

The story of Freud's conception, his misunderstanding of women, one might almost say his ignorance of the feminine, shocks us, coming as it does from a man of such innovative, creative genius. His attitudes and conclusions are completely culture-bound and reflect the male-dominated society in which he lived. But by now this is not new to us. Nor should it be a surprise that, focused as he is on the role of sexuality in human development, Freud calls the young girl's emotional attachment to an older woman "homosexual." Finding another woman to idealize is so common in the struggle of an adolescent girl to separate from her mother that we usually refer to this transitory phenomenon as the girl having a "crush" on the object of her affections. It is not that the terminology in itself is of such importance, but there is something ominous in the way Freud uses the term "homosexual." It always connotes pathology, a point of view that informs much of Freud's theorizing.

The challenge to Freud's strictly normative position on sexuality and his overemphasis on sexual development—in other words, on libido theory— and on the nature of sexual experience as primary in personality formulation comes from two sources: first, from anthropology and sociology, and second from those psychological theories that emphasize the development of the self as primary and consequently place great weight on the interpersonal experiences of early childhood, especially those with the mother.

Reviewing a book by David Greenberg entitled *The Construction of Homosexuality* (1988), Don Browning (1988) writes that "homosexuality is not a static condition; it is not for the most part even a deep-seated psychological orientation." Further, "homosexual identity is a special label. Special classification both creates the homosexual phenomenon and contains the evaluative frameworks by which it is judged, whether as deviant, tolerable, approvable, or admirable." In the case of the young girl whom we are discussing, whatever the individual psychodynamics of her situation, the extreme social intolerance of homosexuality became apparent despite the fact that Freud refers to her as "genitally chaste." The social opprobrium came to her in the form of her father's rage, which most likely made matters worse by reinforcing the inverted emotions. Human sexuality is extremely plastic and innately nonspecific with regard to sexual objects, and all of us, according to Greenberg, have the capacity to be sexually attracted to members of the same sex. Whether or not these feelings are labeled as such and organized into overt behavior and lifelong identities is a result of a wide combination of social and cultural dynamics. Freud was aware of what he called human bisexuality. In this very paper he writes, "a very considerable measure of latent or unconscious homosexuality can be detected in all normal people" (p. 230). By expressing the plasticity of human adaptation along the dimensions of conscious and unconscious, and normal and abnormal, Freud destroyed the very concept of plasticity by neglecting the environmental, social factor that is implied in the term "plasticity." It is ironically as if he himself, when speaking of the unconscious, of repressed impulses, had forgotten that they too basically derive from social factors.

From an anthropological point of view Greenberg has pointed out that "the idea of a static homosexual orientation or essence simply does not hold up against the huge variety of homosexual, bisexual and heterosexual patterns." Differing cultures have varying patterns of sexual orientation, and often among those patterns there is room for homosexuality. In fact in certain primitive societies homosexuality is ritualized. During an early phase of adolescence among boys, it is practiced preparatory to sexual relationships with women.

The anthropological-sociological dimension plays no role in Freud's explanation of homosexuality. It is true that in this particular case the cultural factor is not causal in any primary sense. However, the negative attitudes toward homosexuality in the society at large, coupled with the denigration of women as a whole and the punitive attitude of the girl's father, could foster a profound rebelliousness in a young person trying to consolidate a self-structure, which might result in inversion.

Such a hypothesis leads us into the realm of the psychological, and it becomes immediately clear that Freud's theory of his young female patient's homosexuality is not only focused exclusively on her sexual development but even more specifically on the outcome of the oedipal phase of that development. Freud concludes that after a relatively normal childhood and early adolescence, the 18-year-old girl developed a homosexual attachment to an older woman when her mother became pregnant with her younger brother. This incontrovertible evidence of the father's love for the mother, and of the fact that he gave a child to her rather than to his daughter, so disappointed the young girl that she turned away from men entirely. She became homosexual and withdrew from the field of competition, leaving it unchallenged for her mother. Instead, and in anger, she flaunted her love for a woman of doubtful reputation who was ten years older. The flaunting speaks for the pent-up hostility that she felt toward her parents, especially toward her father, and is one way of releasing it. The choice of a love-object whose sexual code of behavior differs from the one by which she was raised also bespeaks rebellion, but is evidence for another important factor in personality development—namely, the selection of a self-object, to use Kohut's term, upon which to model and structure the self. In this particular choice the young girl is expressing the wish not to be like her mother, but also is searching for a woman with whom to identify. It is when her resentment toward her father leaves no possibility for her to identify with his values and aspirations for her, and when the woman whom she loves rejects her affectionate involvement when she learns of the father's vehement disapproval of the relationship, that the young girl's self is left without a home, as it were, and without further nutrients for its growth. It is in the despair of this situation that she makes a serious suicide attempt.

Freud's explanation for the suicide attempt is framed exclusively in terms of the need for a release of hostile impulses. It is at once a "punishment fulfillment" and a "wish fulfillment." Death wishes must have existed toward her parents, especially the father, who failed to fulfill her wish for a child. These wishes were turned against the self and resulted in the attempted suicide.

It is interesting to address some of the technical issues in the case. Freud describes the young girl as a person participating in the therapy on a purely intellectual level, as is the wont in cases of obsessional neurosis. She remains untouched emotionally in spite of marked progress in analytic understanding—a phenomenon often witnessed in classical analysis in which the emphasis is primarily on the acquiring of insights as a way to change and cure. Since she was undertaking her treatment only to please her parents, and not because she felt burdened by the nature of her choice of sexual object or wanted help either with changing or successfully adapting to it, there was no working alliance with the therapist. In fact, Freud complains about the absence of a transference reaction and then corrects himself, describing the transference to himself as characterized by the same antipathy that she felt toward her father and that became generalized to include all men. At this point Freud does not analyze the negative transference, but instead recommends, if indeed it be thought worthwhile to continue treatment at all, that therapy should be carried out by a female analyst. Since the young girl stopped any communication with the "Lady," Freud leaves us with the impression that not very much more can be expected from the treatment.

Once having decided that the origin of the young girl's homosexuality lay in the failure to overcome the Oedipus complex successfully, he seems to have succumbed to countertransference reactions and to have lost interest in the case entirely. It is as if the whole subject of homosexuality, especially in a woman, irks him in some way and as if he wanted as little to do with it as possible. Essentially we have in this paper scarcely any data to either confirm or refute Freud's oedipal theory of the psychogenesis of the homosexuality. He refers vaguely to the fact that he bases his conclusions on dreams that the patient has reported. But except for the final, compliant dream in which the patient anticipates the successful conclusion of her treatment, and a happy life thereafter—a dream that Freud did not trust and referred to as hypocritical—there are no reported dreams. But more than this omission, we know nothing about the interactions between patient and therapist. What did they talk about? What interpretations, if any, did Freud make, and how did the patient respond?

We know very little about this young girl's behavior in the outside world or of her interactions with friends and family members. Except for the fact that she went through a period of strong maternal feeling toward very little boys, that she retained a significant attachment to an older brother and had a passionate attachment to the woman she loved, and that she was rebellious and defiant toward her father who had so little regard for her as a woman, we do not have data nor a portrait of her as a person. What were her fears, her general likes and dislikes, her interests, her goals, and ambitions? These issues pertain to the nature of the self rather than to her impulses, and we are unlikely to find more than hints about them in Freud's writings.

Freud (1920) concludes, in spite of his oedipal hypothesis about the origins of this young woman's homosexuality, that she was "a case of inborn homosexuality which, as usual, became fixed and unmistakably manifest only in the period following puberty" (p. 229). He expands his understanding of homosexuality, however, by differentiating between object-choice and mental sexual character. They do not always correspond. An individual may choose a love-object of the same sex, and yet his or her way of loving may not reflect this choice, but may be characterized either to correspond to his or her own sex or may evince a character style of the opposite sex.

Freud characterized his young woman patient as not only having chosen a woman as love-object but also as loving her like a man; perhaps, it is this congruence of object-choice and way of loving that made him decide that the homosexuality was so deeply anchored as to warrant calling it inborn.

A way of loving is an expression of the nature of the self. In the development of psychoanalysis, except for the writings of Otto Rank, concern with the self came after 1920, so that we would not expect Freud to look to the dimension of the structuring of the self for an explanation of the psychodynamics of the homosexual development of the young woman whom he was treating; yet, homosexuality, as it arises in large part out of the nature of the quality of interpersonal relationships within the family, defines the coloration of the self. We are told that the young girl under discussion was particularly rebellious and willful. Perhaps this was so because of innate temperament, but perhaps she became unusually willful because her processes of individuation were inhibited by the conventional social attitudes that surrounded her, as well as by the stern and autocratic behavior of her father. In the absence of sufficient social affirmation of her person and a lack of others to be idealized, emulated, and internalized to become part of her self-structure, the young girl became oppositional, i.e. she expressed her individuality through negative will, as Rank would call it. Such an oppositional attitude could in part account for her homosexuality—she became "opposite," as it were, to the biological role assigned to her by nature. The psychodynamics of such a process are not to be confused with Freud's notion that out of envy and competitiveness all women suffer from penis envy. Hers was an existential issue, one that plays a role for men and women alike; for in the inevitable need to become individuated, the will plays an important role, since it represents the very essence of uniqueness. However, if its function becomes distorted and exaggerated by strong pressures for conformity or compliance, it may become so oppositional as to challenge biological destiny itself. This would, of course, include an individual's gender.

We have learned from a perusal of this period piece of Freud how very complex are the origins of homosexuality. The title of his paper, it seems to me, should perhaps have been "Some Possible Factors in the Origins of Homosexuality in the Case of a Young Woman."

26

Some Observations
Regarding Men's
Contemporary Views
of Women

Except when based on experimental data, comments on psychosocial issues must begin with a disclaimer. First, the observations made in this chapter are based in part on a very small sample indeed, namely my current male patients who number five. In addition there is approximately an equal number of male students whose work I am supervising. Of course I also hear about male attitudes from women, both patients and students. These sources, plus general impressions derived from my social life, form the basis of my observations. The data are rendered still more unreliable by subjectivity on all sides—my own, as well as that of those reporting on themselves and others. In addition, the data derive from a limited and atypical sector of the population of Western society—a highly sophisticated, generally intellectual, middle-class urban group. Furthermore, the data are contaminated by the fact that in the case of several members of the sample we are dealing with well-defined psychological conflict, not to speak of pathology, that has its origins primarily in the experiences of childhood. Yet, with a full awareness of these drawbacks, it seems worthwhile noting my observations, which have been made against a background of my own historical life experience. They confirm the influence of recent and rapid social change on individual psychology.

There can be no doubt that the social and psychological position of women has changed radically within the last two decades. The change is more gradual than it would seem, and many factors that go further back in time played a role in bringing it about: (I) technological advances—both labor-saving and birth-control devices—freed women from the exclusive use of their time for domestic work and child rearing, thus enabling them to give expression to other interests; (2) two world wars in which women participated in many roles made clear that their talents and capabilities extended well beyond their familial functions; and, (3) women's suffrage made their participation in the social and political life of the nation inevitable. These are but some of the factors contributing to the so-called liberation of women. However, most important is the inevitable human striving toward autonomy and self-realization, which led women to struggle for equality with men. They no longer wished to be the possessions of men, but rather to be independent persons in their own right.

However, in human affairs emotions are never pure or one-sided. The wish for autonomy is balanced by the wish to be cared for and protected. And so it is with women's wish to be independent of men. The degree to which one or the other aspect of this wish will predominate is a highly individual matter. Yet the overall sociological picture makes it clear that, regardless of individual preferences, the position of women in relation to sexual mores, economic independence, motherhood, career, and self-image and their relationship to and expectations of men have undergone change and are in fact still in transition. Socioeconomic changes and psychological changes go hand in hand.

It is inevitable that the psychology of men, especially as it reflects attitudes toward women, will also change. Long before men begin to interact with women in the adult world, they are boys in the familial setting, and their attitudes toward the opposite sex are shaped by their interactions with their mothers or mother surrogates and by their experience of the interactions and attitudes of parents toward one another. In my experience, many men still carry the burden of the legacy of maternal attitudes that stem from another era. Often they have been idolized, catered to, and spoiled by mothers whose personal ambitions outside of motherhood have been frustrated and who have sought vicarious gratification in the lives of their sons. These men turn to the contemporary world of women with mixed emotions. On the one hand, they hope for a repetition of the indulgences experienced at the hands of their mothers; on the other, they strive to get away from this imprint and choose women as companions and partners who are self-sufficient and whose gratifications come from a fulfillment of their own self-expressiveness.

There is a strong tendency on the modern scene for both men and women to separate the gratification of sexual impulses from affectional bonds and needs for companionship. Classic psychoanalytic theory regarded this tendency as symptomatic of pathology, or at best of developmental arrest. However, the phenomenon is so widespread as to render such a judgment meaningless. Certainly, the changed position of women does not explain it entirely. Yet, this change, along with a generally less stringent sexual morality, is an important causal component. In the transitional phase of the struggle for equality with men, women, especially the more militant individuals, have sought to imitate what has generally been regarded as acceptable male sexual behavior. The result on male psychology has been an expectation of ready sexual acquiescence from women with little (if any) commitment to a relationship.

On a more positive note, and despite instances of discrimination and occasional expressions of contempt, an increasing number of young men regard women as their equals and share their work and love lives with them on a more egalitarian footing than ever before. They share with their female partners the domestic tasks of everyday life and participate in the rearing of children, often enjoying fatherhood far more than did the men of previous generations. Within the limited sample of my experience, I have been struck by men's dependence on women to create a home and to hold the family together when their marital or familial status is threatened. Perhaps contrary to expectation, they seem to do less well alone than do women.

With a more egalitarian relationship between the sexes manifesting itself in greater respect and consideration for one another, there is a notable diminution of specific fears for the individual. In the case of men, this becomes apparent in a decreased fear of the more feminine aspects of their personalities. Despite some prevalence of the "macho" syndrome, many men permit themselves more softness, tenderness, and enjoyment of aesthetic pleasures than was previously the case. It is as if the identification with the mother is no longer experienced as such a dangerous threat to masculinity and is therefore less repressed. Greater acceptance of some feminine identification on the part of men is bound to enhance the mutuality of sexual life since it results in an empathic understanding of the female experience. Of course, the same is true in reverse when women are able to empathize with men.

It is important to realize that social and psychological changes, especially in a transitional phase before they have become consolidated and stabilized, although manifesting positive results, also produce anxiety and ambivalence. Thus, men are bound to resent and fear the loss of dominance, yet to enjoy the fruits of equality. What becomes outstandingly clear even in these brief and cursory observations is the extent to which social factors influence psychological patterns, both in behavior and attitude. This is a relatively new dimension in psychoanalytic theorizing, for in the past the emphasis in explaining the psychology of the sexes, at least in the classical theory, has been on the psychosexual development of the individual. It is fortunate that the contemporary social scene with its many changes in the ways of human thought and interaction provides us with a laboratory in which we can observe the interdependence of the social and the psychological in varying contexts.

IV

PERSONAL JOURNEY

The six chapters in Part IV, "Personal Journey," originated as talks that were presented in various places. They are completely personal in the sense that they describe my own experiences and reactions in the early days of psychoanalysis when I was a student in Vienna. They are not all happy tales, for from the beginning I experienced some doubt and disagreement with Freudian theory and procedure, as well as a certain disillusionment with the character of some individuals identified with the psychoanalytic "movement." The frequency with which I have been asked to speak on this subject by students of analysis has made me wonder whether this fascination with the past is a search for professional roots or whether to some extent, in view of my reputation as a psychoanalytic dissident, it is a search for a way to gain some freedom of thought within the confines of a rather constricted theory. One's history can indeed be a tale of the past, as well as a guide to the future.

27

My Analysis
with Anna Freud

As I contemplated writing this chapter I sometimes wondered why I had accepted the difficult assignment of writing about my former analyst, Anna Freud. The task is difficult because my feelings are by no means entirely positive, nor indeed are they strongly negative. Even the word "ambivalent" does not apply because it is as if—and I write this with no wish to be arrogant, but merely to describe my existing feeling—*I have outgrown her.* The extent of my detachment was made palpably clear to me as I sat down to begin writing this chapter. It occurred to me that I should know the publication date of Anna Freud's classic work, *The Ego and the Mechanisms of Defense.* It appeared shortly after my husband and I returned to this country after five years of psychoanalytic study in Vienna. I wanted to confirm the date of the book's publication, and so I turned to my bookshelves. I found the volume, but to my amazement it was in German. Its yellowed pages had been thoroughly read; there were underlinings and marginal comments. The date of publication was 1936. We had left Vienna at the end of November 1934. As I held the book with its frayed binding in my hands, I had a feeling of estrangement from the memories it evoked. This, it seems to me, is partly due to the fact that the subject matter of Anna Freud's book, the defense mechanisms, has become public domain.

The names of the defense mechanisms have become as much a part of our language as the Oedipus complex, and thus they fail to evoke personal memories and feelings. But in addition, the focus of my psychoanalytic orientation has changed. I no longer feel identified with classical psychoanalytic thought. Its literature and language seem remote to me. Needless to say, this was not always the case. In fact when my husband and I went to Vienna in 1930 I was full of enthusiasm for and curiosity about the new science and imbued with an idealization of its adherents. Anna Freud headed the list of those whom I idealized.

It is a great responsibility to write about an historical figure. In the absence of any possibility of a communicative interchange with a person no longer living, in order to correct some of one's own misunderstandings one also opens oneself to misunderstanding by those who view history and its characters from a different perspective. The relativity of historical truth becomes palpably clear. Fortunately, I am not alone in this effort to draw a portrait of Anna Freud.

In my book *Appointment in Vienna* (1989), there is a chapter about Anna Freud, about my experience as her analysand over a two-year period. I tried simply to tell the facts. But clearly the "facts" were perceived differently by different people. An old friend who called me after reading the book said, "She's certainly not your favorite person." A student just beginning psychoanalytic training told me she could not restrain her tears when she read about some of the ways in which I was treated by Anna Freud. However, most people thought I dealt evenhandedly in my portrayal of Freud's daughter.

She was indeed her father's daughter and was hopelessly attached to him personally, devoted to his theories and to the movement he founded. There is an anecdote that illustrates this attachment, which I have told to many of my students. It occurred in the early weeks of my analysis in 1930 when I was a passionate young idealist in my early twenties and Anna Freud was about 35. I was conscientiously trying to follow the fundamental rule: "What bothers me about psychoanalysis," I began, "is that there are so many splinter movements—Jung, Adler, Rank. If you are all searching for the truth about human personality, why can't you work together?" Her reply came quickly and unhesitantly. "Nothing is as important to us as the psychoanalytic movement," she said. Much later I learned the full impact of that statement, for in England she sought militantly to preserve her conception of "the movement" and to keep it free of contamination by other ideas. But even in the Vienna of the early 1930s her answer offended me. Would she sacrifice the "truth" for the movement? I think that her life demonstrates that she would. But such is the way of movements and ideologies whatever their content, be they political, religious, sociological, or psychological. Their existence depends on the suppression and distortion of new ideas, of some truths, and of progress in general. Anna Freud was the victim of an unhealthy attachment to her father.

In those early Vienna days I did not know a number of facts that have emerged since her life has been reviewed by biographers. If indeed it was known among a few of the inner psychoanalytic circle that her father was her analyst, it was certainly not general knowledge. Nor did I know of the condescending atmosphere that existed in the family around the figure of Anna's mother, with whom it appears she had considerable difficulty. I was unfamiliar with the fact of Anna's very limited education. (She was trained as an elementary schoolteacher in a two-year teacher training school.) She had never attended the university. These are not facts to be held against her. Rather, they reflect her father's attitude toward women in spite of the fact that several of his most prominent followers were women; however, in most cases their professional careers were already set before they made Freud's acquaintance. In a letter to Wilhelm Fliess written on the day of Anna Freud's birth, Freud writes: "If it had been a son, I would have sent you the news by telegram, because he would have carried your name. Since it turned out to be a little daughter by the name of Anna, she is being introduced to you belatedly" (Masson 1985, p. 153).

It is hard to believe that it was only the issue of the naming that prompted Freud to respond so much more matter-of-factly to the birth of a girl. Anna was a substitute for the wished-for son, and in many ways she fulfilled that role. She was the only one of Freud's offspring to become a psychoanalyst—albeit at first she only practiced with children. Her identification with her father was profound, as was her love for him. She served him on every level: intellectually by advancing and contributing to his theories and personally by devoting her life to him at the expense of her own.

It was this giving up of a personal sexual and erotic life of her own that was particularly difficult for me as her analysand. I was a recently married young woman, in love with a somewhat older husband, away from home for the first time, making adaptations to the culture of a foreign country and to a new, intimate relationship, who needed to feel in her analyst an understanding of erotic feelings and of the adjustments that are required in the context of sexual interactions. Anna Freud provided almost none of this understanding. Instead she came across as an ascetic, virtuous, and conscientious schoolgirl—comely and with a certain charm and grace—but asexual. I had to project onto her person fantasies of a sex life in which I could scarcely believe. I must say that it is a tribute to the human imagination that I was able to grow on this rather restricted diet.

There were also good features about our relationship. At the time of my analysis, Anna Freud was much less rigid in the application of psychoanalytic technique than many of her colleagues and was certainly more humanistically oriented than the classical American psychoanalysts. She was most generous in matters of money, and knowing of our limited financial resources she helped me obtain a job as a substitute teacher of English in a small school for children who were in analysis and would not have done well in the public school system. She also helped me obtain some work doing private tutoring in English. When I complained of digestive troubles caused by the very rich Viennese cuisine, Anna Freud took a very pragmatic and practical view of the situation. She did not jump to the conclusion that this was a psychosomatic response to conflict, but instead told me that she knew through an American friend (I later learned that the friend was Dorothy Burlingham) that the excessive fats and sugars in Viennese cooking were not always easily tolerated by Americans. She referred me to a health food store where we could buy foods more congenial to our digestive needs. This was a great help when, despite the housing shortage, we were finally able to obtain living quarters with a kitchen of our own.

These human reactions to the realities of living softened her otherwise strict analytic stance and made her very Freudian interpretations, for which there was often scanty evidence, more palatable. My need at the time for a female figure to look up to created a powerful transference from which it was not easy to extricate myself. Was my analysis with Anna Freud helpful to me emotionally? This is a question I sometimes ask myself, and it is a difficult one to answer because life itself can promote growth and it is not always easy to know to what one should attribute one's progress. I can say unequivocally that I learned a great deal from her—not about feelings, not about human relationships, but about what a classic analysis is, about the interplay of impulses and defenses, and about their unraveling. I learned about the mechanism, almost the mechanics, of a traditional analytic process that is set in motion by a contrived and artificial situation in which two people meet—one the patient enjoined to trust the other with his or her most intimate thoughts and feelings, the other the analyst enjoined to decode those feelings in terms of a previously learned hypothesis and to communicate the decoded answer to the patient. This process may or may not be helpful to the patient in learning how better to live. But whether positive or not, I am convinced today after many years of experience in working with patients that the outcome does not depend primarily on the interpretation and that a positive outcome does not correlate with the correctness of the interpretation. What is most crucial for the patient's growth is the positive nature and authenticity of the relationship to the analyst, and this in turn depends on the personality of the analyst. Anna Freud did not help me mature as a person; she did not foster my creativity; she did not help make human relationships easier and more joyful for me. She was critical of my anxieties, intolerant of my passions, and judgmental of my tastes, my interests, my goals, and to some extent my values. Were it not for a second analysis with Willi Hoffer while I was still in Vienna, I would have returned to the United States perhaps a bit wiser but no less shackled emotionally by an unhappy relationship with my mother than I had been when I left. Anna Freud had little understanding of me as a person, and I believe the narrowness and limitations of her own life were responsible for this lack. She was born into the psychoanalytic world, and she remained embedded in it, devoted to her father and to "the cause," as he called it.

There is a tragic irony in the fact that the discoverer of the dynamic unconscious, the man who supposedly understood the instinctual forces operating within the familial nucleus, should have failed to see that, in fostering too strong a love, too deep a bond, and too loyal a devotion on the part of his daughter, he had deprived her of her personal life. Her strength lay in the fact that she was able to use her intellectual gifts, her identification with and compassion for children, and a certain joy and vitality in living, to overcome the deprivations that the relationship with her father had cost her. But exacting this price from her was her father's responsibility. She was not a free agent given the situation into which she was born and the character of her father for whom, too, nothing was as important as the psychoanalytic movement. I see Anna Freud, despite the fact that psychologically and emotionally she was not particularly helpful to me, as a tragic and heroic figure. Rather than be a victim, she created a rich life for herself within the narrow limits of the world in which she lived by making important contributions to psychoanalysis and enjoying a deep and loving relationship not only with her father, but also with a contemporary who was not a member of her family but who provided her with a substitute family, namely Dorothy Burlingham.

28

Psychoanalytic New York in the Thirties, Forties, and Fifties

Before describing my experiences in the 1930s, 1940s, and 1950s, it is important to explain that Freud wrote *The Question of Lay Analysis* (1927) in defense of Theodor Reik who was being sued by a patient as a "quack." Reik, of course, survived that suit, as well as Hitler's Europe. He came to the United States, only to be denied membership in the psychoanalytic community. Freud's brilliant brief on so-called lay-analysis did not legitimize Reik to the New York Psychoanalytic Society. These medical analysts operated on a principle of selective orthodoxy in which the economic motive superseded the tenets of Freud's thinking. But Reik turned adversity into a productive enterprise—namely the training of non-medical analysts and the founding of the National Psychological Association for Psychoanalysis (NPAP).

I am grateful for the opportunity to present in this chapter some living history of the past half-century of psychoanalysis, for indeed not only has the world of psychoanalysis and psychotherapy changed but also the cultural climate of the world as a whole is so different from the way it was in the 1930s that I myself am sometimes startled by the fact that in one lifetime I have experienced so much change. In the late 1920s when I was still a college student majoring in the hard sciences, I became interested toward the end of my undergraduate studies, in the humanities and especially in psychology. But although the courses were of some interest, they were limited and barren of any concern for the deeper processes of human emotion, conflict, will, or imagination. By chance, through a classmate I was introduced to Freud's writings, but on campus it was necessary to wrap Freud's *Introductory Lectures* in a brown paper cover lest one arouse the ire of one's psychology professor. Such were the attitudes toward psychoanalysis as William Menaker, my late husband, and I stood on the threshold of our psychoanalytic training, which began in 1930. Parenthetically, some years later as students in Vienna it was also necessary to hide one's so-called deviant interests. In the psychology department at the University of Vienna one did not dare reveal one's interest in psychoanalysis, and at the Psychoanalytic Institute one had better not be caught reading such a revolutionary dissident as Otto Rank. The custom of papal indices seems still to haunt us, as in our pursuit of knowledge we try to avoid ideologies.

Nevertheless, despite the general skepticism about psychoanalysis in the 1930s—and perhaps even because of it—and the difficulties in obtaining training as non-medical people, my husband and I were so interested in and committed to psychoanalysis that we were determined to obtain such training. In this resolve we were much encouraged by Dr. Fritz Wittels, one of the early analysts who came to the United States in the 1920s and 1930s, and taught at the New School. Unfortunately, he is almost unknown among younger analysts today, in part I think because he was not a theoretician, but also because of his somewhat ambivalent history in relation to the psychoanalytic movement. He was much more than a psychiatrist. He was a writer of poetry and fiction as well as a writer in the field of psychoanalysis. There were times in his life when he was part of the psychoanalytic community and other times when he withdrew from it. But the breadth of his interests resulted in his having a favorable attitude toward the training of non-medical candidates, and he actively helped us be accepted for training at the Vienna Institute.

In the 1930s, there were no psychoanalytic training institutes in the United States. There was a New York Psychoanalytic Society, but I doubt very much whether there were societies in other cities before the European psychoanalysts came to the United States to escape the Holocaust. This meant that we had to go to Europe for training. Although there were islands of antagonism toward non-medical analysts and their training among some Europeans, in general the attitude was more liberal than in America. Because of the discrepancy between the American and the European point of view, a compromise had to be reached within the International Psycho-analytical Society. This compromise agreement required an applicant for train-ing at a European Psychoanalytic Institute—either in Vienna, Berlin, or London (Budapest and Paris had a few analysts, but not enough to constitute a for-mal institute)—to be at least 34 years of age, to have had training and experi-ence in a field related to medicine, and to have the approval of the Society of the country of his or her origin. By mere chance and a fortunate confluence of circumstances, William Menaker (Bill) met these criteria. He was 34 years of age, had been a dentist for ten years and a social worker for approximately three years, and managed with some difficulty to win the approval of the New York Psychoanalytic Society by convincing A. A. Brill, who insisted that Bill could make more money in dentistry, that making money was far from a primary goal for him and that he was sincerely interested in becoming a psy-choanalyst. Yet, as I look back at the New York Psychoanalytic Society's track record on such issues, especially at that time, I doubt very much that they would have honored the international agreement (although Bill met all the criteria) were it not for another circumstance.

It so happened that in May of 1930, an International Congress of Mental Hygiene met in Washington DC. Several European analysts attended, among them Helene Deutsch, Franz Alexander, and Rene Spitz. Subse-quently, they came to New York to lecture and to participate in the activi-ties of the New York Psychoanalytic Society. Among these events was an admissions committee meeting at which our applications for training in Europe were being considered. As we heard from Dr. Wittels subsequently, it was the presence of the Europeans at this meeting that forced the Ameri-cans to honor the international agreement and to pass Bill for training, since he met all the criteria for admission to European training.

At the time of all these negotiations, I was completing my training as a social worker at the Pennsylvania School of Social Work. I had a working fellowship and was affiliated with a child care agency. My primary interest was to become a child analyst. As far as I knew, there was but one psycho-analytically trained child analyst in New York at the time, so that by all standards one could scarcely consider the field to be threateningly com-petitive. However, the New York Psychoanalytic Society was completely uninterested in me. They never interviewed me; they had no notion of my qualifications, my education, my personality, or my work experience. Helene Deutsch—who offered herself as Bill's analyst—arranged for my analysis with Anna Freud. Thus, despite the fact that at the Vienna Institute training in child analysis was a subspecialty of work with adults, and in the educational process the analysis of adults was a prerequisite for work with children, one could say that I entered the Institute by the back door. In my case, as far as the New York Psychoanalytic Society was concerned, the absence of any economic threat operated in my favor.

In the early years after our return from Vienna I did actually work with children, but I had been trained to do psychoanalytic work with adults. Gradually, with the passage of time my practice shifted to include primarily adults.

Such were the struggles in the early 1930s in acquiring training if one wanted to become a psychoanalyst. But they were not particularly personal struggles, they were circumstantial—built into the existing system in the United States. They were the byproduct of the issue of the practice of psychoanalysis by non-medical people, and although the prejudice against such practice was strongest in New York, there were reverberations that reached Vienna despite Freud's views. I am rarely inclined to consider economic factors among the major motivations in the development of historic events, although I am aware that in certain circumstances such factors are of outstanding importance. The situation in Vienna in the 1930s was such a time. Vienna had not recovered from the First World War. The demise of the Austro-Hungarian Empire had left Vienna poverty-stricken, a city without a country to support it, either in terms of agriculture or industry. Although the Viennese analysts were certainly not poor compared to the general population, they depended for much of their income upon the United States. Patients came from America; psychiatrists came to Vienna for training. Therefore, they could not oppose their New York colleagues too energetically. In this situation we, as non-medical trainees from New York, were at a disadvantage, for the Viennese hesitated to support us as soon as we showed any inclination to deviate from existing theory or to question any aspect of analytic procedure. We arrived in Vienna with an idealized image of the analytic community as a haven for freedom of thought in the psychological world. In the course of time, this image was heavily tarnished.

The story of our experiences in Vienna, of the discrepancy between our expectations and their realization, of our joys and disappointments and of what we learned about psychoanalysis and the analysts and the world of central Europe at that time is told in *Appointment in Vienna* (Menaker 1989). However, the focus of this chapter is the struggles that Bill and I experienced upon our return to New York—struggles to survive economically, establish ourselves as analysts, and find colleagues with whom to share ideas and a forum for our thoughts.

As might have been expected, the New York Psychoanalytic Society did not welcome us upon our return. Dr. Abraham Kardiner, with whom Bill had an interview, told him that the county medical society would make trouble for the New York Psychoanalytic Society if they admitted non-medical people or in any way supported their practice of psychoanalysis. The logic—or illogic—of this stand was based on a recent court case in which a Christian Science practitioner was sued for malpractice for treating a case of encephalitis. Kardiner advised us to move to Nebraska. Freud's monograph on lay analysis, despite its convincing argument that psychoanalysis is not a speciality of medicine such as surgery for example, did not succeed in influencing the New York analysts to change their opinions or policies.

Not having moved to Nebraska—and I am not sure what Dr. Kardiner thought that state would have to offer us, except that it was far from New York—we were completely on our own. We lived on what I earned at the Jewish Board of Guardians as a child analyst while Bill tried gradually to build a small private practice. A few referrals came from friends or from non-orthodox analysts like Izette De Forest or Frankwood Williams, and a few were relatives of orthodox medical analysts who did not trust their own medical colleagues to respect the privacy of their family affairs. Gradually, Bill's patients began to refer their friends and relatives, and a slowly growing practice began to develop. However, we were practically isolated professionally. Fortunately, we had each other and the library of psychoanalytic books we had brought back from Vienna. Such was the situation for non-medical analysts in the late 1930s.

The catastrophic events that took place in Europe in the late 1930s and 1940s changed much in the lives of many people as well as in our own. Hitler's rise to power, the persecution and extermination of the Jews, and the beginning of the Second World War brought many European analysts to these shores. Bill and I helped many of them come here by acquiring affidavits of support for them. Most were medical analysts who depended on the support of the New York Psychoanalytic Society—and by this time there was an Institute in New York as well—so that in practical terms they could be of little help to us, since they could not openly support the practice of analysis by non-medical persons. But they did provide an opportunity for the professional exchange of ideas. Among our friends of that period were analysts who became well-known later on and who made significant contributions to analytic theory. There was also a small group of non-medical analysts. Theodor Reik was one of them. Some years before NPAP was founded Reik led a small discussion group in which we participated. In fact, it was Reik who encouraged me to write; and it was at this time, in the 1940s, that I produced my first papers. We also participated in another small discussion group consisting of European analysts: Charlotte Feibel, Berta Tumarin, Lise-Lotte Heiman, and Lydia Baumgarten, the sister of Rudolf Lowenstein. We met at least once a month to discuss cases. These people also formed the nucleus of our social life at that time. Our isolation was over, but as time went on we found ourselves in disagreement with some of our colleagues on theoretical as well as clinical grounds. Their identification with their European origins and with Freudian psychoanalysis that grew out of its soil was deeper than ours. On one occasion when we were discussing the difficulties of our situation as non-medical analysts, Berta Tumarin expressed the view that we were obviously inferior to the analysts of the New York Psychoanalytic Society since, if this were not the case, we would all be members. This status-ridden non-egalitarianism did not sit well with us, and it was at about this time that I became deeply interested in the problem of masochism. However, some things die hard, for there are still signs among us that some people prefer to emulate the medical analysts rather than find, develop, and create their own identity.

It is a true but unhappy irony that the Second World War—especially when the United States entered it—was of benefit to us as non-medical psychoanalysts. The medical analysts were frequently serving in the armed forces, and civilians in need of mental health services were discovering the capacities of non-medical people. In the army, the discovery was also being made that psychologists were able to do psychotherapy successfully and were often taking the place of psychiatrists, since the need was great and there was not a sufficient number of medical therapists.

It was in the 1950s, shortly after the war, that our own practices grew, that licensing for psychologists was passed by state legislatures after a long struggle, and that psychology departments within some universities dropped their rigidly academic stances, became more clinically oriented, and began teaching some depth psychology. In addition, institutes for psychoanalytic training for non-physicians began to spring up. In fact, there were even choices for individuals seeking such training. In approximately twenty years, the situation for would-be lay analysts changed from having to go to Europe for training to having a choice of training centers. Certainly, the early struggles of non-acceptance and isolation were over.

But there are new struggles. Or are they really new? The struggle over the legitimacy of the practice of psychoanalysis by non-medical persons—a cause that Freud defended so eloquently—is basically over power, prestige, and economics. Unfortunately, within the non-medical group of analysts, the same struggle for dominance that formerly existed between medical and lay analysts still persists, either in the form of competing ideologies within psychoanalysis itself or in the setting up of criteria for training and for acceptance as an analyst. The legitimacy for being an analyst should depend on ability, talent, and proper training, but what constitutes proper training is still being disputed. Criteria are being set up, but as before, some individuals of talent, dedication, and creative imagination within the lay-analytic community are disenfranchised because they fail to meet some technicality that special groups, considering themselves elite, have set up. It is extremely difficult if not impossible for human groups to organize themselves so as to avoid the unproductive hierarchies of upstairs and downstairs. Should we not better tend to our work, advance our knowledge, and help people lead more integrated and productive lives? These are things worth struggling for.

29

Continuity and Change
in Conceptions of
the Psychoanalytic Situation

Historical interest had all but died out in the 1960s, but recently there has been a resurgence of interest in the past, a search for roots, origins, and connections. We all hope to consolidate our personal identity both through a link with the continuity of the past and through an awareness of our unique difference. These two aspects of life—continuity and change—characterize the evolutionary process, be it the evolution of personality or of a professional skill, a point of view, a philosophy of life, or a conception of therapy. Generally, however, when we think of evolution, we focus on the aspect of change and progress, neglecting a full appreciation of the importance of the stability provided by continuity. For it is only from a stable entity that we can expect ordered and progressive change.

Both aspects of evolution have occurred in my own professional life. I work differently now with patients and students than I did over forty years ago, and so I am very aware of change. Yet, recently as I reviewed some of my old papers and notes and reflected upon the development of my ideas, I was struck by the consistent and persistent presence of certain themes, certain concerns and interests, and by the way in which new ideas had emerged from the old, original ones. I ask myself: What is the nature of this continuity in my own life, in my own personality? For one thing, I was born with an insatiable curiosity. My constant "whys" and "hows" were at times a great burden to my mother, and she used to say, with more annoyance than appreciation, that I was born with the word "why" on my lips. The continuity of this trait, coupled with a certain healthy skepticism, was not always looked upon kindly in analytic circles. I tended not to be a true believer, and an absence of awe, except for things cosmic, ultimately led to innovations in my analytic work. Perhaps it was the insistence on the expression of my own individuality that imbued me with a profound respect for the uniqueness of each individual and made me aware of the vulnerability of each patient's self-esteem, especially in the therapeutic situation. This awareness and an emotional expressiveness and candor have characterized my analytic work from the beginning.

But while these traits stood me in good stead in academia and in most of my human relationships, they got in my way in my early encounters with psychoanalysis. It is partially in answer to the question of why and how these personality characteristics were unwelcome in the psychoanalytic world, as I knew it in its early days, that I came to grips with the implications of some of the premises of psychoanalysis and with its conception of the psychoanalytic situation. Thus, a bit of adversity became the spur for the development of my own ideas.

In 1930 when I began my analytic training, the conception of the psychoanalytic situation—its goal, its task, its format—was relatively simple. The neurotic symptoms for the relief of which individuals sought analytic treatment were understood to be compromise formations between unacceptable thoughts and impulses that remained unconscious through repression and the conscious, censoring part of the personality. If these repressed impulses could be made conscious, went the theory, the functioning part of the personality (later defined as "ego") would be free to find a new adaptive solution for the previously unacceptable impulses. The task then was to make the unconscious conscious through the method of free association, but since there would be inevitable resistance to the lifting of repression, the focus of the analytic process became the analysis of resistance and the use of transference phenomena to make both the unconscious impulses and the unconscious resistances palpable. This is still the conception of analysis in many quarters, and even with the advent of ego psychology in the psychoanalytic system of thought, the emphasis in the classical approach has been on the exploration of the unconscious aspects of the ego. In the name of this goal it was thought best to reduce the reality of the relationship between analyst and patient to a minimum, so that the analyst might become primarily the object for the emotional projections of the patient. In the course of my training, I followed this procedure; in fact for some time thereafter, this conception of the analytic situation persisted in my work.

As I look back upon the analysis of my first patient in Vienna, I am appalled at how little I knew about the really crucial aspects of her life, especially about her early relationship to her mother. She was a young woman in her twenties who came into analysis because of sexual acting-out, unsatisfactory relationships to men, a general feeling of meaningless-ness about life, and very low self-esteem. Since I was instructed to await her free associations, I hardly interacted with her, asked scarcely any questions, and consequently learned very little, since most of her conversation was a description of her sexual exploits. My contrived interpretations about penis envy to account for her promiscuous, sexual behavior had no effect, as one might expect, either on her behavior or on her general chronic, low-grade depression. She was so vulnerable to feelings of inferiority, especially in regard to her body, that for a very long time she hid from me the fact that she had a curvature of the spine—a condition, she was told, that would worsen in time. However, at the time that I treated her, it was not apparent. She was, in fact, quite attractive, and the discrepancy between her subjective body image and the objective fact was quite striking.

This patient had been selected as a training case by the clinic of the Psychoanalytic Institute, although acting-out patients were not considered good candidates for analysis. Thus, when things did not progress well, an explanation was readily at hand—she was not suitable for analysis. Fortunately for the patient, my inept attempts to tamper with her unconscious came to an end with my return to the United States.

Aside from my regret at not having been helpful to this young woman, I was troubled by the limiting conception of psychoanalysis—a conception that still persists and one that is consistent with the logic of any attempt to build a general psychology of human personality from a preselected sample suited only for a specific method of observation. For while one may be justified from the therapeutic standpoint in pursuing a given method for specific problems—that is, for special diagnostic categories—from the standpoint of a general understanding of human psychology, one is not justified in making generalized deductions from a sample of individuals already categorized by specific selective procedures. Therapeutically, a case could be made for this medical model for the psychoanalytic situation; scientifically it cannot be justified. It is significant that many of the most important psychoanalytic advances in our understanding of personality have come from those therapists who have been willing or forced by circumstances to work with "unanalyzable" patients—with psychotics, borderline patients, narcissistic personality disorders, children, or delinquents. The needs of these individuals have called for modifications in goals, in the conception of the therapeutic procedure, and the role of the therapist in it. Through the creation of a new field of observation, we have been able to deepen our understanding of personality.

And so from the beginning of my analytic work, there was always a certain uneasiness with the contrived and artificial aspects of technique that seemed to put up a barrier to therapeutic effectiveness rather than to facilitate it; these aspects frequently threatened the reality perceptions of the patient, thereby weakening rather than strengthening his or her ego. In fact, the fostering of transference reactions—projections—through the artificial "neutrality" of the analyst deprived the patient of his most urgent need, namely to make good the initial developmental deficits in the structuring of the ego by using the therapist as an object for new internalizations that will eventually, through gradual assimilation, become part of a restored self.

This conception of analysis, so beautifully conveyed in Kohut's (1977) book, *The Restoration of the Self*, is something that I also felt early on, but had not yet conceptualized. At the time I was treating an adolescent boy at the Jewish Board of Guardians for *pavor nocturnus* (night terrors). He had suffered from these terrors from early childhood. His very religious Orthodox parents had taken him to a "wunder rebbe," a man with magical powers, who said some prayers over him and provided him with an amulet to be worn as a protection against the evil powers of fear. The medicine worked until the old rabbi died, at which point the night terrors returned. It was then that he was brought to me—he was 15 at the time—and I found myself in competition with the occult. As I worked with him in the more or less classic manner—interpreting his oedipal wishes, his castration anxiety, his fears of his sexual impulses, and the guilt surrounding them—it soon became clear that for him my interpretations were not insights but amulets. When the terror would strike him at night, he would repeat what I had told him in the manner of a ritual and would derive comfort and relief from the repetition of my words. From the standpoint of a conception of the psychoanalytic situation as one in which unconscious drives are made conscious, and the new knowledge is consolidated and worked through by an analysis of resistance and transference, this use, by my young patient, of interpretation as a defensive, ritualized incantation was clearly a resistance. I was aware of this and made some tentative attempts to analyze the resistance. These he brushed aside, preferring to insist on the value of my magic. The therapeutic importance of his belief in my omnipotence exceeded the value of the uncovering of unconscious impulses. In fact, what I communicated to him in the language of my psychoanalytic knowledge was important, not as content, but as an offering of help to him. He kept me in the role of a "wunder rebbe" despite my femaleness, and one could speak of his cure—for cured of his night terrors he was—as a transference cure. But there was more to be learned from this experience than that it was an illustration of "faith healing," consistent with his culture. From time to time since his therapy, over a thirty-five-year period, he had kept in touch with me: for example, when he went into the army during the Second World War and when he returned. He had married happily and raised three daughters. One of them had become a librarian, and it was she, who having read of my late husband's death some years ago, had called her father's attention to it. He called me to offer his condolences. Clearly he had spoken of me to his children; he must have spoken on some level of his own problems and conflicts and of the help that I had given him, and he must have spoken with some admiration and gratitude.

At the time of his treatment I did not yet think in ego psychological terms, nor in terms of the significance of the early, pre-oedipal relationship to the mother nor about issues of separation and ego building. But I respected how he was able to use treatment without condemning it as inconsistent with preconceived psychoanalytic goals; I respected him as a person and conveyed a sincere wish to free him of his anxieties. In other words, I was more concerned with the individual needs of the patient than with carrying out the prescribed psychoanalytic method.

In retrospect, I am certain that it was this focus of concern that was curative. Today it could be conceptualized as the positive effect of a relationship to an affirming mother surrogate, resulting in the opportunity for and the permission to idealize the person of the analyst. Both of these processes as transitional phenomena within the therapeutic process help strengthen the ego, consolidate the self, and raise self-esteem, thereby making it much more possible for the individual to deal with those fears that may indeed arise out of unconscious drive needs.

It was becoming increasingly clear to me that the psychoanalytic situation, as an encounter between two individuals, represented much more than the opportunity to discover the nature and content of the patient's unconscious. There was the reality aspect of the situation itself; then there was the particular way in which an individual patient used that reality. As we now know, my adolescent patient was impelled to construct out of the authority situation a priest-rabbi image of the analyst. This is more than a transference reaction, since the analyst is indeed in reality in a position of authority.

The patient about whom I wrote my first paper on masochism—"The Masochistic Factor in the Psychoanalytic Situation" (Menaker 1943)—was actually the daughter of an autocratic rabbi, and it is not surprising that she tended to make of the analytic situation an authority situation in which every interpretation was perceived as a directive for action. But this construct too contained elements above and beyond its obvious transference implications. The set-up of the analytic situation was determined by the analyst. The time, the procedure, and the frequency of sessions were determined by him or her. Insights were arrived at through his greater knowledge and understanding. The analyst was captain of the ship. This is a necessary and inevitable aspect of psychoanalytic therapy, but the effect of this actual duplication of childhood dependency had not been accounted for. For it is not only the patient's need to regress to childhood patterns that brings about transference phenomena but also the actuality of the psychoanalytic situation that, to some extent, duplicates the childhood situation of the patient. It is this mixture of projection and reality that blurs the validity of the content of interpretations of the unconscious and reduces their efficacy in terms of change or cure for the patient. But there is more: if the reality dimension of the analytic situation is unaccounted for, if interpretations are made solely in terms of the transference—a procedure in which the analyst can indulge because of his position of power and one that he can justify because his goal is the exploration of the unconscious— then the narcissistic vulnerability of the patient is unaccounted for and his self-esteem is inevitably reduced. It was this dimension of the analytic situation to which I was sensitive, primarily because I instinctively felt the overriding importance of ego growth as distinguished from the secondary importance of the uncovering of unconscious impulses. When I formulated some of these thoughts in the early 1940s, I thought in the terminology of existing psychoanalytic theory, and I called the inevitable built-in contrast between the authoritative, power position of the analyst and the needy, dependent position of the patient "the masochistic factor in the analytic situation." Although I still think that the observation is valid, today I might choose a title more clearly descriptive of ego processes.

In writing about my development as an analyst in those early days, I cannot fail to mention two people whose confidence in my abilities and whose affirmation of me as a person greatly encouraged me. One was Dr. Van Ophjuisen, with whom I often discussed cases at the Jewish Board of Guardians; the other was Dr. Theodore Reik, who urged me to publish my first paper on masochism and who generously gave me the benefit of his critical appraisal. On a more personal level, my late husband with whom I shared many discussions on psychoanalytic questions was also of great help to me. In addition, the positive response of my patients to my work with them, the tangible effect of my empathic understanding, cannot be underestimated as a factor in strengthening my confidence in my independent and often controversial point of view.

When one begins to work in the analytic field, one usually treats very disturbed patients—patients who fall into the general category of borderline cases and whom established analysts, who can be more choosy about their cases, would turn away as unanalyzable. But it is precisely from these patients that one learns more about the development of personality than the recognized psychoanalytic theory can teach us. It was during my work with such a patient that my understanding of moral masochism deepened. I began to understand it not as a drive phenomenon, but as an aspect of ego psychology in which a denigrated self-conception, initially mirrored to the child by the mother, is tenaciously held on to in order to diminish the fear of separation from the mother. The price for the maintenance of this bond is a greatly diminished ego autonomy and a tendency toward self-destructive behavior, defeatist attitudes, a disturbance of interpersonal relationships, and distortions in the perception of reality. The separation anxiety is overwhelming, and the masochistic stance of the ego acts as a defensive reaction to it. Thus, I conceived of the defensive use of a masochistic self-image, not directed toward unconscious impulses but toward protecting the ego from the fear of individuation attendant upon separation from the mother. This insight led to the inevitable question: What is the origin, developmentally, of such overwhelming anxiety? The answer lay in the nature of the early mother-child relationship, in which the mother's failure to affirm the child, to react positively to its growth—in fact, her need to do the opposite, to be constantly critical and belittling—led to the child's fear of his own growth and to an incorporation of his mother's denigrating attitude toward him. The resulting self-image undermined the child's secure sense of self and eventuated in an ego deficit that affected the functioning of the total personality.

It was not hard to see that, with the realization that one was dealing with a basic faulting in early ego development, the therapeutic task could no longer be conceived of as the uncovering of unconscious drives, but rather as the creation of a situation in which the initial deficit could, at least to some extent, be made good in the reality of the patient-therapist interaction. Thus, the conception of the psychoanalytic situation inevitably changed. It was my work on the masochistic self-image and my attempt to correct it through affirmation of the patient's self that led me to minimize the archeological model of the psychoanalytic procedure, and to view the psychoanalytic experience as a new opportunity for growth for the patient in a relationship that did not repeat the ego-deficit-producing aspects of his early childhood. In the carrying out of this task, a constant sensitive awareness of the individual's narcissistic vulnerability is essential. One finds this awareness, as well as a therapeutic philosophy that places the self-conception at the center of the therapeutic undertaking, in the work of Heinz Kohut. True, he confines his innovative recommendations to what he terms "narcissistic personality disorders." In my clinical experience, however, the narcissistic injury effected in the early mother-child relationship that results in a masochistic self-conception and a consequent deficit in ego development is so ubiquitous as to justify the emphasis on a restructuring of the self as the main task of therapy in practically all cases.

Soon my interest in masochism met with another long-standing interest of mine, namely in animal behavior. I had read Lorenz's charming book, *King Solomon's Ring* (1952), which takes its title from the legend that King Solomon possessed a ring, a turn of which enabled him to understand the language of animals. Lorenz did indeed understand animal communication in terms of movement, gesture, and behavior, and he placed it in the context of its evolutionary, adaptive function. In reading his work more extensively, as well as that of other ethologists, certain similarities between animal and human behavior impressed themselves upon me. These similarities were in the nature of analogies and did not imply the existence either of any causal connections between them nor of any evolutionary hierarchical relationship between the similar modes of behavior. Yet, the species survival value for certain animals—for example, wolves and turkeys—of specific movements on the part of vulnerable individuals, calculated to inhibit the aggression of their more powerful counterparts, suggested a pattern much like that of the masochistic ego stance that developed in the belittled and dependent child who was afraid of separateness. Such similarities alerted me to the evolutionary continuum of all living things and led me to the conclusion that the formation of personality was essentially an adaptive process that represented the human advance over the built-in, instinctual behavior of animals. For the human ego, which is the agent for behavior, action, thought, and feeling is characterized by flexibility and the capacity for making choices, whereas in the animal world behavior is largely predetermined by genetic patterning and its individual variability is exceedingly limited. Yet, certain primitive precursors of human awareness and behavior are present in the animal world, especially among the higher mammals, and most especially in those animals whose way of life involves a clearly defined social organization. It is, of course, highly significant that the analogies to human behavior in the animal world—adaptive, defensive behavior, such as masochism, or processes of internalization that suggest the earliest forms of identification—are to be found in animals capable of relationships to one another.

An awareness of the evolutionary process in all of life leads inevitably to a realization of its advance to higher levels of organization. The reverberation of this evolutionary movement in human personality is manifested in the striving character of ego development. It was the awareness of this striving on the part of ego for object relationships, for synthesis, for a higher level of efficacy, competence, and integration, for increased creative expressiveness, as I saw these phenomena in my clinical experience, that provided for me an additional basis for the affirmation of my patients. For just as the normal development of a child requires that the mother enjoy his or her growth as it eventuates in increasing differentiation, individuation, and autonomy, so the therapist's enjoyment of the patient's striving for progress in all the ways that I have mentioned is reflected back to the patient as affirmation of the self and is crucial for his betterment.

I can already hear objections to this view: first, because it violates the analytic rule of neutrality, and second, because, by revealing the analyst's pleasure, it feeds into the resistance of those obsessive-compulsive patients who are driven into a contrary stubbornness, calculated to defeat the therapist, to deprive him of the satisfaction of successful work even if it means their own defeat. In response to the first objection, the rationality of rules depends on the goals at which they are aimed. When the psychoanalytic situation was concerned with the uncovering of the unconscious, the focus was on the id, with a minimum participation of the ego. To this end, perhaps the relative neutrality of the analyst was helpful, although in my judgment it resulted in serious secondary problems. These problems in turn derived from what to me is a false premise—namely, that the essence of cure resides in extending the boundaries of consciousness by adding to it what was previously outside the limits of awareness. For me—and this has been a growing awareness with time and experience—the essence of cure resides in the consolidation of an as yet not fully synthesized ego, and to this end the affirmation of the therapist is essential.

In response to the second point, there are, of course, patients whose defenses take the form of oppositionalism and for whom any resistance to the analyst's interpretations is much more than a derivative of the small child's opposition to toilet training—which would be the Freudian, libido theoretical view; such negativism attests to a fundamental ego insecurity, to an identity that can define itself only in the negative. But such patients, no less than others, need the affirmation of the therapist in their struggle to reconstitute a secure self. Admittedly they cannot accept such affirmation until the anxiety against which the oppositionalism is a defense has been analyzed—that is, made conscious in all its implications, ramifications, and effects. But during the analytic procedure and certainly when the defenses are beginning to yield, the patient must feel the analyst's affirmation as a backdrop for whatever else is going on.

In describing the oppositional patient I referred to the fact that he can "as yet" only define himself in the negative. The "as yet" implies development and progress for it is future directed. The therapeutic undertaking itself attests to the patient's motivation to change; yet, he or she is caught in what Otto Rank would call an expression of negative will that inhibits the cohesion and fulfillment of the self's potential. In connection with the striving character of psychological growth and development, and with the uniqueness of each individual who strives for the fulfillment of this differentiation, the issue of will is of the utmost importance. It is a dimension that has been neglected—even condemned—within the deterministic framework that has characterized psychoanalytic thinking. But the act of willing is a primary function of the ego; it is that which distinguishes human behavior from that in the rest of the animal world. It is that which makes change and progress possible. True, we are not free to will everything: true, there are psychodynamic reasons for inhibitions in willing—and it is to this latter factor that psychoanalysis originally addressed itself, without realizing that it was attempting to free the will.

In the history of psychoanalysis it was Otto Rank who was the first to be concerned with the will and who finally, when he perceived the fundamental difference between his philosophy of therapy, both in goal and method, and that of psychoanalysis, called his treatment will therapy. He saw the aim of psychotherapy as an aid to the consolidation of an individual's identity—what Kohut would call the cohesion of the self—through the ability to will positively, rather than to live with a false sense of self through negative assertiveness. And he saw the realization of this aim as dependent upon the therapist's ability to convey his affirmation of and respect for the patient's unique personality and of his right to express his own positive will. I was exposed to the influence of Rank's thinking early in my career—in fact, before my psychoanalytic training—through my studies at the Pennsylvania School of Social Work. Even today I am not certain as to how much of this early influence has lain dormant, only to be revived in the course of my analytic work and to result in a conception of the psychoanalytic situation much like that of Rank's, or how much has been arrived at through independent thinking about my analytic experience with patients. Probably both factors are operative. But the question is really irrelevant.

My current conception of the analytic situation—and that of a few others in the field who are unaware of any debt to Rank—is much like his. I see the analytic situation as an interpersonal interaction between patient and analyst in which early deficits in the formation of a cohesive ego—and therefore in the ability to will—are made good by the analyst's affirmation of the patient's self, thereby restoring the capacity for positive willing. The emphasis in such an approach is clearly on providing a corrective experience for the patient, on creating the proper soil for the felicitous growth of a clearly synthesized sense of identity. But it does not exclude the analysis of unconscious drives and defenses when these appear as obstacles to the acceptance of the therapist's affirmation or to other processes that are crucial for the growth of the ego.

A word about affirmation: it is almost impossible to describe verbally a process that has its origins in the preverbal period of mother-child interaction and that can then be echoed in the therapist-patient interaction. Affirmation refers to the conveying of an emotion of appreciation and acceptance of the unique individuality of the person that enables him or her, through the internalization of this feeling, to nourish his or her self-esteem. This raising of self-esteem eventually mends the early narcissistic injury that is responsible for the faulting in ego development and synthesis.

It is clear that, in a conception of the psychoanalytic situation that emphasizes reparative ego processes rather than unconscious drives and defenses, interpretations will be differently focused. A recent experience with a patient illustrates my point. A middle-aged man who had had psychoanalytic therapy some twenty years ago consulted me because of current marital difficulties. His loss of sexual interest in his wife, as can be imagined, created much disharmony in their relationship. He was a person of unusual intellectual ability, but more than this, he had an unusual gift for psychoanalytical insight and understanding. Throughout the many years of his married life he had made good use of his first therapy, arriving at new insights on his own and augmenting his understanding of himself by reading in the field. (His first therapist was no longer available to him because he had left the country.) At the time of his first therapy, when he was a young man in his twenties, he had been a homosexual. The accepted goal of that therapy by both patient and therapist had been the overcoming of his homosexuality. In this aim the therapy had succeeded. He overcame his fear and envy of women sufficiently to initiate a relationship with a young woman who eventually became his wife. However, his masculine identity was not sufficiently nor reliably consolidated in a way to withstand his wife's needs for mothering. It was an increase in her dependency needs, caused by psychological problems of her own that are irrelevant for this discussion, that resulted in his distaste for her as a sexual partner. I learned this very early in the therapeutic undertaking.

Yet on the basis of my rather scant knowledge of his life I ventured an interpretation: namely, that her dependency spoke to the feminine, the mothering part of himself of which he was afraid since he felt that it threatened his masculine identity, I suggested that his life itself had confirmed his masculinity and that there was no reason to fear a return of his homosexuality—no reason to fear mothering his wife when it was appropriate to do so. The effect of this interpretation was dramatic. He was able to accept my affirmation of his masculinity, to respond to his wife's dependency needs, and to have a satisfying sexual relationship with her. However, I was under no illusion that the problem had been securely solved. In the ensuing weeks he brought to the analysis many of the emotional reactions surrounding his relationship to his mother—her dependency upon him to supply her with security and self-esteem and to repair her feeling of being the injured party, a need that grew largely out of a bad marriage; he expressed his bottomless rage at being so used and thus deprived of his childhood. Certainly, these emotions and their relationship to his present life and current relations will have to be analyzed and worked through. But the reparative process is primary and begins with my appreciation and affirmation of him as a person and, in this case, also as a man. It is this nourishing of the self-esteem that makes possible the ultimate consolidation of a secure identity. The historical analysis of his psychological development provides the sense of continuity that every individual requires in order to establish a clear self-image, but it is not this analysis that provides the material for the rebuilding of the nucleus of the self. For this rebuilding, the psychoanalytic situation must take as a model the early mother-child relationship in which the anticipatory affirmation by the good mother of all manifestations of growth in the child enhances his or her physical and psychological development.

I have taken you on a long odyssey of my own personal–professional development, specifically the development of my thinking about a particular psychoanalytic problem: the conception of psychoanalytic goals and methods. In the spirit of my own philosophy let me encourage you to enjoy your own adventure in our professional work: to observe, to explore, to think; where possible to innovate; but above all, while respecting your psychoanalytic heritage as well as all the relevant learning of the past, not to be intimidated by the shadow of existing doctrines nor by the enormity of our tasks and questions.

30

Being Seventy-Five

Perhaps you can imagine my astonishment when I was asked to give my approval to a celebration and a *Festschrift* (a volume of writings in honor of someone—a kind of offering, in other words) in honor of my upcoming seventy-fifth birthday. I had not thought about the upcoming milestone, but I would not deny it. Somehow, becoming 75 was an overwhelming thought. Those high numbers are intimidating. Seventy was a landmark, but it could still be accommodated. But 75! Of course I approved the plans for a celebration and a *Festschrift*. I felt flattered and honored, yet puzzled. How did I come to deserve this honor? I just went on being myself, doing what came naturally—it is hoped with a minimum of injury to others—and getting older! It is only in childhood that getting older seems like a real achievement: "What a big girl you've gotten to be; how you've grown! You're almost as tall as I am," say the proud elders. But the latter-year equivalents—"What big teeth you have, Grandma!" or "Haven't you gained some weight since we last saw you, Mom?"—are scarcely calculated to give one a feeling of accomplishment. Yet we all seem to take the biblical three score years and ten very seriously, and those who wrest more time from Fate are celebrated as if it were their own achievement or as if they had some secret formula for long life. This is hardly the case, for whatever we do to prolong life—and of course there are ways: some medical, some related to lifestyle, emotional, and psychological—the primary factors are a mixture of genetic good fortune and luck, sometimes referred to as the grace of God.

In connection with the age-old question—what does it feel like to be 75—let me discuss the human relationship to time and to the self-feeling in time. Much is said in developmental psychology about *object constancy*, but equally important is *self-constancy*, and so although one experiences change in oneself over time, in a very basic way one knows oneself to be the same person, the same one who has changed. For example, I was extremely shy as a child, and while occasionally remnants of that shyness reappear, I know that I have changed greatly; I am no longer so timorous. Yet I am the same self and experience myself in a continuum, so that to be 75 on one level feels no different from being any other age, and yet on other levels, I am aware of changes. This seeming paradox of sameness and change characterizes the human relationship to time, for we live not only in the three dimensions of past, present, and future but also in a constancy of self within which there are variations that depend in some measure on the time dimension. Obviously our relationship to the dimensions of time changes; in childhood and adolescence there is more future than past, yet the present is most important because the future is too amorphous, unknown, and unpredictable and becomes therefore a source of anxiety. In adult years the relationship between past and future is more evenly balanced, but there is a growing awareness that the future diminishes quantitatively, and in old age we know that the future is minimal.

I use the words "know" and "awareness," but this is the rational side of our "being in time" and it is my belief that no one could live successfully by keeping these realities constantly in the conscious mind. The defenses that are so often denigrated in psychoanalytic theory and practice, however, denial and repression, serve a good purpose in relation to aging. If one is fortunate enough to be able to go about the business of living and of doing productive, perhaps even creative work that is fulfilling, then one can deny age. Just as small children play at being grown up—or at least they used to before this age of sophistication—and deny the reality of their station through make-believe, so the elderly can play at being young if they have been lucky enough to have had grown-up involvements in personal, professional, vocational, or creative events previously. I feel very lucky in this respect: to have had a good marriage that lasted forty-two years, to have had children and a profession that gratified me, and to be able to continue those satisfactions in personal life and work is to look back on a past and to contemplate a present that contains much fulfillment. And what of the future? However long or short it may be, for me it is limitless in the sense that I am involved in exploring the world of ideas and in having young people join me in this enterprise. The world of ideas and the creative imagination are infinite, and this is where it is good to live as one gets older. If there is any magic secret about how to stay young in feeling, it is to pursue a commitment to the exploration of ideas, for it is such activity that brings about change and inner growth.

Often, in an attempt to master and to make peace with the basic tragedy of life—namely, that it ends in death—we project a concrete model or schema to represent it metaphorically. It helps to envisage an objective order of things that is universal, and of which each of us is a part. For Shakespeare, as a dramatist, the world was a stage and all its men and women merely players. For me, who tends to think evolutionarily, life, in terms of a very homely metaphor, is like a gin rummy game, a mixture of randomness and planned orderliness. I am not much of a card player, but I must admit that I play a good game of gin rummy. The hand that one is dealt is of course random, but the optimal exploitation of its possibilities, as one tries to build sequential order, is a planful matter of the judgment of probabilities, of alternatives, and of risks. That is also the nature of life, and wisdom lies in accepting the cards in one's hand and doing the best one can with them. An outstanding bridge player whom I knew many years ago made a point of telling me that he never complains about the cards he has been dealt. That is, of course, much more easily said than done, especially if one is dealt too many bad hands. But it does say something about responsibility for building one's own life, and in our field we tend to think too much in causal terms and to assign responsibility to cause, especially to past events, confusing the two. I do not want to give you the impression that wisdom is the prerogative of age, although it helps. But I suppose that one aspect of the wisdom of old age is to be open to the wise innovations of youth. I try to be so.

Many years ago there was a musical on Broadway called *Bloomer Girl*. It was a milestone in the women's liberation movement. One of its important theme songs, sung by a wonderful comedienne named Joan McCracken (it is amazing to me that I, who do not know one actor or actress from another, should remember her; this is a comment on the subjective, selective aspect of memory), was called "Can't Say No," and one of its unforgettable lines was "I'd rather have something to remember than nothing to regret." Although the double entendre in this line is obvious, one could profitably attribute a broader meaning to it. "Seize the day!" it says. I find that a good motto, but I would add: "wisely."

As one advances in years, one experiences a new set of anxieties or at least so it seems until one examines them more closely, and then one sees that they are really fundamentally the same as those of childhood: fear of loss and separation and fear of autonomy or individuation. It is only the content that differs at varying levels of growth and development. However, as age advances and one experiences some loss of strength and physical capability as well as the loss of one's peers through death, anxiety tends to intensify. As psychologists and psychoanalysts, we are lucky to be able to know and accept anxiety as a natural aspect of life and thus to make efforts at its mastery, instead of denying it or projecting or distorting its effects in fruitless ways. I earlier advocated the denial of fact and the denial of feeling. In the first case the denial helps one transcend the reality; in the second case, in order to master the feeling, one must know it and denial therefore becomes counterproductive.

In general I would say of myself that at 75 I have more humility, more wisdom, more tolerance, and more humor about life than I had earlier on, and I enjoy these facts about myself. Perhaps this is the tertiary narcissism of old age.

31

A Contribution to the Study of the Neurotic Stealing Symptom

In the course of two years I once had, either in analysis or under analytic observation at the Jewish Board of Guardians, a group of six cases, all boys, ranging in age from 7 to 19 years, each one of whom had gotten into difficulties as a result of chronically recurrent stealing episodes. Treatment had not been completed in any of these cases at the time this chapter was written. In addition, I was given the opportunity to evaluate reports submitted by psychiatric social workers of six other stealers. I have utilized the material derived from the cases I have treated and those summarized by the social workers in an attempt to formulate the pathognomonic mechanisms and developmental maladaptations responsible for the repeated, uncontrollable impulse to steal.

In each case studied, the stealing was the most clearly circumscribed symptom and the factor responsible for the boy's referral to the agency. In addition, however, each case presented feminine character traits, work or school maladjustments, and disturbed familial relationships. The cases were all characterized by oral and anal involvements. An analysis of their sexual lives revealed that there was no normal masculine genital expression commensurate with their age levels. Since we know analytically that a symptom represents, in part, unconscious wishes that cannot be expressed otherwise, we can assume that, in the case of the boys who steal. repressed memories have been incorporated into the structure of the stealing symptom. Our study has shown that the content of these wishes that lie behind the symptom is of a specific nature for stealing and is constant for the cases that we investigated. This can best be illustrated by the following case.

Ben, who came for analytic treatment at the age of 15½, was a fearful boy with a furtive, guilt-laden glance and extreme bodily restlessness. He had been brought to Children's Court on a charge of stealing. A study of the case revealed a long history of stealing that probably began at about the age of 6. The family set-up presented neither social pathology nor severe economic stress. The father was a compulsive neurotic character, whose exaggerated altruism and humanitarianism represented a reaction formation against powerful aggressions. He was a skilled worker, a man whom the members of his trade looked up to. He lived a happy marital life with his wife, who was an attractive, rather narcissistic woman. Ben was the oldest child. A sister, three years younger, followed, and a baby brother of 3 is the youngest child.

For about three years before treatment, the boy had been a chronic stealer. According to his own reports, he stole several times weekly. Although the objects he stole varied, his stealing generally followed a specific pattern. Usually he would break into cellars and steal from the superintendent of a building. Books, magazines, newspapers, tools, and bicycles were the things he took chiefly. He sold the things he stole and used the money to buy sweets and to attend the movies.

The treatment revealed two foci of conflict. First was a hatred of the opposite sex. This was expressed in attitudes toward his younger sister. She was, according to him, a fat, unattractive girl whose appearance disgusted him. He was particularly disturbed by the fact that she flirted with and teased the boys—leading them on, never really caring for them, and always letting them down. In school she was much more successful than he and, in spite of the age difference, had caught up with his school grade. It was inevitable that she became the good child in the home and was held up to him as a model. This hatred was further expressed by his feeling that women could do him harm. He held a woman responsible in each instance that he was caught stealing. In the language of the detective stories that he was so fond of reading, he said "girls are rats."

Second was his inability to accept his father as an ego-ideal, coupled with his need to find in books, the movies, and in his friends the kind of man whom he admired and whom he strove to emulate. These heroes were powerful males—gangsters who were so clever that they could outwit any detective, detectives who could solve any crime; magicians like Houdini who could escape from impossible situations. He complained that his father did not understand him, made him feel worthless and inferior, and made a sissy out of him by fighting his battles and nagging him about his appearance and his eating habits. The boy showed marked ability in drawing. The father was anxious that he become an artist, and although Ben enjoyed drawing, his conflict with his father often made him throw down his pencil and say that being an artist was a sissy job and he would never draw again.

If we examine the early history of this boy, together with the material that he brought to the analysis, we will learn something in regard to the origin and nature of his conflicts. Let us first take his hatred of women. Ben's mother told us that he was nursed until he was 14 months old and kept on a bottle until 3 or 4 years of age. He refused to give up the bottle and was resistant to the introduction of new foods. She described him as having a feeding problem from a very early age and said that she herself had to feed him the things he did not like until he was 12 years old. Thus, we see that her unconscious ambivalence led her to overindulge his infantile oral demands on the one hand and to violate his oral wishes on the other. There are still many quarrels in the home because of food that Ben refuses to eat. The mother, in discussing his anal training, spoke with satisfaction of the fact that Ben was toilet trained at the age of 6 months. It is significant, however, that he has been constipated ever since.

It becomes clear that, even before he reached the genital level, Ben's experience taught him that his mother was a depriving person who took instinct pleasures away from him Instead of being a predominantly maternal, giving person, his mother was a masculine, demanding one who took away oral and anal gratifications, that is, she castrated him on these levels. This experience was confirmed when he reached the genital level and began his masturbatory activities. He recalls during the treatment that she threatened to take his penis away from him if he continued to play with it.

His fear of castration is expressed during the analysis in various ways. For example, the normal fear that he experienced as a small boy in connection with an abscessed ear continued in the neurotic fantasy of having to undergo a mastoid operation, from which he could not free himself. At the basis of his castration fear lies the idea of the woman as castrator. This is indicated in his repeated statements that he is afraid women will do him harm. He tells us the nature of this harm and the reason he fears women in the following incident that occurred during the analysis. While attending school, he would come to my office with his school books. Instead of putting them aside on a table during the hour, I noticed he always held on to them very tightly. I called his attention to this action and asked him why he did it. He said he was afraid he might forget them. I remarked that it seemed strange he was so afraid of losing the very thing that he most frequently stole from cellars, namely books. He became quite angry at my remark, denied any connection, picked up a pencil, and began to sketch rapidly. When he had finished, he confronted me with a drawing of a woman who was so masculine looking that it was hard to distinguish it from a picture of a man.

Obviously he was saying to me, "You are the masculine woman who wants to take away my books." The woman who deprived him of something was always the masculine woman, as we see from the picture. When his teacher took away a watch charm with which he had been playing during class, he expressed his antagonism by making cartoons of her as an ugly woman with a prominent nose.

During the analysis I observed a connection between feelings of disappointment and deprivation in the transference situation and the occurrences of stealing episodes. He had fantasies about stealing things from my room. On several occasions he stole from the cellar of our building. Ben spoke about his impulses to steal as representing an outlet for feelings that he could not control and that had to be relieved. This, together with the pleasure that was derived from the stealing episodes in terms of the accumulation and discharge of tension, made clear the instinctual nature of the act.

In our discussions regarding masturbation, it became clear that Ben had frequent and strong impulses to masturbate, that often he gave in to them, but that he suffered from a violent fear of the consequences. Not only had his mother threatened him with castration if he masturbated, but Ben also reported that his father had told him he would become sterile if he persisted in this practice. These explicit castration threats, plus the implicit castrating atmosphere, were partially responsible for a regression from the phallic level. But it must be borne in mind that this regression had been prepared for and fortified by the primary oral and anal mother denials that created, as a result, oral and anal fixations. It is significant that the boy had overt homosexual experiences with an African-American in which the man performed fellatio on him. He claimed he got no conscious pleasure from these activities, but said directly that he did it because it kept him from masturbating. It is obvious that he is repressing the pleasure derived from the homosexual act because of fear of his passive, receptive wishes, charged as they are with the castration threat. From the standpoint of ego defense, he expresses in his homosexual activity an attempt to retreat from masturbatory practices in which he had indulged, because of the same fear of castration. On the other hand, the id impulses, fixated as they are at the oral level, are expressed in the fellatio.

Analysis of homosexuality has given us an insight into the structure of this perversion. An inability to tolerate the fact that the woman possesses no penis, because of an overpowering fear of being similarly castrated, leads the homosexual to hold on to the fantasy of the woman with a phallus and, in his sexual activities, to identify with her.

It would be advantageous at this point to examine the material of Ben's analysis from the standpoint of the stealing symptom. It is important that he stole principally from cellars and that he sold the things he stole to a shoemaker with whom he gambled, whom he admired greatly, and who taught him many skills and tricks. His bond to this man was clearly a homosexual one whether it was overtly expressed or not. In his analysis his first stealing fantasies that pertained to the transference—that is, his desire to steal things from my office—were associated with this man. He wanted to bring him the articles that he wanted to steal from me. During this period he spoke contemptuously of women, reiterating his hatred of them. It was also at the time when he was fantasizing about stealing from me, that he expressed the fear of losing his books in my office—an incident that we have already described and attributed to his fear of castration by a masculine woman. Shortly thereafter he actually really stole from the office. This sequence of events would lead to the conclusion that in the act of stealing he does to me that which he is afraid of having done to himself. In other words, by stealing he identifies with his image of me as the masculine depriving woman, which is a transference of his concept of his mother. With his stolen goods he then goes to the man, to enjoy with him the homosexual relationship in which he is again the woman with the phallus. By becoming the woman he can succeed in winning the man away from the woman—the father away from the mother. *Just as the homosexual activity, so also the stealing represents an attempt to retain the concept of the woman as having a penis and to avoid castration by identifying with her.*

We must remember that from the beginning Ben's mother was for him the powerful person who could deprive him of oral and anal satisfactions and who actually did so. When he became aware of the possibility of genital pleasures, he believed that his mother could deprive him of these too. This was confirmed in reality by her threat of castration if he masturbated. In his fantasy he thought of a person who is so powerful that she can deprive him of oral and anal gratifications and of his penis, as well as possessing one herself.

He brought a dream to the analysis at the time of his homosexual relationship with the African-American, which indicates his concept of the woman with the penis. He dreamt he was alone in his house with an African-American maid whom his mother had employed. She approached him and said, "I'm going to show you something." She lifted her dress and exposed the lower part of her body. The maid is identified with the homosexual African-American, and the lower part of her body has the same characteristics, namely, the penis.

He remarked once in an account of his stealing exploits that he is so deft, that once when in a cellar, he succeeded in stealing a radio from under a woman's skirt. Again we see that he is stealing from a woman and that he is stealing something—namely the penis—from the lower part of her body. *The stealing represents an attempt to retrieve from the mother those objects— breast, feces, penis—and the satisfactions that they represent that he feared she had the power to deprive him of and that he wants to steal back. In stealing he identifies with the phallic mother who, he feels, has robbed him.*

In the case of the perversions, for example, overt fetishism, the concept of the phallic mother and the identification with her, is based on the fact that this fantasy represents an attempt by the boy to deny the woman is castrated, thereby escaping the possibility of castration for himself. We would add from our study of the stealing cases that the introjected image of the phallic mother has its origin not only as an attempted solution of the castration complex, but also that the boy's pregenital experience with the mother is already one in which she is felt as depriving and castrating, thereby creating a prototype of the later image of the woman with a penis.

In the case of Ben, the problem of identification was further complicated by the personality of his father and the nature of his relationship with him. His father loved him intensely, but was ambivalent toward him and loved him in a narcissistic, unconsciously homosexual manner. He could not tolerate any expression of aggression on the part of the boy, and his usual method of handling it was to deny its existence. When situations arose that could no longer be denied, he would plead masochistically with Ben on bended knee to behave himself for his father's sake. At times, on the other hand, he could be extremely severe and castrating. This inconsistency in the father's attitude heightened the boy's ambivalent feelings toward him. We know already how Ben's pre-oedipal history predisposed him to feminine identifications. In the analysis of his relationship with his father, he expressed resentment because he did not enjoy the kind of love from him which his mother and sister enjoyed. Rather than be like him, Ben, who was fixated in a pregenital manner on his mother, wanted to be loved by his father as his mother was. Failing to get this he revenged himself on his father by taking this love—by stealing.

We see Ben's stealing therefore as having two determinants in the unconscious: (1) to get back from his mother those gratifications that she deprived him of and (2) to get from his father those satisfactions that he denied him. The stealing is an expression of the wish to retain the bisexual satisfactions to be both the possessor and the recipient of the penis.

In another case of an adolescent boy who stole, we were able to see how this need to retain the image of the mother with a phallus is acted out in transvestite practices. He was found in the bathroom masturbating while dressed in his stepmother's undergarments, thus substantiating Fenichel's (1931) contention that the transvestite conceives of his mother as a woman with a penis, identifies with her in the transvestite act, and unconsciously wishes to receive the love of the father just as she does.

We know that the expression of the bisexual wishes—the desire to be like the man and like the woman—is a normal expression of our bisexual constitution, that it is clearly expressed in the pre-oedipal phase, and that it is only when development has successfully passed the oedipal phase that the sexual wishes that correspond to the anatomic structure predominate.

In the case of Ben and in other cases that we studied, we found the stealing to be an expression of unresolved bisexual wishes. This led us to investigate the nature of the fixations that made the normal development of the Oedipus phase impossible and to determine the reasons for them. The history of each of the boys studied showed disturbances and strong fixations of the oral level. Most of the children suffered oral deprivation from the beginning of life either in terms of a mother who withheld oral satisfactions, or one who expressed oral aggression by forcing the child to eat, or in terms of traumatic physical disturbances that interfered with the normal ingestion and digesting of food. It is significant that in many cases the stealing began in early childhood as a stealing of sweets that were forbidden.

In some cases, the disturbance on the oral level expressed itself in an unwillingness on the part of the child to give up the bottle. George, who was 7 when he came to me for treatment, refused to give up the bottle until he was 4. In stories that he made up in the course of treatment, he identified himself with a little boy whose mother refused to give him bread and jam and milk after school.

It is characteristic of boys who steal that their wishes are insatiable and that they demand immediate satisfaction. This is typical for psychopathological states having a strong oral fixation as their basis and bespeaks the almost exclusive operation of the pleasure principle in these personalities. The degree of anal satisfaction that the stealing symptom represented was directly proportional to the extent to which the personality of the boy with the stealing symptom approached that of the compulsive neurotic character. For example, David, who stole sporadically, was definitely such a type. His mother informed me that his toilet training was very difficult, that he soiled himself until the age of 3 and wet the bed until he was 5 or 6. He was 6 when he came to me and presented no symptoms other than stealing. However, when stealing occurred it was almost invariably connected with obtaining money in order to add to a stamp collection or other objects that he was interested in at the time. Collecting was one or his hobbies—filing was another. We see in these interests evidences of his strong anal character.

Whether the satisfactions derived from stealing were predominantly oral or anal, in either case they were, in part, of a pregenital nature, and the symptom therefore represented an attempt to retrieve such pregenital gratifications of which the patient had been deprived or that had not been successfully relinquished. Fenichel (1931) has made it clear in this connection that the infantile attitude of the kleptomaniac is a reaction to deprivation that says: "If you won't give it to me, I'll take it myself." This attitude is directed primarily against the mother.

In this fixation on a pregenital level, the stealing cases show a strong resemblance to the perversions. Freud indicated that the perversions are the opposite of the neuroses—that those unacceptable instinctual wishes that are repressed in the case of the neuroses are lived out, and the gratification is experienced in the case of the perversions. Whereas it is true that the ego has accepted the satisfaction of the partial instincts to a much greater extent in the case of the perversions, even here the deepest wish is disguised and the satisfactions experienced replace others, namely, those connected with the repressed oedipal wishes. We found the same thing to be true in the case of the stealing symptom. There was actual gratification for these boys in the act of stealing. The stealing, however, represented in its deepest meaning the satisfaction of and defense against wishes that remained unconsclous.

The destiny of the oral and anal phase in these stealing cases was such as to preclude the possibility of a successful outcome of the Oedipus experience. The mother was experienced as the predominantly depriving person. Actually, in all our cases, the mother was either a dominating, masculine woman or an overnarcissistic one. Since the deprivations came primarily from the mother rather than from the father, as is the case where we have a normal development of the Oedipus situation, and since the father was, as a rule, the weak, feminine, masochistic type, the major identifications were made with the mother. In addition to the pre-oedipal fixations, there is the over-development of what is known as the negative Oedipus complex. This implies an unconscious wish on the part of the boy to be loved by his father in the same way as his mother is. We saw in the case of Ben that one of the determinants in the stealing symptom was to steal this love of the father since he could not actually experience it.

An important consideration in regard to the stealing symptom is the role played by the superego. In the case of every symptom, each one of the three parts of the psyche—the id, the ego, and the superego—is involved. Stealing, because of its asocial nature, has been evaluated predominantly from the superego side. An artificial dividing line was drawn between neurotic symptoms and asocial behavior. Asocial behavior was described as an innate personality defect. Such an approach breaks the continuity of our psychological thinking. The asocial behavior, just as the perversions, represents a differing interplay of the same psychic forces that operate in the creation of what we know as the neurotic symptom.

We have shown how the stealer is the victim of a conflict of identifications. It follows therefore that the development of the superego cannot take place normally. We have seen this clearly in the case of Ben. He does not accept his father as an ego-ideal, and because of the nature of his passive homosexual attitude toward him, he does not identify with him, but wants to be loved by him. On the other hand, he attempts to achieve his masculinity by identifying with his mother, who for him is the phallic woman. We know that the superego depends for its normal development on the conflict-free introjection of the parent of the same sex. For stealers, as exemplified by Ben, this is not possible because unconsciously they neither know who possesses the penis nor have they decided whether to be male or female. So that just as their personalities represent a fluctuation of identifications, so the superego, as a precipitate of these identifications, becomes, instead of a more or less stable psychic entity, an oscillating one. This unstable superego does not imply, however, an absence of a sense of guilt. On the contrary, where an identity conflict of such proportions is present, guilt must result from the juxtaposition of opposing wishes. Furthermore, we can characterize the stealing symptom as an autoerotic activity in which the pregenital wishes, as we have already described them, are satisfied by the patient himself without relation to a real love-object. We must expect the presence of guilt wherever such activities are present, since in fantasy every gratification is received from the introjected love-object without the giving of any love in return.

The presence of guilt is confirmed empirically in the cases that we studied. Sometimes this guilt was consciously experienced as such. Most often it was evidenced by a welcoming attitude toward punishment after stealing, by self-reproach for this type of behavior, or by tendencies toward self-debasement and feelings of inferiority.

Up to this point we have described what we have found to be the unconscious content of the stealing symptom and the resultant malfunction of the superego, but we have not yet explained the specific causation of this particular symptom. Why did the cases we studied become neurotic characters, with stealing as an outstanding symptom? When we examined the personalities of the parents of these boys, as well as the kind of relationship between parents and children and between the parents themselves, we found in each case what we have called a psychopathological family situation. This is meant in a psychological and not in a social sense, for the cases that we studied, almost without exception, came from a milieu that was in no sense socially delinquent nor was there real economic stress. A psychopathological family is one in which the parents' personalities are of such a nature that the child is subjected from the beginning of development to trauma so constant and extensive that normal emotional development cannot take place. Among the twelve cases we studied, we were able to differentiate four psychopathological family types. First is the family in which the mother is definitely masculine, in which she assumes the authoritative and dominating role in the family and acts toward the children primarily in the role of the restricting, depriving person. The father in such families is usually a weak, ineffectual person, with strong latent feminine drives that express themselves indirectly in his handling of the boy child. The second type of psychopathological family situation is the one in which the mother is a neurotically narcissistic woman and the father generally is a tyrannical person. The third and fourth type of psychopathological families represent situations in which one of the parents is missing. We had two cases of this type. These families all have one element in common as far as the emotional development of the boy is concerned, namely, that because of deprivations that the boy suffered from the mother, either because of her masculinity, her narcissism, or her absence, or due to the absence of the father, she had to play the role of father as well as that of mother, the deepest and most important identifications took place with her. At the same time the aggressions toward the mother for these deprivations expressed themselves in a revengeful, active *taking* of those things that were not *given*.

In the case of Ben that we have already described, the mother was a narcissistic woman who, if we are to judge by her oral and anal upbringing of Ben, was herself fixated on these levels. The father's relationship to the boy was also a narcissistic one, colored by strong unconscious homosexual impulses. The result was a feminine personality in the boy and a reversal of the passive desire to receive into an active taking. This reversal of a desire to *get* into one to *take* characterizes the stealing. The tendency of the psyche in the face of deprivations is to seek satisfactions in terms of the gratification of the opposite of the original impulse.

The polarity of reactions—the desire to get, and its opposite, the impulse to take—depends for its intensity on the original strength of the instincts. In the cases of stealing, in addition to the psychopathological family situation, we were dealing with individuals whose personalities were burdened with unusually large quantities of instinct need. This burden consequently reduced their capacity to tolerate deprivations and, hand in hand with the family situation, created the soil for the development of the symptom.

Our findings in the crises of twelve boys presenting stealing as a central symptom led to the conclusion that in all cases the unconscious content of the symptom is an attempt to retrieve from the mother those things of which she deprived the boy, namely, oral and anal satisfactions and the possession of the penis. In doing so, the boy identifies himself with his concept of the mother as the phallic woman. In identifying with his mother he expresses a desire to be loved by the father as she is. The symptom is thus an attempt to solve the desire for bisexual gratification. However, it serves not only the gratification of unconscious wishes, but as every symptom, is also a defense against the coming into consciousness of these pregenital wishes. Just as the libidinal wishes fluctuate between the poles, masculine-feminine, so we found the development and organization of the superego to be impaired by the fixation of these boys on the pregenital level, and their inability to successfully complete an identification with the father figure that would have been the normal outcome of the oedipal phase. The failure to form a normal superego is concomitant with the development of stealing as a symptom, but is not the cause of this development. The cause lies in a pregenital fixation on the mother that most probably results from a conspiracy between powerful, constitutional oral and anal instincts and a weak ego, which is the result of the operation of libidinal forces in a psychopathological family constellation.

It is to be hoped that an understanding in fine detail of the etiologic mechanisms responsible for the stealing symptom will serve to orient the future development of psychotherapeutic techniques and enable us to analyze more intelligently the problem of a child from its own family.

32

Hypermotility and Transitory Tic in a Child of Seven

The following case of a 7-year-old girl whom I treated psychoanalytically is of particular interest for an understanding of the complex overdetermined role that motor behavior can play in expressing the emotional conflicts of childhood. It is important for psychologists to understand theoretically the psychodynamics of motor manifestations and ultimately to arrive at some generalizations and norms that may make it possible for parents and teachers to evaluate correctly the motor behavior of the children they are handling. In the case of Alice, there was not only an overtolerance for her hyperactivity in the prekindergarten and kindergarten years but even an admiration of it, which precluded the possibility of its being understood by her parents or teachers as the expression of neurotic conflict. Only when the demands of reality were sterner and her behavior, by contrast, became more than ever crass, unadapted to, and interfering with the activities of a normal school group did it become clear that Alice was expressing in her bodily movements, and in the animal-like vocal sounds that she made, unresolved emotional problems.

At the time that she entered analysis, Alice, an attractive, physically well-developed child of high normal intelligence, was a great burden to her teacher. She was not quite 7 and attended the first grade in a progressive school in the city. She had moved recently from a quiet, country town where she had been accustomed to a small outdoor play group with practically no restrictions of her motor activity, so that the existing school situation, with its larger classes and more formal atmosphere, represented, together with all the other changes in her external living conditions, a new and threatening situation. She reacted largely with uncontrollable, asocial motor behavior—sometimes with depressive moods, unhappiness, crying, and a clinging to her mother.

The school day always started badly. Alice went to school in a taxicab with a group of other children from her neighborhood—most of them older than she—who teased her unmercifully. On arriving at school, Alice got out of the cab on all fours and entered the school building barking like a dog. Then the ceaseless bodily activity in the classroom would begin. She walked on tables and chairs, climbed on window ledges, and crawled under desks and into corners. Her motor activity was accompanied by hilarity that infected the other children in the class, so that often there were parades of children walking across work tables or benches. Not only was Alice's behavior uncontrollable, for she did not submit to the authority of the teacher, but also the entire classroom situation got out of hand. It was at this point that the child was referred to me for analytic treatment.

During almost an entire year Alice's analysis took place in pantomime. This intelligent 7-year-old girl related practically nothing in words—nor was hers an "acting-out" of the conscious "let's pretend" variety. The body musculature, whether through the use of the large muscles or those involved in the production of sound (non-representational), was the exclusive organ of expression. Her body movements had an infantile, unorganized, repetitious, purely instinctual character. The movements had the character of symptoms in that they represented the motoric carrying out of some unconscious wish, much as a dream is the realization of unconscious wishes largely in terms of visual and verbal imagery, as well as the defense against the fulfillment of the wish. The problem of the analysis was to understand the language of this motor conduct and to make it conscious to the child.

It is worth noting that in the first two analytic sessions this otherwise violent and impulsive child displayed an overcompensated politeness, a studied reticence, and a compulsive care of the objects in my office. Her mother reported that Alice's behavior in company was equally polite, that she had the reputation of being a "perfect lady," and that her actions were in sharp contrast to the boisterous tomboyish child they knew at home.

Early in the analysis it became clear that the impulsions were set in motion by the least postponement of gratification. If Alice had to wait for even a short time in the waiting room, she was unable to tolerate the tension, the psychic content of which had many aspects. She reacted by shouting, whistling, making loud animal noises, bouncing on cushions, or sliding on the arms of chairs. Waiting meant that I was devoting my attention to someone else, that I was depriving her of time, that the pathway between her wish—for example, to play with the toys or to get some candy—and its fulfillment was not direct and immediate. She knew that such behavior in the waiting room was unacceptable, that it was disturbing to the work with other patients. Her persistent use of her hypermotility in this situation represented therefore not only a release of tension and gratification through movement but also an aggressive act directed at me. Sometimes her aggression was verbalized in a compulsive preoccupation with the clock and arguing about time, with a minute spent figuring out exactly how many minutes I owed her. Incidentally, Alice, whose reading was much retarded for her age level and intelligence, was very good at figures. The more aggressive her attitude, the more her motor behavior changed from pure impulsion and approached the vocal or facial tic. She would come into the room grunting, barking, or grimacing at me.

Jealousy of other children played an important role in Alice's emotional life. Her only sibling was a brother four years her senior. In the course of her analysis an extremely ambivalent attitude toward him was disclosed. At times she was loving and admiring, almost worshipful toward him. She followed him like a shadow and attempted to emulate him. Since, for obvious reasons of age and sex differences, she was unable to copy her brother's performances, she picked out and distorted some of the less attractive aspects of his behavior. Her frustration in not being able to be like her brother resulted in hostility, which was expressed less in relation to him than in contacts with other children. She would, either through her bizarre appearance and bodily movements or through her grimaces and vocal mannerisms, provoke children into teasing her much as her brother did, and she would then react aggressively with increased motor expression, which finally became so intolerable to either adults or children in the situation that she called down on her head the wished-for punishment. This pattern was repeated over and over again in the analysis. Whether it was a child or adult whose analytic hour followed hers, she would refuse to go when her time was up. She never expressed this refusal in words, but would throw herself on the floor, wave her arms and legs about like an infant, and make grunting sounds, often attempting in addition to expose her genitalia and masturbate simultaneously. She was completely unreachable through any attempt to reason with her at such times, but would react aggressively, either violently throwing cushions around or dropping to the center of the floor like an inert mass and refusing to move. It was sometimes necessary literally to drag the child from my room in order to get her out.

The understanding of this behavior as an unadmitted jealousy reaction, an unwillingness to share me with anyone else, a desire to possess the mother person exclusively herself, was the first big step in the analysis. It brought with it a diminution of the impulsive behavior, but temporarily, at least, a definite facial tic, which consisted of a twisting and drawing up of the mouth to one side of the face. The development of this tic was coincident with a decidedly better adjustment at school, the beginning of a successful learning experience, and the first meaningful verbal expressions in the analysis.

It is significant for an understanding of the meaning of motor expression that the tic, which represents, as do all true neurotic symptoms, a compromise solution for the ego between the impulse and the demands of the superego, should have partially replaced the impulsions when Alice was able through analysis to accept as inevitable the demands of reality, both in school and in the analysis, and to make some more or less successful adjustments to them. Significantly enough, her behavior at home during this period became much more difficult than it had been hitherto. She displayed there the same impulsive, uncontrolled hypermotility that had previously characterized her behavior at school and in the analysis. It was necessary for her parents to retrace their steps in upbringing and to place restrictions on unacceptable motor expressions that they had tolerated too long previously.

Alice's impulsive use of motor activity, her barkings and gruntings were an expression of frustration in relation to the problem of jealousy. It soon became clear that other frustrations also caused this behavior. For a child of 7, Alice made at the beginning of her analysis an extremely limited use of materials. She refused to draw or color or to make things of clay. Gradually it became clear that the main reason for this refusal lay in the feeling that she could not do it as well as I could. She had set a standard of perfection for herself that she could not meet. On a deeper level the relationship with her older brother was certainly the determining factor in the creation of this attitude. She could neither do what he did nor be what he was, namely, a boy. Therefore, she felt utterly worthless and ready to give up in defiance. Through her emotional conflict, integration of the motility function was impaired, and her performance ability was lagging far behind the unorganized motor function. This lag in turn added to the impatience and emotional dissatisfaction of the child. Her attitude was one that said, "There is no use in doing anything." As a result there was an actual retardation in the performance function of her ego, which secondarily acted as a cause of frustration, the primary frustration in this instance being the denial of her wish to become a boy. Occasionally she would attempt to draw something, would become discouraged in the attempt, would scribble over the entire page, would finally destroy the entire paper, and would then find expression in the completely uncontrollable motor discharge that has already been described as so characteristic of her. It is conceivable that these bodily expressions afforded not only gratification and a release of hostile impulses but that they also represented magic gestures whose unconscious purpose it was to bring about the fulfillment of the unconscious wishes (to be in her brother's place) that were thwarted through the inability of the performance function of the ego to bring about their realization.

As the analysis progressed, she achieved some insight into this mechanism and began more actively to make use of paints and crayons as a means of expressing her thoughts and fantasies. One day she herself volunteered the following: "I know why I wouldn't draw or color before. I was jealous because you could do it so much better." She began to be willing to accept her role with its normal limitations and possibilities as it really was. Interestingly enough, however, one of her first drawings was of a house that was tall and tower-like in structure, had no doors or windows, but only a chimney on top with some smoke coming out. It seemed quite obviously a penis symbol and represented one of the first attempts to express and symbolize the unrealizable unconscious wishes through the performance activity ego, rather than merely to discharge the energies arising from such wishes and their frustrations through diffuse, impulsive hypermotility or through the compromise formation of the symptomatic tic.

There was a very important aspect of Alice's behavior in the analysis that might perhaps be called the counterpart of the energy discharge through hypermotility. Sometimes she responded to difficulties with authority—for example, being scolded by her teacher for misconduct—or to unhappy experiences with other children in play with a mixture of depression and sullen contrariness that was acted out in her motor behavior. I always knew when she had experienced some difficulty or disappointment during the day by the manner in which she came into my room. First of all, in appearance she looked as if she were portraying a disreputable, delinquent character. Her hands were grimy, her face streaked with dirt, her hair disheveled and streaming over her eyes, her shoelaces untied, a button torn from her dress, and her belt trailing behind her. She was a frightening sight, and actually several adult patients who met her in the waiting room at such times, even those who had had experience with children, remarked that they were afraid of her, that they would not know how to handle such a child, that she was like a little beast. She thumped her way from the waiting room into my office with slow, heavy, partially uncoordinated movements as if she were intoxicated and threw herself in a heap on the couch.

Instead of throwing herself about, as was her habit in her hyperactive states, she curled into a fetal position and lay still, sucking her thumb. Often she crawled into a corner of the room, preferably under some furniture or sometimes even under the couch, and would remain in a knee-chest position for long intervals, almost always sucking her thumb. When she emerged she literally unfolded as if she were representing the act of birth. Taking a cue from *Alice in Wonderland*, she referred to this behavior, which assumed during phases of the analysis a repetitive and ritualistic character, as going "down the rabbit hole." Like Alice in the story, she returned to a land where many wishes could be magically gratified without the efforts of the conscious ego. Any attempt to make contact with the child, to bring her back to the world of reality as it existed for her actual age level, met with a most aggressive petulance—a grunting of negative sounds and a violent shaking of the head.

The quietest and most integrated periods of Alice's analysis followed long vacations during which she spent much more than the usual amount of time with her mother. She would return, communicative and happy, without the usual symptoms of hyperactivity or vocal sounds, a typical little girl of 7. She enjoyed most playing with dolls during these times, and always the game was "tea party," in the course of which elaborate care was taken to bathe and dress the dolls for the tea party. When the actual party took place, however, Alice often forgot her mother role, failing to pretend to feed her dolls, and identified completely with her doll children, greedily eating all the food herself.

Much of Alice's motor behavior was of a decidedly erotic character, not only in the sense that the bodily movements as such were erogenized, but in that she literally masturbated while tossing or throwing her body around and while performing acrobatic feats; in addition, many of the movements were consciously intended to stimulate erotic sensations of the genital parts. She would straddle the arm of a chair, for example, and rub her body back and forth along it. She was extremely active in attempting to draw adults into her sexual play. She liked to sit on people's laps, fondle collars or beads, rub her hands along one's legs, or stroke one's hair. This was characteristic of her behavior in the analysis and also at school with her teacher (she had been transferred from her original school situation to one in which she was fond of the teacher). Her teacher reported a great deal of sexual play in the school situation. Several little girls, of whom Alice was one, were unable to sit still in the classroom. They would run out and congregate in the bathroom, where they indulged in "secret games." For some time this behavior was so persistent that it presented an acute problem to the teacher.

Certainly, Alice gave the impression of an oversexed child. Her actively seductive behavior, plus the fact that it was characteristic for her to turn experiences that for her were passive into ones in which she played the active role, would lead one to conclude that she had experienced some form of sexual seduction—perhaps at the hands of her brother—as a much younger child.

The psychic picture that Alice presents and that expresses itself in hypermotility and in vocal and facial mannerisms of a transitory nature is that of a child whose ego has been overwhelmed by a flood of sexual as well as aggressive impulses. The ego has not proven strong enough to cope with the violence of the impulses themselves nor with the frustrations that must inevitably follow in their wake, and the kinetic function of the ego—motility—has been chosen as the organ for the discharge of the energies deriving from these unconscious sources. The fact that the motor apparatus became the seat of the symptom picture is an expression of the infantile character of the personality and its strongly regressive tendency. Alice is a child who remained fixated at a primitive level of ego organization at which all impulses were most easily expressed through unorganized, diffuse motor discharge. The ego was not strong enough to have attained even a 7-year-old level of control against indiscriminate motor gratification. The motor function of the ego in itself is not integrated, in that the expressive motor function (gestures—affectomotility) predominates, whereas the performance and locomotor functions lag far behind.

This psychic picture might be accounted for in two ways in the case of Alice: first, she is a child who probably is constitutionally burdened by an excessive motor drive, and second her exaggerated affectomotility was mistaken for the expression of free, emotional creativity and physical

prowess by her parents, becoming for them a source of narcissistic pleasure and finding therefore special approbation in their eyes. As a result
they failed to restrict the motor expressions sufficiently during the early
years when the ego should normally begin to exercise controls over indiscriminate motor discharge. The motor organization of the child thus became libidinally overcathected and readily became the point of anchorage
for the expression of neurotic conflict.

Alice's motor behavior became an expression of inner conflict for her
and was perceived as a symptom by her environment when increasing repres-
sive influences appeared in the reality situation. Up to the age of 5½ she is
described as a very active, happy child, well liked by both children and adults.
The only clues, from any material I was able to obtain, to the coming difficulties were contained in a statement by Alice's play group teacher that
she noticed that occasionally there was a peculiar moodiness and an un-
accountable contrariness in the child's behavior that were in contradiction
to her total personality picture. At the age of about 5½, when most likely
she was at the height of her oedipal attitudes and the problem of the consolidation of the identification processes was of the utmost importance, three
things happened in her life that were inevitably traumatic in their effect.
The family moved from their country home, where Alice had enjoyed an
extremely free life, with space and grounds giving much opportunity for
physical play, to a city apartment; simultaneously her brother was sent away
to a boarding school. Shortly thereafter she entered a school situation that
was not only new but that also imposed restrictions on physical outlets and
made demands in terms of adjustment to routines and to a large class group.
The previously available avenues for the discharge of emotional energies—
namely, through affectomotility—were partially cut off, and the resultant
conflict expressed itself in a flooding of the motor apparatus, manifested
in hypermotility and a transitory tic.

The diffuse character of the motor behavior, its ceaselessness, and
variety of form have their analogy in the amorphous character of the child's
ego and are inextricably bound up with problems of identification. It is as
if Alice had attempted to solve the problem of identification by the magic
of gesture—of imitation. The language of her motor behavior tells us all the
things she would like to be: a dog, a baby, a boy like her brother. That she
found no other way of expressing these wishes or of getting beyond them
to a successful identification with her mother is a measure of the primitivity
of her ego, its weakness in relation to the force of the instinctual drives,
and of the overcathexis of the motor apparatus.

33

Conversations with Esther Menaker

The following interview, comprising three conversations between Esther Menaker and Claude Barbre, took place in January 1994. It was conducted over a period of several weeks at Dr. Menaker's office in New York City.

B: In Chapter 30, *Being Seventy-Five,* you describe yourself sharing your antiquity with others in what you refer to as the "tertiary narcissism" of old age. At 85 is it still tertiary?

M: Still sharing my antiquity! [Laughs.] At 85 I've become increasingly aware that I often feel more open to experiences, and this has helped me realize more acutely that in allowing things to happen, going with the moments, one can use the opportunities that are, in turn, allowed by what occurs. A chaotic moment has more opportunity than I think I realized earlier on. Ideas are not just cognitive; there is a creative way in which they are born. In a way this is a nod to Jung's understanding of synchronicity: an awareness of more vital correspondences. One becomes more open to this kind of presence. I think I share this feeling with many others; by the time you get to be 85, you think, "What more can happen?" and "What's to lose?" There's nothing to lose but to live; you don't know how many years are left. The result is that you live more freely without—with much less—anxiety, certainly about how people are going to react, whether people

are going to like or not like what you are about. I have found that
even as I experience the anxieties of some loss of strength and physical agility there surges a kind of vigorousness, given you by the permission age gives: you let yourself be more forceful at times, even
more definitive in what you might say.

B: You remark that these anxieties are fundamentally the same as those
of childhood—fear of loss and separation and fear of autonomy or
individuation, and yet you suggest that your life work has helped you
know and accept anxiety as a natural aspect of life, the acceptance of
death as a natural aspect of life?

M: I think that one may deny the reality of death, which helps one transcend that reality as we live; yet, in order to master the feelings associated with the awareness of death, to deny those feelings hinders
that transcendence. There is a kind of acceptance of death even as
one continues as if it didn't exist. Otto Rank resonates with this experience when he speaks of "the volitional affirmation of the obligatory"—
a wonderful phrase. The obligation here is death. For Rank himself
this acceptance of death effected a "zest for life" and creative will.
From this experience so much of his work evolved. I remember when
I was a child—speaking of childhood—of 6 or 7. I recall realizing that
there was no way out of life except death. I remember trying to figure out ways in which one could avoid it—I was always a problem
solver! [Laughs.] Realizing there was no solution, no avoiding it, this
led me to allow the obligatory, understood then as solution. Perhaps
allowing is the stage before affirming.

B: Do you think that your work, in part, explores the conflicts associated with allowing and affirming new ideas?

M: I think I have been sensitive to this issue since I was quite young.
My mother was an outspoken suffragist, and I no doubt identified
with some of her willingness to question unchallenged values. My
family included several scientists, one of whom was my father. The
spirit of inquiry and investigation fueled a quizzical nature. . . . Although I am thinking of a story once told to me by my father about
living in Russia: a chicken they were planning to eat jumped up on
the table and drank from a pitcher of milk, and thus my father was
sent to the rabbi to learn if it was all right to eat the chicken since it
drank from the milk, if the chicken was still kosher. [Laughs] I'm
not sure how scientific that was! Nevertheless (laughs), my father later
became a research scientist and taught me a great deal about scien-

tific inquiry, not to mention the influence of culture! Later, in the course of my psychoanalytic training, I tended to be more skeptical and more critical than my husband Bill—a fact that did not particularly endear me to the Vienna psychoanalytic establishment. Often my unwelcome questions, which appeared as question marks in the margin of the Freud papers that I was reading, also came out in my analysis with Anna Freud as doubts about the validity of certain theoretical tenets. Did women, for example, always and inevitably experience penis envy in the course of development? Was it always resistance to the analyst if one failed to agree with the analyst's interpretation? Was intensity of emotion inevitably a defensive maneuver to disguise the opposite feeling? These were some of my thoughts that found expression in the "free associations" of my analysis.

B: An ongoing interrogative spirit—and these questions led to observations, as you chronicle in *Appointment in Vienna* (Menaker 1989).

M: Once the psychoanalytic movement had solidified, new ideas were often viewed as dissident. For instance, early in my analytic work in the 1930s I was struck by the impact that the set-up of the psychoanalytic situation itself had upon the psychology of the patient. For example, the position on the couch, the relative silence of the analyst, the fact that the time and duration of the session were largely dictated by the analyst helped reinforce a hierarchical situation in which the analyst could easily become an unquestioned authority, thus catapulting the patient into the dependent, submissive position of early childhood. Around 1942 I wrote about this as a problem in structuring a therapeutic milieu in a paper entitled "The Masochistic Factor in the Psychoanalytic Situation." This was the beginning of the expression of my interest in issues concerning the position of the self in relation to the "other" as these became manifest in the interactions that occurred in the psychoanalytic exchange between two individuals. In the therapeutic situation, it is important, I concluded, to affirm a patient's growth potential by creating an atmosphere of utmost equality in the human sense, thereby nurturing his or her self-esteem. To diminish self-esteem by placing the entire emphasis on the patient's unsuccessful attempt to resolve conflict between unconscious impulses and superego censure was not therapeutic, I reasoned. Again, affirmation of the person's growth potential by allowing an ambience of mutuality.

B: The book you wrote with your husband Bill—*Ego in Evolution* (Menaker 1965)—developed this thinking in that you emphasize that the ego is primary?

M: At the time we wrote the book, and that was thirty years ago when the idea was born—an idea anathema to analysts at that time—that the ego is primary, as you mention, that it strives to fulfill its potential, that growth and the wish for growth are what fuels, directs, awakens the human being to life, to balance, that the ego is not exclusively or by any means primarily sexual as described in Freudian thinking of the time, this kind of thinking was a departure from many of my colleagues at the time. I think that even today there are too few psychologists and analysts who would see the motivating force in human life as the need and wish of the self to fulfill itself and to grow. I think that Kohut's thinking came closest to that area we explored then, and it is in that sense primarily that I think *Ego in Evolution* was at its inception ahead of its time . . . and after all, self psychology and Kohut's writing are still being heavily disputed in analytic circles, so I don't think the more orthodox psychoanalytic world is ready to receive it today.

B: In the book there is a keen acknowledgment of the influence of social forces on the psychological development of the individual.

M: And on the structure and character of groups. This influence has enlarged the framework within which human beings are being understood, so that a concept of psychosocial evolution is no longer so alien. We argue that the structuring of the self—which we have termed "ego" in our work—this structuring to ever higher levels of integration and complexity as it interacts with the environment is more readily perceived as the creative expression of the evolution of life itself.

B: You posit such an evolutionary movement within the structure of personality?

M: Yes. Viewing as we did such evolutionary movement within the structure of personality seems to gain credence from the most recent work in physics in which the exclusive universality of the Second Law of Thermodynamics has been challenged by the discovery of new structures that function locally as "open systems" and are not subject to increases in entropy. For indeed, if there are open systems within the non-living world that do not "run down" but evolve to greater complexity, then it becomes more plausible to assume that human personality, which exists within an "open system" of life itself, is also constantly evolving.

B: Is this "open system" of life a model for psychological evolution in contrast to what you consider a more closed system found in psychoanalytic theory?

M: Well, since evolutionary theory emphasizes both stability and change in the world of biological organisms as they interact with the environment, we posit the same dichotomy for psychological evolution, yes. This inevitability creates a new framework for processes of individuation, which are no longer understood solely as developmental processes occurring within the limits of the familial experience, but as influenced by changing and evolving social and cultural forces, which indeed affect the very nature of the family itself.

B: The therapeutic task then is to facilitate the growth and evolution of the individual in a way more consistent with such a philosophy?

M: It is important to be aware of the fact that changing values and social change, as well as psychological change, exist in a highly complex interactional system. We cannot always know which is cause, which effect, for changing values effect social change and vice versa; and both interact with psychological changes in personality. Yet the entire dynamic syndrome expresses the essential nature of humankind's psychosocial evolution. So, to address your question, an opportunity for the observation of this process as it is revealed in depth is offered us in the psychotherapeutic situation. We are able to study a kind of comparative psychopathology in which either our own experience or a study of the classic cases of the past, or both, give us a basis for drawing conclusions regarding changes in personality and its malfunction.

B: The cultural influences are given a more prominent place in your work.

M: Certainly the tenets of Freudian theory were derived from observations made during the late Victorian period of patients of middle-class origin presenting definite symptomatology. It was an historic period dominated largely by sexual repression, especially for women, by a patriarchal family structure, and by a sense of individual responsibility for conduct. The value system of the individual, as an outcome of social inheritance, resided in the superego; the ego-ideal, as we know from its secondary place in Freud's writing, played a relatively minor role in the creation of conflict. The ego's strength was

sapped and neurotic symptomatology was created by the conflict between instinctual impulses and superego prohibitions, as well as by
its own defensive operations. Now, current social changes and corresponding changes in values have created new forms of conflict. For
example, greater sexual permissiveness, a more egalitarian relationship between the sexes, a change in life goals and a radically different attitude to authority are not only the hallmarks of progress but
also the causes of specific imbalances in the formation of personality.

B: These new forms of conflict affect the emergence of our personalities within an evolutionary continuum, what you speak of as a "psychosocial ecology"?

M: I speak of a "psychosocial ecology" in which the introduction of new
elements into the psychosocial environment disturbs individual and
societal balance. . . . In the case of the individual imbalances that we
observe in psychoanalytic treatment, the disturbance lies, in a very
general sense, in the area of a definition of self. Change in the societal authority system has shifted the formation of ego from processes
that in the past depended primarily on individual identifications to
ones that seem to define the self through alignment with ideologies.
Our patients are often those who fall between these two processes.
This has frequently resulted in a loss of individual centeredness, of a
sense of individual responsibility, and an ego structure dependent upon
a collective ideology for its existence. In terms of psychopathology this
has meant the sacrifice of autonomy to a heightening of narcissistic
cathexis, with a consequent impoverishment of object relationships.

B: This dependency upon a collective ideology when it leads to a loss of
individual centeredness, as you say, is reminiscent of Winnicott's
definition of "false self" organization—a compliance rather than an
experience of aliveness.

M: That characterizes one dynamic. I explored the presence of masochism in this loss of self, in that the individual may become subser-
vient to an image provided by familial and social imperatives, to the
point that he or she submits to a referential, provisional self rather
than a more cohesive self. This issue of masochism continues to interest me.

B: Do you think that your exploration of masochism in regard to cultural and familial influences anticipated the current focus on the effect these influences have on the development of the self?

M: I think our work concerning masochism and the development of the self was more than a question of emphasis. We continued to develop these areas in a larger context.

B: Could you say what influenced the development of these ideas you mention?

M: *Ego in Evolution* and my papers on masochism? Certainly there are many emotional and intellectual factors. I'll tell you what immediately comes to mind. In a way I think I could say that *Ego in Evolution* was born out of a conflict of values. Years ago I went to a meeting on ethology and psychoanalysis where I first met Winnicott, Sutherland, Weigert, and others, and at this meeting I was amazed to learn that I had been mentioned at the conference as having written a pioneering paper in the field! Well, you might imagine my excitement. I was both surprised and elated. I ran into Willie Hoffer, an analyst I had worked with some years before, and told him of my experience. He was quite detached and disinterested—in a way an extreme form, I think now, of his past focus on my children and not on my professional life, the life of my career. He did not acknowledge, in the slightest, anything I said to him and the experience so infused me with frustration that I grew creative [laughs]—I believe this might be a character trait. As long as I can remember, when I get angry, my mind tends to become more lucid rather than muddled! I remember soon after that I met Bill coming out of the meeting with Anna Freud, and I told him of my interest in planning a book! A week later we were in northern Italy, sitting on a mountainside, and Bill and I began talking about what later became *Ego in Evolution*.

B: A creative will sparked from a counter-will!

M: Your reference to Rank is indeed relevant, and Rank was and continues to be an important influence on my writing and work. When you mention "creative will" I am reminded of earlier influences on my creativity. I recall clearly that I wanted to write a book when I was 12! I didn't have the vaguest notion about what I wanted to write—it was more the *idea* of writing a book.

B: Speaking of Rank: when you say " the idea of a book" I hear echoes of Rank's remark that before one can create one must appoint him- or herself an artist. You saw yourself as a writer.

M: Yes, that's true . . . but the influence of another supports the creative endeavor. For me that support was my father who encouraged me—I think he set the idea in motion. I was in eighth grade in junior

high school, the first junior high in the eastern part of the country—
an experimental school. We were assigned in English to do a compo-
sition of our choice. You know, when you have that kind of freedom
it can be difficult to find your direction. I remember being a bit upset
with what to do, what to write. I talked about it at home, and my
father said he would help me; although English was not his first language, he dictated a quite fanciful story, more a picturing of a wonderful landscape to me, and of a child dreaming or meditating or
fantasizing in this landscape with the clouds and the wind and the
birds—it was all very beautiful. He gave me a start, a beginning, and
I continued the story from his initiatives.

B: A kind of Squiggle game to prompt your own play!

M: That's right! But I felt a bit strange at first because it wasn't entirely
my work. But then I thought, what a wonderful thing he did. Even if
it side-stepped the perceived rules, it began, through encouragement
and initiative, my writing, and the subsequent idea of writing a book—
and it wasn't so much emulation, but inspiration, a spark toward
creating.

B: The feeling of a father creating beautiful pictures, showing how one
might have access to the experience—a true selfobject phenomenon,
don't you think, a function you have often written about?

M: Absolutely, a selfobject illustration. There were identifications on
many levels, with his poetic sensitivity, especially his love of nature.
You must realize that my father read from Pushkin's poetry Sunday
mornings at breakfast the way a religious person would read the Bible.
In fact, I still have that volume from which he read, though I'm still
working on my Russian alphabet! So, yes, many identifications with
my father.

B: Since you mention identification and selfobject function together,
do you differentiate between the two terms?

M: Identification to me means internalization of the selfobject—not as a
defense as Freud so often uses the concept—but as a function that
leads to self building, as a part of the growth experience, and I think
that's what my father did. It was an experience of inspiring, and in
the very act, and I would add, in the impulse that produced the act
on his part, there is expressed a tremendous amount of trust and faith
that I could and would create in turn, that I could do it if he showed
me the way.

B: What you say intimates your analytic perspective: your writings articulate the importance of communicating to the analysand a trust and faith that he or she can incorporate toward creative autonomy.

M: I think that's true. Autonomy is one kind of emphasis, creativity that is the expressiveness of the self is another, and in my father's interaction with me as I described it in the story, he inspired both.

B: In your memoirs you mention that Theodore Reik encouraged you to write.

M: In a way he did. My first contact with him was around a paper I had written, and he made it very clear to me that in the paper I showed to him I had two papers in one, and he helped me lift one from the other. One was "Masochism—A Defense Reaction of the Ego" (1943) and the other embedded in that one and separated out was "The Fate of Mario's Masochism"—a story taken from Thomas Mann's tale of the effect of a hypnotist on this particular individual and even the audience, which inspired me to write the paper. I had already begun to write, but he helped me bring my writing to clarity, guided me in the writing. He was the first analyst who was encouraging to me on that level.

B: Again a kind of affirmation that helped separate out your own voice.

M: Through the interaction and affirmation of another. . . . Yes.

B: You mentioned earlier Willi Hoffer's emphasis on your children and not your career. Was that a prevalent attitude you encountered after all your training in Vienna?

M: When I was wondering if perhaps *allowing* is the stage before *affirming*, I thought of a story then, and your question makes me think of it now. I remember Edith Jacobson saying to me: "The trouble with you is that you don't have enough *resignation.*" [Laughs].

B: Meaning?

M: A story as response. I learned to drive a car late in life mostly because of practical reasons: we didn't have a car at the age I could have learned to drive. Anyway, I was in my forties by the time I learned to drive. When I took the first driving test, it was the first time in my life that I failed a test! Well, I was thrown by this. Since Edith was a confidant, I called her and said how miserable I was about this failure [laughs]. She said,"Well, after all, driving a car is a masculine thing." Imagine! It sounds funny today. And so she concluded that my misery "must have to do with [the fact that] you haven't made peace with the fact that you are a woman." She was quite serious. Recalling this exchange, I think she was talking about renunciation in the Freudian sense: women must make peace with the fact that they can have a child instead of a penis and so on—renunciation. Hoffer's focus on my children was not out of interest, but in the spirit of pedagogy. Both of these stories echo the Freudian theories of the psychology of women that I encountered. . . . Stemming from the exclusively male orientation of that time, women were universally thought to suffer from penis envy as an inevitable part of their development, to have a lesser degree of intelligence than men, to possess an inferior superego, and to be generally unstable if not hysterical. This led to attitudes that are now a matter of record. I remember an episode that took place in my student days in Vienna. I was pregnant with my first child, and while somewhat frightened at the prospect of childbirth, I was extremely happy in the anticipation of motherhood and very far from complaining about my role as a woman. Yet, somehow seemingly out of the blue the following remark came from my analyst: "I don't know what women are complaining about, when they complain about being women. They have on the inside what men have on the outside!" Please note the anatomical reference, the emphasis on structure rather than function, the concern with what one *has* rather than what one *is*, the exclusive focus on sexuality, the masculine measure of value, of what one should be satisfied with, and the implication that women should not complain because while she is not a man, she does indeed have second best. This list constitutes my criticisms of my analyst's remark, which are echoes of the usual criticisms of Freud's theories and certainly of his theory of feminine psychology.

B: You describe the Freudian theories that inform the psychology of women as a reinforcement of social attitudes.

M: Indeed, and the social attitude that was reinforced mandated an *exclusively* domestic role as the norm for women—hence, Hoffer's focus on my children and Edith's emphasis on renunciation. When this mandate becomes entrenched as an inviolable value and belief system and cannot be adhered to by individual women, much needless suffering, conflict, and guilt are created. Women have always had many roles: from the woman whose baby is on her back as she works in the fields to the contemporary woman who combines her daily work-life with the care of her child when she is at home.

B: What you say again underscores prevalent themes in your writing—that sociological factors meet psychological ones.

M: The task of integrating the masculine and feminine ways of being into a successfully functioning self is a common human task. It is not only a woman's issue. For all human beings, integrating a self-structure is a creative process that is ongoing throughout life. It is based on the internalization of perceptions and of experience—experience with significant individuals and groups in the course of life. It is thus that values and beliefs are absorbed, and attitudes, ways of behaving, and a sense of self develop. I have stayed the course of this theme from early on: if the environment, the societal demands, and strictures of a culture are at too great a variance from individual developmental needs, the process of internalization and therefore of self-structuring is inhibited. Otto Rank's writing explores this reality. Over the many centuries that women have been dominated by men, one must conclude that in general the social environment was not friendly to the growth of the feminine self and to the fulfillment and expressiveness of that self as a separate and total personality. Only recently have we experienced some incremental changes.

B: Along these lines, what changes have you noticed in regard to your work?

M: Let me give you another illustration of the extent to which Freudian analysts, in the early days of psychoanalysis, thought of women, and therefore of their women patients, as individuals who must learn *resignation*—resignation to the fact that they were born female and must accept substitutes for their lack of a penis [see Chapters 22 and 23]. In the late 1940s I was treating a young scientist for certain sexual difficulties—premature ejaculation, occasional impotency, plus generally low self-esteem and profound feelings of insecurity. These difficulties, as one might expect, were reflected in his marriage. His wife, who also had a career in the field of science, expressed the need for some psychotherapeutic help and asked me for a referral. It was a time when many European analysts had come to the United States seeking refuge from the Holocaust, and I was eager to help them establish themselves. I also respected their training. Therefore I referred my patient's wife to a middle-aged female analyst from Berlin whom I had met and who had become part of a small discussion group that we had organized for non-medical analysts. For many months I heard nothing about the patient's progress. Then one day I had occasion to

phone my colleague on another matter and used the opportunity to
ask her how my patient's wife was getting along. "Oh, she's doing
very well," said my colleague. "She has finally resigned herself to
being a woman and accepts the idea of having a child instead of a
penis." I thanked her for the information and withdrew in a state of
shock. Could anyone still seriously believe that a basic and primary
conflict for women was dissatisfaction with her biological role, that
is, with her biological structure? Certainly women—individual women—
might experience dissatisfaction and wish they had been born men.
But such feelings arise out of the social position of women, out of
the strictures of society, out of the fact that until very recently they
were confined to prescribed roles, that they had so little freedom of
choice, and were so limited in the ways they could fulfill their potentialities. The fact that a therapist could impose her psychological
beliefs, her values, her view of life upon a patient so completely as to
make her give up her career and devote herself entirely to the domestic scene was shocking indeed. Unfortunately, the ultimate outcome of this situation was not good, for no one can live successfully
with a false self built on the ideology of another individual upon whom
one has become dependent. . . . A more current example: just yester-
day I heard about a young woman who had a nervous breakdown
during the first year of her first child's life, after having given up a
good and interesting job in the business world to devote herself exclusively to the care of her baby. She had been trying, out of guilt and
a sense of obligation, to live by what she perceived to be the dictates
of society rather than by what represented her own wishes and inclinations. Fortunately, her very wise physician suggested that she go
back to her job and arrange for some help with the care of the child.
Certainly, if a woman is discontent with the full-time job of caring for
her child, neither her emotional needs nor those of the child are being well served. When women are clear and definitive about their own
needs and are secure in their ability to love their children as well,
children adapt quite well to the part-time absence and part-time presence of their mothers. It is the quality of the time spent together, rather
than the quantity of time that is important. . . . I think the change in
woman's attitude toward her self, her awareness of her rights and
her expectation that society will provide an opportunity for the exercise of those rights has inevitably changed the psychology of men.
We are therefore in a critical, active, transitional phase of social devel-

opment in which the nature of the tension and the character of interaction between the genders are bound to change.

B: You mention the importance of Rank's work. Will you elaborate?

M: I had been somewhat exposed to Rank's way of thinking at the Pennsylvania School of Social Work long before I was a psychologist. But
Rank's followers and analysands in Philadelphia, Jesse Taft and Vir-
ginia Robinson, taught Rank indirectly by paraphrase and without
necessarily mentioning his name. It is to my late husband Bill that I
owe my exposure to Rank. He had been interested in his writings
when we were in Vienna in the early 1930s. I remember a small incident that occurred one evening when we were attending a class of
Helene Deutsch's that was held in the same building that housed the
Psychoanalytic Press—the publishing house for those psychoanalytic
books that were acceptable to the movement. In an adjacent room
on several tables were displays of available psychoanalytic books, some
recently published, some of an earlier vintage. Bill, who loved to
browse in bookshops, was looking over the books and leafing through
a book of Otto Rank's (published when he was still a member of the
Vienna Psychoanalytic Society) before our class began. Helene Deutsch
happened to walk by. "That's a very bad book," she said in her limited English. Bill bought it and several other Rank books nevertheless, and as a result of his adventurousness and open mind, I own
several of Rank's books in German and I have acquired an abiding
interest in Rank ever since. But you know, even today when I mention Rank to colleagues who are unfamiliar with him, there comes
over their faces a look of uneasiness as if they feel that either they
should know something about his theories or that I should not have
mentioned someone who has been discredited by the psychoanalytic
community!

B: Another kind of resignation?

M: [Laughs.] I suppose . . . but more often than not the uneasiness I
mention is not at all based upon his contributions, which are extraordinary, quite singular.

B: Like Rank you began your training as a Freudian and developed new
ideas from that beginning. Can you say what it is about Rank that
drew you to his work?

M: So many reasons. Rank's own creative impulse shaped his life, and I
suppose I resonate with that immensely. For Rank viewed the human
personality as an open system, capable of growth and change, able to

create itself as well as products expressive of that self and to have an influence on the outcome of the interaction between the self and the environment. In my book on Rank, *Otto Rank: A Rediscovered Legacy* (Menaker 1982), I describe in detail his creative odyssey, his work with Freud, his theoretical development. Certainly there was much good fortune in this beginning; but we should not underestimate the importance of Rank's initiative, of his striving, of what he later came to call "will," for it is his emphasis on the creative will that finally informs his conception of personality and of therapy. And it began with his experience of himself.

B: Freud's theory also emerged in large measure from himself.

M: Yes, specifically from the attempt to understand his own dreams and those of his patients. But in its emphasis on unconscious factors as primary determinants in human behavior, and on repressed sexuality as crucial in the formation of neurotic symptoms, as well as on the superego, Freud's theory reflected the scientific materialism and reductionism of his time. This point of view inevitably influenced the nature of his therapeutic interventions. In the spirit of the Newtonian conception of the universe that prevailed at that time, human behavior and its aberrations were thought to be reducible to their primary elements, and the understanding of the interaction and interrelationship of these elements offered a causal explanation for the particular behavior. As we all know, in his search for causality, Freud discovered the dynamic unconscious. In his work on dreams, on parapraxes, on hysterical symptoms, it became clear to him that there were factors operating in the creation of these phenomena that were not directly observable. Their influence could only be deduced indirectly from their derivatives. If one could, however, make appropriate deductions one could understand in causal terms the otherwise unknowable, that is the unconscious impulse. Since neurotic individuals suffer from impulses that remain unconscious through repression, the task of treatment is to lift the repression and make available to consciousness what was previously unconscious. In order to make this possible, Freud devised the analytic procedure as we know it, with its emphasis on free association and on the interpretation of resistance and of transference. The hope was that the conscious knowledge of the impulse—that is, insight—would do away with the neurotic symptom or change the neurotic character structure. Freudian psychoanalysis is therefore essentially an appeal to rationality in that it seeks the curative factor of therapy in the unearthing of causality, and it assumes that once an individual has understood the reasons for his or her pathology, he or she will relinquish it. Why this should be so lies in a complex theory—Freud's so-called economic theory—involving shifts of energy from unconscious to conscious aspects of the mind. It is as if change is thought of as taking place automatically once certain parts of the mental mechanism have been altered in their nature and in their relationship to one another. The will, or the choice, or the participation of the individual is omitted—at least theoretically—as a factor in the outcome of the therapeutic endeavor. While Freud's emphasis was on understanding and insight, Rank's was on separation of the individual from the maternal matrix, thus freeing the will to express itself creatively. Will, in Rank's sense, is that force through which the individual ego expresses itself. It is inevitably creative in that it forges a unique personality in each instance as the individual seeks to emerge from the oneness of the mother-child relationship.

B: This separation Rank conceptualizes as an act of will?

M: For Rank the emergence of each personality is a creative act, one that is largely determined by the individual will. It is an act, yes, rather than the result of the deterministic operation of environmental forces. This does not mean that Rank disregards the importance of external influences, nor that he eschews the usefulness of insight. But he views the central and lifelong task of each person as that of separation and individuation, and he places the responsibility for the outcomes of this task upon the individual. This distinction from Freud was an important ingredient in the history of psychotherapy and affected my work and writing.

B: You agree with Rank that Freud minimizes the potential of free will.

M: Let's put it this way: I was teaching two chapters recently from the Ernest Jones biography—one chapter on Freud's metapsychology and the other on Freud's view of the mind. Jones begins that last piece by describing Freud's determinism and his absolute nonbelief in free will. It is not that I did not know this—I remember my training well. But when you encounter it again, it is like coming up against a stone wall—the implications of which are quite profound. Not so much in regard to constitution, the drives, the imprint of the familiar influences and culture—the point is that the mind is immutable. There is no free will, you can only change the relationship between the unconscious and the conscious by making the unconscious conscious. Therefore, according to him, you free up the ego as if it had choice, more choice than it had before, because *it knows more* than it did before, because one knows more what one feels; but it is not a template that includes the possibility of moving out of a position and growing into something different, or *taking in anything new* that would facilitate that growth process and further it. . . . And although many contemporary Freudians have amended this thinking, this position is still held officially in Freudian theory, although the models have undergone many changes.

B: In your collected papers you make connections to more current models and schools of thought—for example, Heinz Kohut's writing and areas of self psychology.

M: Yes. Just as Rank influenced my thinking, so Kohut's work has activated a number of papers and presentations. Rank and Kohut were both great thinkers, and both were responding to limitations in classical psychoanalytic theory. However, I do not think Kohut would have been particularly happy with a comparison of his thinking with that of Rank. His acquaintance with Rank stopped, like that of so many others in the psychoanalytic field, with Rank's *The Trauma of Birth* (1914), the reasons being discussed at length in my forthcoming essays on Rank. Thus, Kohut failed to follow the development of Rank's thinking, from a narrow concern with a paradigm for the origin of anxiety in the birth experience to the broadest and deepest understanding of the significance of separation—that is, birth in the metaphorical sense—in human life.

B: Your writings nevertheless explore salient similarities in their attitudes about the self.

M: Both Rank and Kohut thought philosophically about human life: Kohut through his conception of Tragic Man, the individual who suffers from an unfulfilled self, and Guilty Man, the man of structural conflict; Rank through his understanding of the human fear of death against the backdrop of the struggle to create the self, and the consequent wish for immortality to preserve that self. Indeed, there is a breadth and profundity in the existential view of both of these great thinkers that transcends the limitations of a view of human psychology that is bounded by a concern with psychic mechanism and functions or by the methodology of therapeutic procedure. For both, the dimension of certain inevitabilities in the nature of life itself,

which do not necessarily point to the existence of neurosis, informs
their writings. Sometimes they use similar terminology with very
different meanings; sometimes the terms are different for similar
meanings; but it is their ultimate feeling for and respect for the individual self that, in my mind, unites them.

B: When you say "an ultimate feeling for the individual self," are you
suggesting an emphasis on empathic attunement to what is authentic in the individual?

M: Yes, the empathic presence as the vehicle for therapeutic procedure.
Kohut in particular experienced the impossibility as well as the inad-
visability for the analyst of attempting to maintain the classically recommended so-called neutral or objective stance in the relationship
with the patient. Since for Kohut the self is primary, disorders of the
personality—borderline states, for example—must be causally attributed to anomalies or deficiencies in the cohesion of the self-structure,
rather than to conflicts, frustrations, and deprivations surrounding
gratifications of the drives. While the core of the self is given from
birth, the growing self needs selfobjects—initially, the primary care-
takers—with whom to identify and to internalize so that they become
part of the self-structure. one might say that the selfobject is the necessary nourishment upon which the development of the self depends,
much as the body depends on food for maintenance, growth, and
development

B: This sense of nourishment corresponds to Kohut's thinking that empathic attunement is oxygen to the self that animates that growth and
development.

M: Precisely. Simply put, if the food is the wrong kind or is insufficient,
the organism will suffer, wither in body or self. Kohut's clinical observation led him to conclude that deficits in the self-structure are due
to lacks in the empathic relatedness of parents to the growing child,
with the result that the internalization of the images of the parental
figures does not take place adequately. . . . In the therapeutic situation this faulting in the self-structure can only be repaired if the analyst
through his or her empathic stance becomes a selfobject for the patient
to replace a destructive internalized imago or to provide a positive
mirror where none had existed before. The *patient* must be understood, which is quite different from understanding some psychodynamic aspect of his or her personality. This emphasis is away from
the cognitive meaning of "understanding" to "being understood,"

within the context of a relationship in which "the other" (in this case the analyst) understands, by virtue of being human and having sufficiently analogous experiences to convey—however subtly—emotional rapport with the patient. The patient's perception of the analyst's empathy, this emotional rapport, is akin to the mother's positive mirroring which through its affirmative character serves to nourish and maintain the child's (or the patient's) self-esteem. When, in the course of the child's development, it is internalized as an aspect of the mother imago, it becomes part of the structure of the self. The analyst's empathy too is internalized as the approving imago of the therapist, thereby correcting insufficiencies in the self-structure of the patient.

B: This notion of repair emphasizes the present experience of the patient, does it not?

M: Rank and Kohut made explicit that the analytic situation should be used as a present experience for therapeutic purposes and that this experience should not confine itself to the reliving of the past. Rank underscored that this transference, as it appears in the analytic situation, is not primarily sexual, but rather a re-establishment of the biological tie to the mother. The tie suggests separation, a reason Rank spoke of the need to set a terminal date for the ending of treatment as a way of effecting separation from the mother—in effect, of bringing about the psychological birth of an autonomous individual.

B: The termination date was not so much a necessary cessation of the therapy; rather it was understood as effecting an experience of separation.

M: Yes—a point often misunderstood, taken too literally. Rank's emphasis on present experience in therapy anticipates Kohut's goal for his patients, which emphasizes primarily the establishment of an integrated, cohesive self-structure through the use of an analyst as a selfobject. Through the present experience of positive mirroring and of permission to idealize the analyst in the name of nourishing the impoverished and faulty self-structure, the analyst may facilitate the restoration of the patient's self. Initially this goal of reconstruction of the self-structure was a process necessitated by and in the service of curing the narcissistic personality disorder; but as Kohut's thinking evolved, the need for the selfobject in the formation of the personality became generalized and was seen as a normal part of human

development. I might add that the emphasis on the current experience of the therapy as crucial to cure would not make sense were it
not that both Rank and Kohut envisaged cure as possible because of
the almost limitless capacity of the human being to grow.

B: What you say again reiterates the idea of a model of growth that you
contrast with Freud's more deterministic model.

M: Historically psychoanalysis arose out of a need to cure symptoms—
that is, out of pathology, as understood in the medical model. In the
course of its development it moved away from a focus on symptomatology and in certain cases regarded the entire character structure of an individual as symptomatic of personality disorder. But even
in the attempt to change character, the Freudian conception of psychological causality responsible for pathology was defined by the notion
of conflict within the structural model of personality, or earlier on,
between unconscious drives and superego requirements. The ego—
or self—was ground down in the millstone position between these two
powerful forces. Cure—that is, the acquired understanding of the
psychodynamics in terms of past history responsible for the helplessness of the ego to make more adaptive choices—resulted from the
making conscious of these dynamics. Well, to some extent the ego
was thus given back its sense of *agency*—to use a term currently in
vogue—and was no longer exclusively the victim of the repetition compulsion. What is clear in this conception of human psychology is that
the self has no primary inherent capacity to grow, no striving to un-
fold embryologically, to fulfill its given potentialities. After the work
of Rank the first hint of such inherent striving of the primary self
was expressed in the work of Fairbairn when he spoke of the fact
that the ego is first and foremost "object-seeking." But initially it was
Rank who understood the innate striving force of the self to fulfill
itself, to differentiate itself from the selves of others, and to express
its uniqueness. As I have said, he called the striving force "will" and
conceived of neurosis as an inhibition of will, thus emphasizing a
function of the self, whereas Kohut addressed its structure. The inhibition arose through a lack of affirmation of the child's will during
developmental years and could be "cured" in the analytic situation
primarily through the analyst's acceptance of the patient's will. Thus,
Rank did not deny the influence of an individual's past in the formation of the nature of his or her current self, but he saw this influence

not in the Freudian terms of libido deprivation, but in terms of self development, especially as this takes place in the relationship and interaction with the mother.

B: So Rank acknowledges a distinction between the cure of symptoms and the care of the self?

M: Yes—I think the cure for such an inhibition of will as Rank understood it is essentially an assertion of self, and is not only the analytic uncovering of the causes and factors responsible for the inhibition, but the constructive use of the relationship with an affirming and accepting therapist who makes possible, through identification with the therapist, the acceptance of one's own will. Perhaps this is what you suggest is more care than cure, and an important difference of focus. In Kohut's terms one would say that Rank saw clearly the need in the analytic situation for the analyst to offer her- or himself or make her- or himself available as a selfobject. And both Rank and Kohut understood that because the self is in a constant process of growing, of renewing itself and of expressing itself creatively through interaction with others, the need for selfobjects is not confined to the therapeutic situation, but is a need that asserts itself throughout life.

B: You discuss in your papers how the striving to separate, to grow, to create, is always guilt-producing.

M: Yes. Rank took an existential view of the inevitable consequences of the psychological growth process. Psychological birth is a separation from the "other"—originally from the mother, that is, from the very "other" with whom one was once united. The result of psychological birth is the creation of guilt feeling in the "newborn" individual. This strange and seemingly paradoxical consequence of individuation is a unique aspect of Rank's thinking, and it rests on his profound understanding of empathy. The distinctively human capacity to feel for another originates in the mother-child relationship precisely because they were at one time a single entity, both biologically and psychologically. Rank refers to this as an "ethical" relationship. It is in fact the beginning of empathic feeling, for one can envisage the emotions of another individual on the basis of one's own, especially if the "other" was initially oneself. . . . It follows then that the process of separation—that is, the creation of a separate self—is felt as rejection of "the other" because one would have experienced such withdrawal on the part of another individual as rejection of oneself. According to Rank, it is the implication of hostility toward another that is inherent in the separation process that gives rise to guilt. He speaks of individuation, of self-expression as an act of will that inevitably must oppose the will of another in order to be separate. And indeed the early manifestations of individuality in the small child are expressions of what Rank called counter-will. Guilt, then, is experienced for the opposition that heralds one's own separate will, but it is made possible because of the capacity for empathic feeling. So within limits guilt is not a feeling to be shunned; it is an existential reality of human life and a manifestation of the human capacity for relatedness. Rank's conception of conflict is essentially that of the opposition of two wills—one's own, and that of another—and to that extent it is a self phenomenon.

B: What you enumerate reintroduces Kohut's distinction between Guilty Man who is fundamentally based on Freud's views of humanity and the supplemental conception of Tragic Man who suffers because he is unable to fulfill completely the expressive pattern of his nuclear self.

M: For Kohut guilt is a matter of excessive devotion to the pleasure principle and therefore the conflict of drives with the superego. The supplementation you note is consistent with Kohut's theory of the bipolar nature of human personality. Drive theory and self-theory are two vantage points from which to observe humanity and are not in conflict. There is an important difference here between Rank and Kohut in the ways in which they perceive the human dilemma. Kohut, consistent with his Freudian heritage, sees conflict and suffering as largely *intrapsychic*, while Rank is more interpersonal and views conflict as a social phenomenon—a struggle between autonomous self-expression, with its accompanying guilt, and the will and needs of another. This is a rather surprising difference, since Kohut is so clear about the individual's need for a selfobject not only in the course of early development but also throughout life. While acknowledging the interdependence of individuals upon one another for psychological nourishment, Kohut does not derive a theory of conflict from this fact, but rather a theory of deficit in the development of the self. It seems to me that this is because he has not transcended the Freudian notion of guilt as primarily the byproduct of the conflict of forbidden drives and wishes with the superego. Thus, conflict remains intrapsychic in origin, and the function of the selfobject is perceived one-sidedly.

B: Winnicott talks about the "use of the object"—can you talk about guilt from this notion of use in Rank or Kohut's thinking?

M: Well, if we bear in mind Rank's idea that guilt arises in the process of individuation in the context of an exchange of opposing psychic forces between two individuals in which empathy is felt for the so-called opponent, then it is not so difficult to imagine that guilt might also arise when one individual "uses" another as a selfobject. This is not pathological or unethical exploitation of another; it is part of the natural process of nourishing oneself psychologically to achieve optimal self-cohesion and expressiveness. The debt to the other is paid off and the guilt ameliorated through what is given back emotionally to the selfobject. The selfobject may be society at large, or particular aspects of culture, in which case the individual who has been nourished can give back what he or she has taken through creative productivity.

B: As in Winnicott's emphasis on the small child's need to *contribute*, which, in part, is the origin of culture?

M: Yes, one could make that parallel. In Rank's theories the structuring, expression, and assertion of self comprise a creative process accompanied by a certain amount of guilt. Reparation for this act of creating and expressing one's separate self is made by further creative acts for the benefit of others. Kohut does not make this point, but one could envisage a parallel process taking place because of the mandatory function of the selfobject in structuring the self.

B: Kohut was asked once if he thought self psychology was too optimistic. What do you think?

M: Certainly not overly optimistic, but optimistic in the sense that the teachings convey an uncompromising belief in life; it is a psychology, if you will, of faith in life that Freudian thinking and procedure in classic form, much of which still survives today, is not. Freud's determinism led him to think of therapy as a rearrangement of energies within the structure of the psyche. . . . He didn't see the psychic life as growing, but just changing the way in which the energies are distributed in the personality.

B: A recent paper you wrote explores the striving quality of the self in regard to the search for the immortal self.

M: For both Rank and Kohut the unfolding and striving qualities of the self are axiomatic. Rank argues that, in the struggle to separate and become a self, the individual becomes increasingly aware of the fini- tude of this very self—that is, of its mortality. Thus, the wish for im- mortality arises and becomes a driving force in the expressions of the self that will lead to its perpetuation. For most people this is achieved throughout the continuity of the self in succeeding genera- tions. For the creative individuals—artists, scientists, writers—it is achieved through their productive works. For others, perpetuity is acquired through a merging and identifying with some larger entity— an ideology or institution, political or religious, for example—that will outlive the individual self.

B: And Kohut?

M: Kohut does not deal specifically with the issue of immortality, but in his [1982] article, "Introspection, Empathy and the Semi-Circle of Mental Health," he is at pains to point out that the competitive atti- tude, which characterizes the oedipal situation for both father and son as Freud described it, is not the only possible attitude toward the succeeding generation. It is, in fact, not a product of normal devel- opment, but of a disintegrative process. By way of contrast, in the story of Odysseus, the father's productive response when the life of his infant son is threatened is the normal intergenerational response. Kohut does not say so, but it is clear that in saving his son, even at the cost of exposing his own fraudulence to the authorities, Odysseus's need for immortality—for perpetuation of self through his son—is thereby expressed and served.

B: Clearly, in your writing and analytical style you have challenged many psychoanalytic theories, especially the classical stance.

M: Even though I initially wrote according to Freudian theory, my way of working was constantly inclusive of others' forms of wisdom—an imperative I still believe must animate our psychotherapeutic train- ing. When I first encountered Rank's notion that the drives are not what motivates human life, rather, it is the life force, I recognized a vital link to my own creative strivings.

B: The life force that is expressed in the individual as the will?

M: Yes. Rank's understanding of the life force, and the life instinct under- stood by Freud are different in that the life force expresses itself in all of life in the universe. The life force is that which inspires all living things. In human beings this forces expresses itself in the will, as you mention. For Freud we all have the same drives. Not so with

Rank. Each will is not the same either in context or intensity. The life force is not impersonal but an expression of our uniqueness as we encounter it in the interpersonal world.

B: You have witnessed many shifts in psychoanalytic history. Can you address what changes in the field you anticipate and your future interests as well?

M: Therapy will always continue because it has always existed—the presence of one person with another. This work is always full of surprises. One thinks one understood something and finds out that one did not. It is the scientist in me that has kept me interested in the field for so long, and that's partly environmental, but it is also genetic, considering my family's background. But I've always been interested in the spiritual proclivities of human life. The psyche or the mind or human behavior—it is not adequately dealt with without the concept of soul. And it is a struggle and a conflict for me to try to grasp that concept of soul that I believe exists—this spiritual side of the human creature—that I would like to describe in the terms that we know in modern psychology while not getting bogged down in the other polarity, the other extreme, and resort to completely mystical notions about the soul. In other words I think the soul plays a role, and an active role, in phenomena like empathy and love. . . . Eventually, I'd like to be able to say more about that.

References

Alpert, J. L., ed. (1986). *Psychoanalysis and Women*. New York: Analytic Press.

Becker, E. (1973). *The Denial of Death*. New York: Free Press.

Berliner, B. (1940). Libido and reality in masochism. *Psychoanalytic Quarterly* 9:322-323.

—— (1947). On some psychodynamics of masochism. *Psychoanalytic Quarterly* 16:459-471.

Blos, P. (1974). The geneology of the ego-ideal. In *Psychoanalytic Study of the Child* 29:43-88. New Haven, CT: Yale University Press.

Bowlby, J. (1969). *Attachment and Loss*. New York: Basic Books.

Browning, D. (1988). Rethinking homosexuality. *Christian Century* 106:911-916.

Chasseguet-Smirgel, J., ed. (1970). *Female Sexuality*. Ann Arbor, MI: University of Michigan Press.

DeForest, I. (1954). *The Leaven of Love*. New York: Harper.

Delderfield, R. F. (1966). *A Horseman Riding By, vol. I. Long Summer Day*. New York: Ballantine.

Dixon, W. M. (1958). *The Human Situation*. New York: Oxford University Press.

Doi, T. (1981). *The Anatomy of Dependence*. New York: Harper and Row.
—— (1985). *The Anatomy of Self*. Kordanska International.
Erikson, E. (1950). *Childhood and Society*. New York: Norton.
—— (1959). *Identity and the Life Cycle*. New York: International Universities Press.
Fairbairn, W. R. D. (1954). *An Object Relations Theory of Personality*. New York: Basic Books.
Fenichel, O. (1931). Perversionen, Psychosen, Charakterstörugen. *International P.A. Verlag*.
Franks, V. and Burtle, V., eds. (1974). *Women in Therapy*. New York: Brunner/Mazel.
Freud, A. (1946). *The Ego and the Mechanisms of Defense*. New York: International Universities Press.
Freud, S. (1895). The psychotherapy of hysteria. In *Studies on Hysteria*, ed. J. Breuer and S. Freud. New York: Basic Books, 1957.
—— (1912). Dynamics of transference. In *Collected Papers*, vol. II. London: Hogarth.
—— (1914). On narcissism: an introduction. In *Collected Papers*, vol. IV. London: Hogarth.
—— (1915a). Further recommendations in the technique of psycho-analysis: observations on transference-love. In *Collected Papers*, vol. II. London: Hogarth.
—— (1915b). Repression. In *Collected Papers*, vol. IV. London: Hogarth.
—— (1920). The psychogenesis of a case of homosexuality in a woman. In *Collected Papers*, vol. II. London: Hogarth.
—— (1921). Group psychology and the analysis of the ego. *Standard Edition* 18.
—— (1924). The economic problem of masochism. In *Collected Papers*, vol. II. London: Hogarth.
—— (1927). The question of lay analysis. *Standard Edition* 20.
—— (1933). *New Introductory Lectures*. New York: Norton.
—— (1953). Dynamics of the transference. In *Collected Papers*, vol. II. London: Hogarth.
—— (1960). *The Ego and the Id*. New York: Norton.
—— (1961b). Inhibitions, symptoms and anxiety. *Standard Edition* 20.
Guntrip, H. (1964). *Personality Structure and Human Interaction*. New York: International Universities Press.
Hartmann, H. (1950). Comments on the psychoanalytic theory of the ego. *The Psychoanalytic Study of the Child* 5: 74-96.

Herrick, C. J. (1956). *The Evolution of Human Nature*. Austin, TX: University of Texas Press.

Grinstein, A. (1956-1975). *The Index of Psychoanalytic Writings*, 14 vols. New York: International Universities Press.

Greenberg, D. (1988). *The Construction of Homosexuality*. Chicago: University of Chicago Press.

Horney, K. (1937). *The Neurotic Personality of Our Time*. New York: Norton.

—— (1967). *Feminine Psychology*. New York: Norton.

Jacobson, E. (1964). *The Self and the Object World*. New York: International Universities Press.

Jones, E. (1953). *The Life and Work of Sigmund Freud*, vol. 1. New York: Basic Books.

Kohut, H. (1977). *The Restoration of the Self*. New York: International Universities Press.

—— (1982). Introspection, empathy and the semi-circle of mental health. *International Journal of Psycho-Analysis* 63:395-407.

—— (1984). *How Does Analysis Cure?* Chicago: University of Chicago Press.

—— (1985). The continuity of the self. In *Self Psychology and the Humanities*, ed. C. B. Strozier, pp. 232–243. New York: Norton.

Lampl-de Groot, J. (1962). Ego ideal and super ego. In *Psychoanalytic Study of the Child* 17:94-106. New York: International Universities Press.

Langer, S. (1967). *Mind: An Essay on Human Feeling*, vol. 1. Baltimore: Johns Hopkins University Press.

Levy, E. (1934). Psychoanalytic treatment of a child with a stealing compulsion. *American Journal of Orthopsychiatry* 4:1.

Lorenz, K. (1952). *King Solomon's Ring*. New York: Crowell.

Mahler, M. (1968). *On Human Symbiosis and the Vicissitudes of Individuation*. New York: International Universities Press.

—— (1975). *The Psychological Birth of the Human Infant*. New York: Basic Books.

Masson, J. (1985). *The Assault on Truth*. New York: Farrar, Straus & Giroux.

Masterson, J. (1988). *The Search for the Real Self*. New York: Free Press.

May, R. (1969). *Love and Will*. New York: Norton.

Megnaghi, D. (1993). *Freud and Judaism*. New York: Brunner/Mazel.

Menaker, E. (1979). The masochistic factor in the psychoanalytic situation. In *Masochism and the Emergent Ego*. New York: Human Sciences Press.

—— (1953). Masochism—a defense reaction of the ego. *Psychoanalytic Quarterly* 12:205-220.

—— (1965). *Ego in Evolution.* New York: Grove.

—— (1979). The fate of Mario's masochism. In *Masochism and the Emergent Ego.* New York: Human Sciences Press.

—— (1979). *Masochism and the Emergent Ego.* New York: Human Sciences Press.

—— (1982). *Otto Rank: A Rediscovered Legacy.* New York: Columbia University Press.

—— (1988). Pitfalls of the transference. In *How People Change: Inside and Outside Therapy.* New York: Plenum.

—— (1989). *Appointment in Vienna.* New York: St. Martin's.

Moulton, B. E. (1931). Some causes of delinquency in relation to family attitudes. *American Journal of Orthopsychiatry* 1:2.

Nurnberg, H. (1932). *Allegeime Neurosenlehre.* Hans Huber Verlag.

Rank, O. (1914). *The Myth of the Birth of the Hero.* New York: Vintage.

—— (1924, 1973). *The Trauma of Birth.* New York: Harper and Row.

—— (1925). *Der Kunstler,* 2nd. ed. Vienna: Internationaler Psychoanalytischer Verlag.

—— (1945). *Truth and Reality.* New York: Knopf.

—— (1958). *Beyond Psychology.* New York: Dover.

—— (1968a). Emotion and denial. *Journal of the Otto Rank Association* 3(1): 11-13.

—— (1968b). The possibilities of therapy. *Journal of the Otto Rank Association* 3(1):39.

—— (1973). *The Trauma of Birth.* New York: Harper and Row.

Reik, T. (1941). *Masochism in Modern Man,* trans. M. H. Beigel and G. M. Kurth. New York: Farrar and Rinehart.

Restak, R. W. (1984). Possible neurophysiological correlates of empathy. In *Empathy,* ed. J. Lichtenberg, M. Bornstein, and D. Silver, pp. 63-75. Hillsdale, NJ: Analytic Press.

Roland, A. (1988). *In Search of Self in India and Japan.* Princeton, NJ: Princeton University Press.

Roland, A. and Harris, B. eds. (1979). *Career and Motherhood.* New York: Human Sciences Press.

Schilder, P. (1951). *The Image and Appearance of the Human Body.* New York: International Universities Press.

Schwing, G. (1940). *Ein Weg Zur Seele Des Geisteskranken.* Zurich: Rascher Verlag.

Spitz, R. A. (1965). *The First Year of Life.* New York: International Universities Press.

Stern, D. (1985). *The Interpersonal World of the Infant.* New York: Basic
    Books.
Takemoto, Y. (1985). *Amae* as metalanguage: a critique of Doi's theory of
    amae. Unpublished paper presented at the Annual Meeting of the
    Association for Asian Studies, Philadelphia, March and at the Annual
    Meeting of the American Psychoanalytic Association, Los Angeles, May.
Tiebout, H. M. (1930). Delinquency: problems in the causation of stealing.
    American Journal of Psychiatry 9:5.
Tiebout, H. M., and Kirkpatrick, M. E. (1932). Psychiatric factors in steal-
    ing. *American Journal of Orthopsychiatry* 2:2.
Weigert, E. (1962). Sympathy, empathy, and freedom in therapy. In *Modern
    Concepts of Psychoanalysis*, ed. L. Salzman and J. Masserman. New
    York: Citadel.
Wheelis, A. (1958). *The Quest for Identity.* New York: Norton.
Winnicott, D. M. (1965). *The Maturational Processes and the Facilitating
    Environment.* New York: International Universities Press.
Wolstein, B. (1974). Toward a conception of unique individuality. *Contem-
    porary Psychoanalysis* 10(3):347-357.
Wu, J. (1994). Therapy with Asian patients. *Contemporary Psychoanalysis*
    30(1):152-168.
Yankelovich, D., and Barrett, W. (1971). *Ego and Instinct.* New York:
    Vintage.

Publications of
Esther Menaker

(1939) A Contribution to the Study of the Neurotic Stealing Symptom. *American Journal of Orthopsychiatry, 9* 368– 377

(1945) Hypermotility and Transitory Tic in a Child of Seven. *Nervous Child*, 4:335– 341.

(1942) The Masochistic Factor in the Psychoanalytic Situation. *Psychoanalytic Quarterly*, 11: 171–186. Also in *Masochism and the Emergent Ego*, pp. 36–51.

(1953) Masochism—A Defense Reaction of the Ego. *Psychoanalytic Quarterly*, 22: 171–186. Also in *Masochism and the Emergent Ego*, pp. 52–67.

(1956) A Note on Some Biologic Parallels Between Certain Innate Animal Behaviors and Moral Masochism. *Psychoanalytic Review*, 43: 31–41. Also in *Masochism and the Emergent Ego*, pp. 68–83.

(1960) The Self-Image as Defense and Resistance. *Psychoanalytic Quarterly*, 29: 72–81.

(1965) *Ego in Evolution.* New York: Grove Press.

(1967) Review: *The Biology of Ultimate Concern.* By Theodosius Dobzhansky. *Journal of the Otto Rank Association*, 2: 93–96.

(1968) Interpretation and Ego Function. In: *Use of Interpretation in Treatment*, E. Hammer, ed. New York: Grune & Stratton, pp. 67–70.

(1968) On Re-reading *Beyond Psychology*. *Journal of the Otto Rank Association, 3:* 66–74. Also in *Masochism and the Emergent Ego,* pp. 273–281.

(1968) Discussion of a Panel on The Emergence of Ego Psychology, *Journal of Clinical Issues in Psychology,* 5:38–42. Also in *Psychoanalytic Review,* 1969, 56: 543–551.

(1969) Will and the Problem of Masochism. *Journal of Contemporary Psychotherapy,* 1: 67–77. Also in *Masochism and the Emergent Ego,* pp. 84–98.

(1969) Creativity as Conscious or Unconscious Activity. *Journal of the Otto Rank Association,* 4: 23–36. Also in *Masochism and the Emergent Ego,* pp. 282– 294.

(1970) The Emergence of Ego Psychology, A Discussion in *The Psychoanalytic Review,* 56: 543– 551.

(1972) Adjustment and Creation. *Journal of the Otto Rank Association,* 7: 11–25. Also in *Masochism and the Emergent Ego,* pp. 295–309.

(1973) The Social Matrix—Mother and Child. *The Psychoanalytic Review, 60:* 45–58. Also in *Masochism and the Emergent Ego,* pp. 151–166.

(1973) Possible Forerunners of Identification Processes in the Animal World. *Identity, Identification and Self-Image.* New York: NPAP Psychoanalytic Monograph I, pp. 1–9. Also in *Masochism and the Emergent Ego,* pp. 167–180.

(1974) The Therapy of Women in the Light of Psychoanalytic Theory and the Emergence of a New View. In: *Women in Therapy, V.* Franks and V. Burtle, Eds. New York: Brunner/ Mazel, pp. 230–246. Also in *Masochism and the Emergent Ego,* pp. 181–201.

(1975) Review: A Book Which Probes The Inevitable Human Dilemma. *The Denial of Death.* By Ernest Becker. *Journal of the Otto Rank Association,* 10: 65–68.

(1977) Creativity as the Central Concept in the Psychology of Otto Rank. *Journal of the Otto Rank Association,* 11: 1–17. Also in *Masochism and the Emergent Fgo,* pp 310–330. Also appears in part in *Psychoanalysis, Creativity and Literature,* A. Roland, Ed. New York: Columbia University Press, 1978, pp. 162–177.

(1977) The Ego Ideal: An Aspect of Narcissism. In: *The Narcissistic Condition,* M. C. Nelson and J. Ikenberry, Eds. New York: Human Sciences Press, pp. 248–264.

(1978) The Effects of Counter-Identification. *The Psychoanalytic Review*, 65: 381–389. Also in *Masochism and the Emergent Ego*, pp. 214–224.

(1979) Issues of Symbiosis and Ego Autonomy in the Treatment of Masochism In: *Parameters in Psychoanalytic Psychotherapy*, G. D. Goldman and D. S. Millman, Eds. Dubuque, Ia: Kendal/Hunt, pp. 127–140. Also in *Masochism and the Emergent Ego*, pp. 99–114.

(1979) *Masochism and the Emergent Ego*, L. Lerner, Ed. New York: Human Sciences Press.

(1981) Morality and Ethics in the Thinking of Otto Rank and their Implications for Psychotherapy. *Union Semiary Quarterly Review, 36:* 109–117.

(1981) Otto Rank's Contribution to Psychoanalytic Communication. *Contemporary Psychoanalysis*, 17: 552–564.

(1981) Self-Psychology Illustrated on the Issue of Moral Masochism: Clinical Implications. *American Journal of Psychoanalysis*, 41: 297–305.

(1982) Female Identity in Psychosocial Perspective. Women and Individuation: Emerging Views, A Special Issue of *The Psychoanalytic Review*, 69: 75–83. Also delivered at a conference on female identity sponsored by the Council of Psychoanalytic Psychotherapists, Oct., 1979, in New York City.

(1982) Otto Rank: Forerunner of Ego Psychology. *Issues in Ego Psychology*, 5: 40–44.

(1982) Review: On Bettelheim's Reflections on Freud and the Soul. *Freud and Man's Soul.* By Bruno Bettelheim *NPAP News and Reviews*, 12 (Spring), p. 7.

(1982) *Otto Rank: A Rediscovered Legacy*. New York: Columbia University Press.

(1983) Self, Will and Empathy. *Contemporary Psychoanalysis*, 19: 460–470.

(1984) On Being Seventy-five. *The Psychoanalytic Review*, 71: 1–5.

(1984) The Ethical and the Empathic in the Thinking of Otto Rank. *American Imago*, 41: 343–351.

(1984) Impressions of the Diaries. *Columbia Library Columns*, 23: 12–20.

(1985) The Concept of Will in the Thinking of Otto Rank and its Consequences for Clinical Practice. *The Psychoanalytic Review*, 72: 255–264.

(1986) Review: Acts of Will. By E. James Lieberman. *Contemporary Psychoanalysis,* 22: 306–310.

(1986) Some Observations Regarding Men's Contemporary Views of Women. *The Psychoanalytic Review,* 73: 210–213

(1986) Review: The Nature of Choice. By Anita Faatz. *The Psychoanalytic Review,* 74: 146–149.

(1986) Women in Psychoanalysis (Foreword). In: *The Psychoanalysis and Women: Contemporary Reappraisals,* Judith L. Alport, Ed., The Analytic Press.

(1987) Otto Rank and the New Story of Science. *The Psychoanalytic Review,* 17: 549– 559.

(1988) Early Struggles In Lay Psychoanalysis: New York In The Thirties, Forties, And Fifties. *The Psychoanalytic Review,* 75(3): 373– 379.

(1989) Otto Rank and Self Psychology. In: *Self Psychology,* Douglas W. Detrick and Susan P. Detrick (eds.) Hillsdale, NJ: The Analytic Press, 1989.

(1990) Transference, Countertransference and Therapeutic Efficacy in Relation to Self-Disclosure by the Analyst. From *Self-Disclosure in the Therapeutic Relationship,* George Stricker and Martin Fisher, Eds. Plenum Publishing Corporation, pp. 103–115.

(1990) Discussion: The Feminine Self. *The American Journal of Psychoanalysis.* 50: 63–65.

(1991) Questioning the Sacred Cow of the Transference. In How *People Change,* eds. Rebecca C. Curtis and George Stricker, Plenum Publishing Corporation, 1991. pp. 13–20.

(1991) On Anna Freud: A Discussion of Personal Analytic Reactions in the Early Days of Psychoanalysis. *Journal of the American Academy of Psychoanalysis,* 19:606–611.

(1992) Review: *Shame, The Underside of Narcissism,* by Andrew Morisson. *Contemporary Psychology,* 37:127.

(1992) Review: *Lingering Shadows: Jungians, Freudians, and Anti-Semitism.* Eds. Aryeh Maidenbaum and Stephen A. Martin. *Quadrant,* 25:105–107.

(1993) The Self-Object as Immortal Self. *Journal of Religion and Health,* 33:81–88.

Credits

The author gratefully acknowledges permission to reprint the following:

PART I SELF-PSYCHOLOGICAL PERSPECTIVES

"The Self-Image as Defense and Resistance," *The Psychoanalytic Quarterly*, 29: 72–81, is reprinted by permission of *The Guilford Press;* copyright 1960 by *The Guilford Press*.

"The Ethical and the Empathic," *American Imago*, Vol. 41, No. 4, pp. 343–351, is reprinted by permission of *American Imago;* copyright (Winter)1984 by Association for Applied Psychoanalysis, Inc., Brooklyn, New York.

"Self, Will, and Empathy," *Contemporary Psychoanalysis*, Vol. 19, No. 3, pp. 461–470, is reprinted by permission from *Contemporary Psychoanalysis;* copyright 1983 by W. A. W. Institute, New York.

"The Ego Ideal: An Aspect of Narcissism" from *The Narcissistic Condition* edited by M. C. Nelson and J. Ikenberry. New York: Human Sciences Press, pp. 248–264 is reprinted by permission from Human Sciences Press; copyright 1977 by Human Sciences Press.

"Otto Rank: Forerunner of Ego Psychology," *Issues in Ego Psychology*, Vol. 5, pp. 40–44, is reprinted by permission from *Issues in Ego Psychol-*

PART II MASOCHISM

PART III WOMEN'S ISSUES

permission from The Guilford Press; copyright 1986 by The National Psychological Association for Psychoanalysis.

PART IV PERSONAL JOURNEY

"On Anna Freud: A Discussion of Personal Analytic Reactions In Days of Psychoanalysis."Journal of the American Academy of Psychoanalysis, Vol. 19, No. 4, pp. 606–611, is reprinted by permission from The Guilford Press; copyright 1991 by The Americian Academy of Psychoanalysis.

"Early Struggles in Lay Psychoanalysis: New York in the Thirties, Forties, and Fifties, *The Psychoanalytic Review*, Vol. 75, no. 3, pp. 373–379, is reprinted by permission from The Guilford Press; copyright 1988 by The National Psychological Association for Psychoanalysis.

"On Being Seventy-five," *The Psychoanalytic Review*, Vol. 71, no 1, pp. 1–5, is reprinted by permission from The Guilford Press; copyright (Spring) 1984 by The National Psychological Association for Psychoanalysis.

"A Contribution to the Study of the Neurotic Stealing Symptom," *The American Journal of Ortho Psychiatry*, Vol. 9, pp. 368–377, is reprinted by permission from *The American Journal of Ortho Psychiatry*; copyright 1939 by *The American Journal of Ortho Psychiatry*.

"Hypermotility and Transitory Tic in a Child of Seven, *Nervous Child*, Vol. 4, pp. 335–341, is reprinted by permission from *Nervous Child*; copyright 1945 by *Nervous Child*.

Index